Museums in a Troubled World

'Intelligent, passionate and provocative, Janes reminds us all that the museum can – and must – play a leading role in building a sustainable future.' – *James M. Bradburne, Director General, Fondazione Palazzo Strozzi, Florence, Italy*

'I commend the book to anyone who wants to share in iconoclastic and original thinking about museums and their roles in society now and in the future.' – *Suzanne Keene, Reader Emeritus at University College London, UK*

'Robert Janes is not only one of Canada's most distinguished museologists but a fine writer. *Museums in a Troubled World* reaches far beyond the exhibition gallery to become a wise and witty critique of the forces that threaten the cultural health of our civilisation.' – *Ronald Wright, author of A Short History of Progress*

'*Museums in a Troubled World* lays out the challenges facing the museum field in the 21st century and issues a clearly crafted, articulate charge for museums "to help create the future, grounded in their unique blend of the past and the present." This is an important work that should be read, and enjoyed, by museum professionals everywhere.' – *Ford Bell, President of the American Association of Museums*

Are museums irrelevant?

Museums are rarely acknowledged in the global discussion of climate change, environmental degradation, the inevitability of depleted fossil fuels and the myriad local issues concerning the well-being of particular communities – suggesting the irrelevance of museums as social institutions. At the same time, there is a growing preoccupation among museums with the marketplace. Museums, unwittingly or not, are embracing the values of relentless consumption that underlie the planetary difficulties of today.

Museums in a Troubled World argues that much more can be expected of museums as publicly supported and knowledge-based institutions. The weight of tradition and a lack of imagination are significant factors in museum inertia and these obstacles are also addressed. Taking an interdisciplinary approach, combining anthropology, ethnography, museum studies and management theory, this book goes beyond conventional museum thinking.

Robert R. Janes explores the meaning and role of museums as key intellectual and civic resources in a time of profound social and environmental change. This volume is a constructive examination of what is wrong with contemporary museums, written from an insider's perspective that is grounded in both hope and pragmatism. The book's conclusions are optimistic and constructive, and highlight the unique contributions that museums can make as social institutions, embedded in their communities, and owned by no one.

Robert R. Janes is the Editor-in-Chief of *Museum Management and Curatorship*, Chair of the Board of Directors of the Biosphere Institute of the Bow Valley and is the former President and CEO of the Glenbow Museum in Calgary, Canada. He is also a museum consultant. His books include *Looking Reality in the Eye: Museums and Social Responsibility*, *Museum Management and Marketing*, *Museums and the Paradox of Change*, *Archaeological Ethnography Among Mackenzie Basin Dene, Canada*, and *Preserving Diversity: Ethnoarchaeological Perspectives on Cultural Change in the Western Canadian Subarctic*.

Museum Meanings

Series Editors

Eilean Hooper-Greenhill and Flora Kaplan

The museum has been constructed as a symbol of Western society since the Renaissance. This symbol is both complex and multi-layered, acting as a sign for domination and liberation, learning and leisure. As sites for exposition, through their collections, displays and buildings, museums mediate many of society's basic values. But these mediations are subject to contestation, and the museums can also be seen as a site for cultural politics. In postcolonial societies, museums have changed radically, reinventing themselves under pressure from many forces, which include new roles and functions for museums, economic rationalism and moves towards greater democratic access.

Museum Meanings analyses and explores the relationship between museums and their publics. 'Museums' are understood very broadly, to include art galleries, historic sites and historic houses. 'Relationships with the public' is also understood very broadly, including interactions with artefacts, exhibitions and architecture, which may be analysed from a range of theoretical perspectives. These include material culture studies, mass communication and media studies, learning theories and cultural studies. The analysis of the relationship of the museum to its public shifts the emphasis from the museum as text, to studies grounded in the relationship of bodies and sites, identities and communities.

Also in the series:

Museums in a Troubled World

Renewal, irrelevance or collapse?

Robert R. Janes

Routledge
Taylor & Francis Group

LONDON AND NEW YORK

First published 2009
by Routledge
2 Park Square, Milton Park, Abingdon, Oxon OX14 4RN

Simultaneously published in the USA and Canada
by Routledge
270 Madison Ave, New York, NY 10016

Routledge is an imprint of the Taylor & Francis Group, an informa company

© 2009 Robert R. Janes

Typeset in Sabon by
Bookcraft Ltd, Stroud, Gloucestershire
Printed and bound in Great Britain by
CIP Antony Rowe, Chippenham, Wiltshire

British Library Cataloguing in Publication Data
A catalogue record for this book is available from the British Library

Library of Congress Cataloging in Publication Data
Janes, Robert R., 1948–
Museums in a troubled world : renewal, irrelevance, or collapse? /
Robert R. Janes.
    p. cm.
    1. Museums—Social aspects. 2. Museums—Philosophy. I. Title.
AM7.J36 2009
069 dc22   2008049311

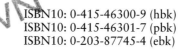
ISBN10: 0-415-46300-9 (hbk)
ISBN10: 0-415-46301-7 (pbk)
ISBN10: 0-203-87745-4 (ebk)

ISBN13: 978-0-415-46300-3 (hbk)
ISBN13: 978-0-415-46301-0 (pbk)
ISBN13: 978-0-203-87745-6 (ebk)

For Peter, Erica, Geoff and Kiran – the hope of things to come

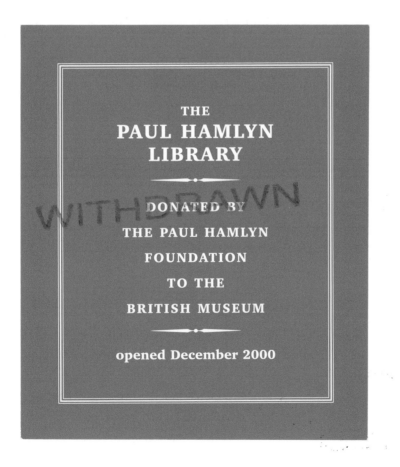

And can we also realize in time that, in many ways, we are ironically but unwittingly poisoning ourselves and the biosphere, psychically and physically, out of our endless and magnificent but unexamined precocity, out of our fear and our greediness, and the cleverness of our minds and our industry and our institutions, cleverness that turns dangerous when we become attached, entrenched, absorbed, delighted with parts but uninterested in wholes and larger wholes?

Jon Kabat-Zinn[1]

Contents

Figures

Acknowledgements

Lengthy book acknowledgements have been criticized recently, but such criticism is uncalled for when one has spent over thirty years in any kind of work, whether it is museums or plumbing, and then writes a book. Those thirty-plus years encapsulate countless interactions, musings and learnings, and it is careless to pretend that one's thoughts and perspective somehow spring full-blown at the moment of writing. Because they don't, I have a number of people to thank for their ongoing expertise and support. Research, reflection and writing are ultimately a collective enterprise and I must mention some of the key participants.

For acuity, collegiality and perseverance beyond the call of duty, I wish to thank Richard Sandell for reviewing the manuscript; his comments and support were instrumental in the completion of this book. I am also grateful to Joy Davis for reviewing the manuscript, as her generous support, her thoughtful comments and editorial scrutiny were invaluable. In addition, James M. Bradburne generously reviewed the draft and provided cogent comments and an international perspective. Writing is a solitary task and Sandell, Davis and Bradburne kept me motivated. I am indebted to the celebrated museologist, Elaine Heumann Gurian, for writing the foreword. Her accumulated knowledge and experience are rivalled only by her generosity in sharing them.

Others reviewed various chapters and provided useful comments and welcome encouragement, including Adrian Ellis, Suzanne Keene, Kathleen McLean, Michael Robinson and Douglas Worts. There are also a number of individuals who provided interviews and guidance, as well as published and unpublished work, including Joanne DiCosimo, Maurice Davies, Elaine Heumann Gurian, Peter Janes, David Klatt, Emlyn Koster, Ruth Lane, Diane Mar-Nicolle, Sylvie Morel, Bernice Murphy, Gabrielle Nammour, Will Phillips, Beatriz Plaza, Marjorie Schwarzer, Charles Stanish, Frank Vanclay and Alaka Wali. I want to thank Rob Ferguson, in particular, for keeping me abreast of relevant literature.

Other colleagues and friends continue to provide ongoing support and encouragement, as well as reviewing various drafts of papers and presentations that have led to this book. I thank Alexandra Badzak, Mary Case, Christine Castle, Gerry Conaty, Michele Corbeil, Ford Bell, Jim Cullen, Clare-Estelle Daitch, Naomi Grattan, Des Griffin, Eilean Hooper-Greenhill, Erica Janes, Joan Kanigan-Fairen, Doug Leonard,

Michael Lundholm, Suzanne MacLeod, Kitty Raymond, Barbara Soren and Ronald Wright. I thank them for their consideration and interest. There are two other individuals who are no longer with us – Michael Ames and Stephen Weil – whom I wish to acknowledge for their ongoing, albeit silent, legacy. I also want to thank the Editorial Board of *Museum Management and Curatorship*, as well as the many authors and referees, for their research, writing and commitment to the journal. All of them are a continuous source of stimulation and insight.

I was able to present and test many of the ideas in this book in various public presentations, and I want to thank the Mid-Atlantic Association of Museums, the British Columbia Museums Association, the 'Tribute to Stephen Weil' hosted by the Cultural Management Program at the University of Victoria (Canada), the University of Leicester, and the Committee on Audience Research and Evaluation/American Association of Museums for generously inviting me to address their organizations. I also thank the Canadian Academy of Independent Scholars and Simon Fraser University for providing financial assistance in the preparation of this book through the Beatrice Gross Independent Scholar Award.

I want to thank those who assisted me with fact-checking and references, including Marc-Andre Anderson, John McAvity, Terry Cheney, Michelle Elligott, Elizabeth Ellis, Chantal Fortier, Graham Kappel and Alexander Pappas. Numerous individuals also generously provided images on behalf of their projects and institutions. Although I was not able to use all of these images, I am grateful for the willing assistance of Adam Blackshaw, Christie DuBois, Maurice Davies, Jocelyn Dodd, Ceri Jones, David Klatt, Ruth Lane, Elizabeth McCrea, Gabrielle Nammour, Mark O'Neill, Madeleine Tudor, Frank Vanclay, Alaka Wali and Douglas Worts. Ron Marsh prepared the digital images for publication, and I thank him for his impeccable work.

My editor at Routledge, Matthew Gibbons, has been involved with this book since the beginning and I sincerely thank him for his unwavering support and guidance. I also acknowledge Lalle Pursglove, who has provided skilful assistance at every turn. I wish to thank Matthew Brown for his expert copyediting and proofreading, as well for managing the many production details. Last, I thank my wife, Priscilla, who has contributed to every aspect of this book while remaining even-tempered, gracious and insightful.

Foreword

Elaine Heumann Gurian[1]

Robert Janes has a fertile mind and an omnivorous delight in learning. He has written and edited books on social responsibility and change in museums. He is an editor of an important museum journal. And it is evident in his past work and in this book that he is brave and has an evident, visible, moral core. He has spent a lifetime championing museums as important institutions, not only because of their collections but also because of their possibilities within the social fabric of society. Bob Janes fervently wants museums to make a difference in every community and in individuals' lives.

Janes can visualize the ideal museum as clearly as he can see the food on his plate, and he wonders why we can't also see it. Having worked so hard to point out museums' possibilities, he is baffled and disappointed by those of us who control museums but fail to change them in the ways he so fervently wishes. He cannot conceive that there are some within the profession who like museums just the way they are. He believes that these colleagues are either misguided or that they lack tools to remake their museums and improve them along the lines of his vision:

> I will argue that the majority of museums, as social institutions, have largely eschewed on both moral and practical grounds a broader commitment to the world in which they operate. Instead, they have allowed themselves to be held increasingly captive by the economic imperatives of the marketplace and their own internally-driven agendas. Whether or not they have done this unwittingly or knowingly is immaterial, as the consequences are the same. It is time for museums to examine their core assumptions. (p. 13)

Bob Janes would argue that he is essentially an optimist though he appears both sad and frustrated. This book serves as a summation of a lifetime of work, thinking, writing and speaking. He hopes it will guide us on the road to fundamental museum reformulation. I must say that I share his frustration. Museums can be stubborn institutions to those who wish for them to change.

This book is an exhortation to us – museum trustees, students and practitioners – to create museums that will make a difference to society in this perilous new century.

He thinks we, with all good but misguided intentions, have persisted with outdated models and have become inadvertently stuck,

> seemingly in a collective inability or unwillingness to generate and sustain a critical mass of purpose and will. Thought and action are largely uncoupled in the museum world – a primary cause of the drift into irrelevance. (p. 173)

The author thinks we have been deceived by the capitalistic world of for-profit management and have charted our success by using the wrong measures:

> Marketplace ideology, capitalist values and corporate self-interest are clearly not the way forward, having conclusively demonstrated their financial fragility and moral bankruptcy. (p. 184)

Janes wrote this book before today's world-wide financial calamity and yet is prescient about the need to turn away from 'the belief that unlimited economic growth and unconstrained consumption are essential to our well-being' (p. 94).

He is even more forward-looking when he poses a new use for our collections which he refers to as 'cumulative knowledge and wisdom':

> The need to revisit this cumulative knowledge and wisdom may come sooner than expected, as the destruction of the biosphere renders industrial technology increasingly malevolent. This record of material diversity may have a value not unlike biodiversity, as we seek adaptive solutions in an increasingly brittle world. Collections will be the key to examining the relevance of this material diversity in contemporary times, and will distinguish museums as the only social institutions with this perspective and the necessary resources. In this respect, museums are as valuable as seed banks. (p. 179)

He wants us to re-examine our fundamentals – what museums are for – and to invent new methods and more humane ways of being with each other. He hopes we will measure success by yardsticks of kindness, relevance, community cohesion and other more psychological markers of good health. He provides many examples of how we can shape an uncertain future and is sure we will figure it out.

The book incorporates models, examples and readings that are in part spiritual, utopian, and harkens back to the 'hippy' days when activists hoped that the world would become kinder. For example, as an admirer of Jon Kabat-Zinn, Janes wants us to be more 'mindful' which he explains as 'moment-to-moment awareness ... cultivated by purposefully paying attention to things we ordinarily ignore,' and wants us to guard against 'chaotic cascades' of endless electronic distractions and interruptions, and practise the creation of ideas that are orthogonal, or at right angles to conventional reality.

Bob Janes has written a personal, passionate polemic. Just the chapter titles are provocative – 'Museums and irrelevance', 'A troubled world', 'Self-inflicted challenges', 'Debunking the marketplace', 'Searching for resilience', 'The mindful museum' and 'Stewards or spectators?'. He hopes that if he can more clearly describe problems, we will feel impelled to work together to remake museums into more useful organizations as he so fervently wishes. And he offers us some fix-it ideas so that we might get started on the way.

While Bob Janes can clearly see the new improved museum in his mind's eye, how to transform our present institutions into these more relevant ones is slightly murkier. He can sense, but not quite fully describe, the next steps. So he gives us many ideas, side readings, excursions into other disciplines, and examples that he hopes will provide some guidance as we figure out our way.

I found the experience of reading this book very like beginning to read philosophy in college: intrigued, but always a little befuddled – almost, but not quite, grasping the point. Nevertheless I see ways that I could apply the ideas, as imperfectly as I understand them, to my own professional life. I find it interesting and useful to meander into the places that Bob has found interesting and try to parse the connections that he so plainly sees. Each of the possible course corrections he offers is unexpected, interesting and worth contemplating. Janes thinks about ecologically sustainable lives, study circles, strategic thinking, new models of shared leadership and sensitive ways of working with community.

> Along with the willpower required to reduce consumption is the greater need to transform the museum's public service persona, defined by education and entertainment, to one of a locally-embedded problem-solver, in tune with the challenges and aspirations of the community. (p. 173)

He wants consultation and organic clusters within our organizational structures, and strategies for quick and nimble responses. He summarizes his aspirations as follows:

> All museums have the responsibility and the opportunity to become synthesizers, and foster an understanding of the interconnectedness of the problems we face, both environmental and social. A mindful museum can empower and honour all people in the search for a sustainable and just world – by creating a mission that focuses on the interconnectedness of our world and its challenges, and promotes the integration of disparate perspectives. (p. 166)

This is not a 'how-to' book. Janes leaves it to us, our passion, and our individual and collective circumstances to create the improvements that fit within our unique community needs.

Robert Janes uses himself as a barometer. This makes for vivid and engaging reading and, as the authentic self-reflection of a fervent practitioner, the book is valuable. The author is someone who is really, really smart, humane and wants us all to succeed. As a reader, you feel that you know him even if you don't. This book is multi-layered, and challenging to absorb in one reading. Chapters have their own internal trajectories. Every paragraph could be turned into a chapter and each of these would be interesting in its own right. Bob Janes reads both far afield and close to home.

The titles listed in the notes for this book are in themselves an excellent guide for personal self-study.

This is an intriguing book so stocked full of ideas and good quotes that I find I have to read and then reread each paragraph and think about it before going on. This is not a book to take on the airplane and glide through on the way to a conference. This is a book so filled with ideas that one wants reassurance that Bob Janes will show up tomorrow morning at early breakfast so you can start a discussion that will range all over the universe (hopefully while you also tramp through hill and dale) and end with exhaustion at bedtime. At the end of each paragraph I want to say, 'But, Bob, what about … and, Bob, I don't agree these are linked ideas but they're important and could lead to a very different conclusion … and, Bob, have you read … and, Bob, …' And so it goes. (And I know Bob personally, so the possibility of having that conversation is not farfetched.)

But for you, dear reader, if you do not know him yet, I suggest you get a highlighter and armed with his email address begin to read while sitting at your computer madly writing questions and rebuttals to him. In today's technological age it is possible to set up such a real dialogue with the author. Alternatively, the best use of this book may be as a book club project, tackling just one chapter at a time. This should not be a superficial bag-lunch discussion but an agenda item for a serious meeting – the senior management weekly meeting, for example.

The chapter chosen for discussion would be the one most related to your museum's current situation. My expectation is that your colleagues will protest the very idea of shared study, arguing that they have 'real work' needing to be done. After reading the assigned chapter, they will become so agitated, so angry at the author, so dismissive or embracing of the ideas embedded in the chapter, that the ensuing conversation will be heated – and sufficiently provocative to unlock a real plan of action that will move the institution ahead in unexpected ways. The results will vary from the book's prescriptions but will fit the needs of the institution, just as Bob hoped they would.

I believe this book will serve as an irritant that causes change – change that has not happened using smoother and more tranquil methods. I predict that joint reading will give rise to new ways of doing things that will prove productive for the institution.

The real usefulness of this book is that, as Janes suggests, we are so comfortable in our shared, but narrow, set of self-referential information that we cannot get out of our collective rut without provocation from thinkers outside our small groups. If used in this way, the book will allow your colleagues to gather insights, marshal refutational arguments and not having Bob Janes around – take each other on in ways that will expand the possibilities of productive change far beyond that imagined by the group before. When this happens, the author's exhortations will bear the fruits he has hoped for and render the book a success.

3 November 2008

Prologue

Time immemorial

By some First Nations accounts, there is a Great Council of All Animals which meets in perpetual session in a cave deep within a mountain, beside a great river.[1] These animals monitor the affairs of humans wherever they are on earth. If a woman or man is in need or in trouble, and humbly asks for assistance, the Council chooses one of its members to help. The representative, whether winged, four-legged, or crawling, then appears to the person and gives something of its own power or advice that should thereafter guide the person's life. It is understood that animals were here before human beings and thus have a recognized superiority over them.

The Council was meeting once again under the large mountain, and there was the usual amount of noise, confusion and odour as the assembly gathered. It has always been this way, even during the magical time before humans, when animals spoke, changed their shapes and did pretty much what they wanted to do. That was also the time when clever animals, like wolverine, could travel great distances by simply folding the earth in half, like a piece of paper, and then taking a few steps to get somewhere far away. Even when humans first arrived, life was fine, mostly because there was an inaugural meeting called by the animals. That first meeting lasted for a very long time, some say several hundred years, because critical decisions had to be made about how they would all relate to each other.

This meeting involved a lot of humans, as well as every bird, fish and animal on the earth. There were far too many insects, so they were allowed to send representatives. All agreed on a number of principles that should govern their relationships, such as letting the humans use all of them for food, providing that humans killed only what they needed to live comfortably and treated their prey with great respect. There was to be no wasting of anything, and the humans were told to always think often and highly of animals, including all the winged, swimming and crawling creatures. This was a continual challenge for humans, and many of the animals simply decided to avoid those people who failed to show them respect. Even when the inaugural conference was over, animals and humans could still talk to each other, especially medicine people and animal leaders. Things worked well for as long as the humans and the animals remembered, until one day a new kind of human appeared, one with

1

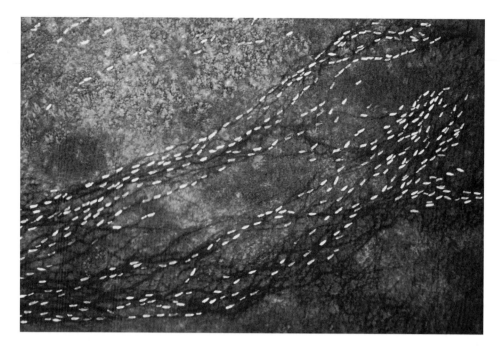

Figure 1 Aerial view of migrating barren-ground caribou in the Thelon Game Sanctuary, Northwest Territories, Canada, 1971.

Photo: courtesy of Priscilla B. Janes

lighter skin and many things in their canoes. Since then, the Council had needed to meet almost continually.

The grunting, whistling and calling was cut short by a booming snort from a barren-ground grizzly, the moderator of these sessions. There are many good reasons to have a bear for a moderator, as it is common knowledge that bears have excellent hearing, are capable of reading human minds and hearing what they're saying, as well as knowing what humans are thinking. Most importantly, bear is known as a good friend and will treat you the same way you treat him. For all these reasons, bear had chaired the Great Council of All Animals since time immemorial. As the meeting was called to order, the cavernous chamber reverberated with the noise of so many creatures, including the marmots, which also use this chamber to make the clouds for overcast and rainy days.

'We have many requests and interventions to consider,' said bear, revealing obvious irritation in the human voice he used for these occasions. Human is the lingua franca for these meetings, acknowledged by all animals as a practical, albeit inelegant, means of communicating. 'It appears that our relatives, the humans, continue on their path of self-destruction – fouling the land, air and water – and many have petitioned us for assistance,' began bear. 'We must determine if we are prepared to assist yet again, as we, too, have been weakened by their artifice and hubris.' Bear noted, as he had done for years, that wolf was in the best position to provide guidance and counsel to humans, on account of her ability to shift her shape into that of a dog – who is said to be the humans' best friend. Wolf refused yet again, ever mindful of the humans' childish view of wolves, imbued as it is with superstition and folklore. Their incessant portrayal of wolf as fierce, rapacious and destructive had left all wolves uncooperative and resolute in their disgust for humans. The wolves in attendance reiterated their intention only to sniff under tails, which humans don't have.

There was general consensus that the current state of human self-absorption made it impossible for the Council to make any appreciable improvements in the human world anyway, even if wolf were to help. The other topic of discussion, and one that had also been on the agenda for centuries, was whether it was now time to collapse the three layers of spiritual energy that surround the earth. This was a perennial question, as the middle layer is not only where all of the animal and insect spirits live but it also allows the Great Council to do its work. This question always provoked intense discussion among Council participants, not to mention cynicism and frustration, as they debated the value of assisting humans. 'Simply close the middle layer,' said wolverine. 'Most humans will not know the difference anyway.' His was still a minority opinion, and the question was once again deferred. The meeting concluded with a decision to provide assistance to a small group of hunters who still made their living in a great forest in the far north. It seemed that alcohol, television, and oil and gas exploration were taking their toll, even among those remote hunters.

The Willow Lakers[2]

This group of humans, with darker skin, call themselves the Willow Lake Dene.[3] They are one of the world's last great hunting cultures and for thousands of years have hunted, fished, and trapped in the boreal forest of Canada's western subarctic. They have survived countless famines, epidemic diseases and the wily ways of the newcomers – in one of the most severe environments in the world. The climate is one of seasonal extremes, with a long winter and a brief, but warm, summer. The mean January temperature for the region is minus 28° Celsius, and temperatures of 32° Celsius are not uncommon in summer. The subarctic ecosystem is very simple or, put another way, it lacks diversity. The low temperatures have a powerful limiting effect, and relatively few living things have successfully adapted to these northern conditions. This simplicity is also associated with a lack of stability, and the resulting cycles of animal abundance and scarcity make this a very difficult place to live.

The community at Willow Lake is a cluster of separate households situated on a spit of land surrounded by rivers and lakes, and is best described as a residential hunting camp. Hunters range out from this location in search of meat, fish and furs on a regular basis, returning after absences of one to several days. Seven families constitute the core group, including 31 men, women and children, ranging in age from one month to about 78 years. The Willow Lake Dene are not directly comparable to

Figure 2 The Willow Lake hunting camp in the Northwest Territories, Canada, 1975.

Photo: courtesy of Father Felix Labat, OMI

their hunting and gathering forefathers and, as yet, there is no unbroken historic link between their cultural adaptation and the prehistoric record of the area. Nonetheless, they engage in activities that can be considered transitional, if not traditional, within the context of the twentieth century.

Many of these activities, such as hunting, meat processing, land travel, hide processing, cooking, water travel, shelter construction, and gathering, as well as their social organization, are forms of adaptive behaviour that have been only superficially altered, or not at all, since Euro-Canadian contact. The Willow Lakers make extensive use of modern technology, such as high-powered rifles, snowmobiles, outboard motors and nylon gill nets, integrating them with an indigenous material culture which includes snowshoes, moccasins and a sophisticated wood technology. Meat (moose, caribou, beaver, rabbit, muskrat, ducks, geese, grouse and so on) and fish obtained in the forests, lakes and rivers constitute the bulk of their diet in the bush.

Individual family patterns vary considerably in terms of the scheduling and duration of their annual cycles, which are marked by pronounced flexibility and mobility. The Willow Lakers exhibit some characteristics of both the local band and the task group. Like a local band, they generally exploit all resources within their own range and are predominantly a spatial grouping of kinsmen. Like a task group, the Willow

Lakers exploit specific seasonal resources at particular locales and share the produce, including ducks, fish and large mammals. A task group is a voluntary grouping of people that comes together for specific economic purposes, and is exemplified by numerous activities such as the many-family fish camp, the many-family meat camp, and the trapping party. The local band and the task group are similar in their tendency toward shorter duration and the freedom of choice to affiliate. One Willow Lake elder noted that 'we move around a lot, just like animals.' The Willow Lakers are a small group culture, and it is in the small group that most habits become shared, modified or rejected. The Willow Lakers' values stress individual autonomy, egalitarianism, decision-making by consensus and limitations on the exercise of power. All of these traditional values continue to be reflected in their social organization and their patterns of leadership.

For a hunting culture residing in one of the world's largest forests, the importance of wood as a raw material cannot be overstated. The number and variety of wooden tools, devices and structures used in prehistory are largely lost to posterity, as a result of the perishable nature of wood in the acidic subarctic soils. With abandonment or discard, it is simply a matter of time before wooden objects perish completely in the boreal forest. The scarcity of collections (both prehistoric and historic) representing these northern hunters is also apparent in museums. *The Athapaskans: Strangers of the North* was the first major exhibition and catalogue devoted solely to the northern Athapaskans of Alaska and northwestern Canada. It was concerned with the material culture of these peoples and combined the best objects from two of the world's foremost collections – those of the Royal Scottish Museum and the National Museum of Man, now called the Canadian Museum of Civilization in Gatineau, Canada.[4] Of the 268 specimens or groups of specimens described in the exhibition catalogue, only 57 of them were made of wood or contained wooden components – amounting to 21 percent of the total collection. More revealing is that 38 of the 57 wooden specimens were collected in the twentieth century, and do not appear to be old.

The curator

She'd been having a lot of dreams lately, maybe because of all the stress and strain at work. The government had cut their funding for the third year in a row; there was a new director and a new board chair – both of whom were being minutely dissected in the museum's rumour mill. The only consistent pattern she could detect was that both of them were strong-willed and difficult. The chair was an entrepreneur, with a net worth of $900 million, who didn't keep an appointment book. The new director was rumoured to be a change agent, whatever that meant, although the cloak of secrecy under which he left his last position could have been the kind that indicated a whitewashing of the incompetence of directors and boards alike. Not only that, but the new director had just denied her request to attend a national conference on the implications of global terrorism for museum collections. He told her to do that on her own time, and it struck her that he had no interest in the collections, or in talking to her about them. This did nothing but deepen her anxiety about the rumoured possibility of a massive deaccessioning program.

She'd been thinking a lot about the collections lately – why they had them and all the work that needed to be done. She was increasingly bothered by her failure to record all that she knew about the tens of thousands of items she had collected, but had never written down. The same could be said of her curatorial colleagues. What would happen when they left or retired and there were only the meagre accession files, usually incomplete, to confound their successors? She comforted herself with the thought that all curators had this problem and, anyway, they salved their collective conscience by dutifully obsessing about these shortcomings at museum conferences, as well as in special workshops funded by government and universities. Oddly enough, these gatherings only produced recommendations, never any plans or resources to actually deal with the situation. The only tangible results were the special issues of prestigious, but unread, journals that documented these curatorial woes. She took additional comfort in the thought that there was never enough money to do every-thing. At times, when she mused that posterity would be forgiving, her thoughts would unravel as she weighed her failed obligation to the dead and those yet to be born.

Contrary to conventional wisdom, she thought, there is actually some urgency in curatorial work, although you would never know it. There were curators with 25-year careers who had never published an article, scholarly or otherwise. You might think that was because of all the collection work – but then you found out that their collections were not even fully registered, much less catalogued. There were always plenty of reasons for the backlog and the lack of publishing. The popular reason these days is the demands of the marketplace and the priority to make money. Ten years ago it was the lack of trained staff. Ten years before that it had been the government's fault – collections weren't a priority. Ten years before that it was a lack of focus because of too much money and too many opportunities to build buildings and go to conferences.

Lately, she was beginning to question the common refrain that 'curators are devoted to their collections.' It was sounding more and more disingenuous to her, and she knew it wasn't true. She knew that her colleagues would rather spend time in other ways. She knew that she did, despite the pretence she had to maintain among non-curatorial colleagues and at professional meetings. All the curators she knew would rather talk to people and visit collectors, than muster the discipline and commit-ment to help those mute objects speak for themselves. It took her 11 years to finish her master of arts degree and that was enough, and she secretly knew that she had no interest in making herself vulnerable by researching and writing for anyone – colleagues or otherwise. Whether it was performance anxiety or fear of failure, she just didn't want the uncertainty and self-doubt that inevitably accompany the life of the mind. With all of these tensions and paradoxes roiling and broiling in her brain, it came as little surprise that she was dreaming a lot lately.

The curator dreamed of a scaffold burial on a stone outcrop polished smooth by the relentless creeping of glacial ice. The surface was like a jumble of stone pillows of different sizes, with countless nooks and crannies. The billowy rock hills were sheathed in multicoloured lichens – from white to black to green to orange, and all shades in between. Scattered among the lichen carpet were other random explosions of colour, including colonies of bearberry, Labrador tea and a profusion of cranberries. Wild roses and fireweed were nearly lost amid this backdrop. The funeral was on this bench of smooth granite, devoid of trees and bordered by a fast flowing stream. The scaffold was made of peeled poles lashed together with strips of green moose hide. The corpse was on the ground next to the platform, completely covered in a beaver skin robe.

'We worked hard for two days to get 'em ready,' the old woman said. 'We washed his hands and feet, just like our people do, and dressed him in new clothes. Wool pants and a caribou skin shirt, with lots of beadwork. New moccasins, too. That's how we do it here.' There was a volley of screams, taken up by many other women. It stopped as abruptly as it started, as two other women drew knives from their dresses and clumsily slashed their legs. Their blood flowed freely.

The curator made her way to the head of the crowd for a look at the body. She was too late, as it had already been placed in a crude box made of intertwined saplings. The relatives and friends had all his possessions, which they were putting in the rough coffin or throwing on a pyre of spruce logs and brush. An ancient woman was directing the division. The curator watched as a Winchester 44.40 and a double barrel shotgun were placed in the coffin, along with a skinning knife, snowshoes, embroidered mitts, a shot bag and a dog whip. A hunter's prized possessions, not to mention a bewildering variety of wooden tools and devices, were thrown on the fire. The old man's snares, sleeping robe, clothing, dog packs and skin tent were also consumed by the raging fire, along with a peg leg that was hanging on the burial scaffold. Half a dozen women were kneeling at the edge of the fire, torpid with grief. Together, they slowly bent their heads toward the intense heat and singed their hair in a matter of seconds. As the coffin was lifted on to the platform, one of the women spoke.

'He has to make fire on his journey. That's why the mens are putting that tea pail by his head. There's dry meat in that basket, too,' she said.

'Hunting will be easy there; there's always lots a animals,' an old man said. 'That's what the old-timers say, anyway. Lots of fat fish and so much goose grease you gotta drink it out of a pot. That's why they put his stuff with him.'

The grieving continued and a line had formed in front of the fire. Relatives and friends were now destroying their own property, from clothing and hand tools, to muskrat skins intended for trade. All the women had singed off their hair, with the exception of their young daughters, who were spared this obligation. Two women flung themselves into the stream and were calmly rescued near the point of drowning. The dead man's hunting canoe was launched into the current with no ceremony, only to overturn and disappear in the fast moving water. The self-mutilation continued, especially among the older women, and their faces and bodies were covered with a ghastly ochre of blood, dirt and tears. The smell of burning hair hung in the air, as did the harsh mix of odours from the destruction of so much property. It was profound, mad and exhausting all at once.

The curator walked to the fire, removed her shirt and flung it in. The same for her watch and sheath knife. The curator unlaced her boots, removed her socks and jeans, and threw them all in the fire. She had nothing on but her underwear, along with a growing sense of detachment.

She awoke instantly, overwhelmed by the fate of all those priceless objects.

The exhibit technician

One winter morning at 8 a.m. sharp, the exhibit technician was waiting in the First Nations Gallery for his boss, Lester, the head of exhibit production. Lester was an impatient, hard-drinking refugee of the religious wars in Beirut, and suffered no fools but himself. They were to remove a sacred rattle and return it to storage because the higher-ups in administration were worried that displaying sacred artifacts would provoke accusations of disrespect by aboriginal peoples. That's what the rumour mill said, anyway. The rattle was apparently used a long time ago to summon some sort of council of animals, and they were waiting for the ethnologist who knew all about those things.

The ethnologist spent a lot of time with aboriginal peoples, learning their language and going to their ceremonies. They had taught him the proper way to handle these sacred things, including those in the museum's collection. That's what the exhibit technician had heard in the coffee room, anyway. By 8:25 there was no ethnologist in sight and Lester was impatient for another cup of coffee. They lifted the top off the glass case, and just as it cleared the rattle and the exhibit mount, the glass top imploded into a million pieces with a loud hissing noise. They stood there speechless, holding the empty frame.

'Holy shit!' shouted Lester. 'You okay?'

'Yeah,' the exhibit technician said, 'and so's the rattle. But we shouldn't have tried to move it without the ethnologist. He said not to.'

'Now you wouldn't be believin' all that Indian spirit stuff, would you? It's nonsense; unreal,' Lester insisted. His bravado was hollow, and anyone could see he was shaken. He was on the walky-talky to the director's office immediately. The exhibit technician was sweeping up the tiny glass shards when the four administrators showed up.

'What's happened here?' the assistant associate deputy director asked Lester. 'You said there was an accident.'

'It don't figure,' Lester said. 'I've never seen anything like it. Our cases are built like brick shit-houses. It just blew up in my hands.'

'I see that,' said the senior assistant deputy director, 'but where's the ethnologist? You were supposed to wait for him.'

'He's home with the flu. I just talked to him,' said Ethel, the senior executive assistant.

'He wasn't on time and we got a busy day. So my helper here suggested that we move it ourselves,' said Lester.

The exhibit technician was used to being blamed, as that was Lester's way of dealing with his own mistakes. Besides, the technician's attention was on the museum director, who was taking deep breaths while his eyes got watery.

The director's voice quavered as he spoke. 'No, you shouldn't have moved it. It was wrong. You must learn to listen,' he said, and abruptly left.

That was the one and only official response to the rattle incident.

The Chief Executive Officer

'What do you do when you're only the mail clerk around here and all you hear are rumours? I never have the chance to talk to anyone about anything. Not even my boss, who doesn't call me by my name. I don't care if I get laid off; I can get this kind of job anywhere, but it won't be as good as here. You can stay for coffee as long as you want and nobody says anything. Not like driving that truck for the landfill. Ten minute break and that's it. Everybody here just sits and sits, half an hour, an hour, who knows? It makes for a short workday, anyway. They got enough people around here to do the work anyway – Christ, I heard that the exhibit they're doing now has been going on for five years! So now I hear one of the curators talking about staff cuts. I don't care anyway, like I said, but it sure pisses me off that no one around here even talks to you. They all think they're so damned smart.'

'How dare he change our titles and collapse all the departments? I didn't spend nine years getting a PhD to be jerked around like some mail clerk. We are the knowledge owners in this place and always will be. So what if we don't publish in scholarly journals – we own that damn collection. We just haven't had enough time and money to get it all written down. And don't talk to me about the educators and marketers. They have too much power and influence, and including them on exhibit teams is stupid. They even use the word "customer." All this talk about accessibility and customers is nonsense. The *sine qua non* of all museums is the collections, and they will still be here long after the business types have sold their last widget. Curators aren't dead. We're just waiting.'

'It's about time there's a shake-up around here. I've been in security here for 19 years and there are still signs in the galleries from my first day of work about artifacts missing because they gotta be treated. Can you believe it, 19 years and there's still empty space? Try that in a department store. I've seen seven directors – queers, drunks, slackers, and eggheads – even a con woman. But I gotta give 'em credit, each one of them's a good talker. Only they never talk to us. No one does, except the custodians. We got a lot in common with them – meet the public every day, hear what they like and don't like, recommend restaurants. You name it. We gotta have the answers or look like idiots. The new CEO said we were the front line. What the hell does that mean – we're the first to be shot? No one ever tells us a thing around here, except to change our name from security to visitor services. What the hell does that mean? Isn't security what we do? You won't find me worrying about all those rumours. We gotta union, and I pay my dues. We got job security here, and overtime, too.'

* * *

The museum's Chief Executive Officer wasn't really surprised to learn that he had provoked that much anger. He had just received a death threat, packaged in a bright white envelope and slid under his office door. It was very late on a Friday night, the end of a 70-hour week. How awkward if the Board and the Management Committee were to find out about this now, he thought, and how lucky he was that they wouldn't. He disposed of the threat in his personal shredder and turned off the lights. This week had been longer than usual, in preparation for the Board meeting tomorrow. He had done all he could to ensure that his orchestration would be flawless, especially his blueprint for change, and that the Board would approve all his plans. Experience had taught him that the secret to getting his way was to ensure that there was a semblance of choice for the Board members, and he never resented the inordinate amount of work that this pretence required.

The Chief Executive Officer had spent the better part of four months designing his blueprint for the future, thinking about it, dreaming about it, and rehearsing the transformation in his mind – cataloguing all that would ensue from his vision. In one of his dreams, he was being presented with an international award for his market-driven initiatives. He was wearing a white tuxedo while waiting for the presentation, mildly content after several scotches. As he leaned over to receive the medal and ribbon around his neck, the master of ceremonies was replaced by his deceased mother, and she told him once again that museums were no place for someone with ambition and drive. He awoke instantly with a scathing sense of loss. He consoled himself with the fact that it was only a dream, and immediately longed for another one in which he would manipulate the outcome.

Some of his colleagues said that organizational change would take a year or more. One of his acquaintances, a dyspeptic thinker from Europe, told him that organizational change was a work in progress and would never be finished. This, too, he dismissed with the usual self-confidence and superiority that had characterized his progressively responsible museum career – from summer research assistant, to a law degree, to the manager of marketing, and then to assistant director – all in the span of seven years and all in different institutions. Never mind that he had been forced to leave his last job for grossly overspending an already fragile budget. Six months later he was a CEO, a new title for him, which heralded the steady march of marketplace ideology into museum board rooms. He liked the business talk and the business values; he found it easier than grappling with the perplexities of museum traditions. He also didn't have to read much, and his board commented approvingly when he used business words or ideas he had picked up in airline magazines.

The title of CEO caused him no anxiety or painful reflection. On the contrary, it was a source of comfort and strength, encapsulating as it did an unambiguous locus of authority that belonged to him alone. Although he never shared this with any of his colleagues, his title and position were also his rationale for limiting the discussion of his plans for change to his vice-presidents only. He wanted nothing to do with the expectations and imperfections which inevitably result when you ask people their opinions. Moreover, he thought happily to himself, why assemble a critical mass of opposition? This latter bit of wisdom came from one of his mentors, a former SAS paratrooper, and now a consultant to the World Bank. The CEO decided, however, to seek the blessing of a high profile director he had briefly met, in the rare event that the Board started asking difficult questions.

'Yes, of course, I will read your plan, she said over the telephone, 'but I need a week to do it. There's too much going on here right now. The Union wants 14 percent and we only have three.'

'I can't wait a week, but I'll call you back in three days. Okay?' the CEO said, clearly impatient with her answer.

She quickly sensed his irritation. 'All right, then, I'll do my best. Talk to you Friday night.'

***

'It's me. 'I'm calling back. Did you read it?' he asked.

'I did,' she said, 'and we have a lot to talk about. This is huge. How many months for Board and staff involvement in the thinking and planning?'

'None, actually. I need Board approval on Monday, with implementation to begin the following day. I have some high-priced consultants lined up and their meters are ticking. It's time to get on with it, and like I always say, there's no use in assembling a critical mass of opposition. The staff knows that major changes are in the works, and there's no way I am giving them any extra time to put the knife in my back.'

'What do you want from me, then?' she asked.

'Your endorsement. You know, your approval. I need it for credibility, and back-up, in case things heat up at the Board table. You've been through this before; you know what I mean.'

'Yea, I have, and that's why I can't do anything useful in three days. Your plan has no process in it, and may well blow up in your face. Someone said the other day that organizational change is a lot like nursing – it takes time and nurturing. You must have some kind of process. What is it?

'Thanks, anyway, but there isn't any. We don't have the time. I gotta run,' he said.

He hung up the phone and stood to acknowledge the silhouette in the darkened doorway, as two rounds from a 9mm Smith and Wesson tore open his heart.

The future

'Spaceship Earth now has 150 admirals. The five admirals in the staterooms immediately above the ship's fuel tanks claim that they own the oil. The admirals with the staterooms surrounding the ship's kitchen, dining rooms, and food refrigerators claim they own all the food. Those with a stateroom next to a lifeboat claim that they own the lifeboat, and so forth. They then have an onboard game called balance of trade. Very shortly the majority of admirals have a deficit balance. All the while the starboard-side admirals are secretly planning to list the boat to port far enough to drown the portside admirals, while the portside admirals are secretly trying to list the boat to starboard far enough to drown the starboard-side admirals. Nobody is paying any attention to operating the ship or steering it to some port. They run out of food and fuel. They discover that they can no longer reach a port of supply. Finis.' [5]

1

Museums and irrelevance

Troubling questions

The Prologue is both fact and fiction, real and apocryphal, and perhaps even a fanciful disservice to the museum world in the eyes of some. There are undoubtedly museum workers who have never encountered any of the characters in this Prologue. I am comfortable with any of these reactions, as the Prologue is intended to highlight some of the uncertainties and difficulties that now directly or indirectly confront museums and galleries, whether they are the fate of collections, the psycho-politics of complex organizations, or our nearly complete separation from the natural world. Of particular note is that these difficulties and uncertainties not only originate in the world at large but are also created by museums themselves. As a result, one must cultivate a respect for uncertainty, especially with respect to the current and future role of museums as social institutions.

By social institutions I mean those that are publicly owned, and thus owned by no one, and engage in activities that are normatively sanctioned. Museums have legislated acts or constitutions, boards of trustees, sources of finance other than shareholders, and are not properties that can be bought and sold.[1] I will argue that the majority of museums, as social institutions, have largely eschewed, on both moral and practical grounds, a broader commitment to the world in which they operate. Instead, they have allowed themselves to be held increasingly captive by the economic imperatives of the marketplace and their own internally-driven agendas. Whether or not they have done this unwittingly or knowingly is immaterial, as the consequences are the same. It is time for museums to examine their core assumptions.

In making this sweeping assessment, I am, of course, generalizing, and I accept this liability as the starting point for reconsidering the underlying purpose, meaning and value of museums. These questions are rarely, if ever, truthfully examined in the museum literature or thoughtfully discussed at museum conferences. On the contrary, museum practitioners and academics are seemingly preoccupied with method and process – getting better and better at what they are already doing well. Over thirty years as a museum practitioner and consultant have sensitized me to the importance of asking questions about the meaning and value of museum work. Admittedly, there is little comfort to be had in asking questions, if one heeds the words of John Ralston

Saul, the Canadian essayist. He wrote that 'to most questions there are many answers, none of them absolute and few of them satisfactory except in a limited way.'[2]

Nonetheless, there are some essential questions worth considering, such as – if museums did not exist, would we reinvent them and what would they look like? Further, if the museum were to be reinvented, what would be the public's role in the reinvented institution? It has been noted that 'the great challenge to our time is to harness research, invention and professional practice to deliberately embraced human values.' The fateful questions, according to scientist William Lowrance, are 'how the specialists will interact with citizens, and whether the performance can be imbued with wisdom, courage and vision.'[3] My main motivation in writing this book arises from the belief that none of the questions posed above have been articulated by the majority of museums, much less addressed by them, despite there being no more important questions than these for both museums and society at large.

The idea of rethinking the purpose of museums is also an oversimplification and perhaps a pretension – the latter in the sense that expanding the purpose of museums may or may not be achievable. The reader will be the judge of that. Revisiting the purpose of museums might also be seen as an exercise in individualism and a refusal to mind one's own business. With this comes a certain amount of risk, such as being seen as iconoclastic and overly critical. I concede that these outcomes are possible, which makes it incumbent upon me to be as fair-minded, constructive and as informed as I can be. The reader will also be the judge of that. I intend to be as analytical as possible, although a certain amount of adjuration is unavoidable, having retained my belief in the unrealized potential of museums as essential social institutions.

I have also chosen to address various challenges that mainstream museums are apparently unable or unwilling to consider. This task is made easier by the fact that there are some splendid examples of purposeful museums, which will be considered later in this book. My worry is that these exceptional organizations have not yet formed a critical mass sufficient to overcome the tyranny of tradition which weighs so heavily on their sister institutions. Interestingly, this tyranny is expressed both in the inertia of past practices and in the uncritical adoption of methods, models and practices from the world of commerce. Examining both of these enslavements is yet another purpose of this book.

I must also be clear about what museums I am referring to, as museums are a nearly universal phenomenon in the twenty-first century. The primary focus of this book is Canadian and American museums, with an obvious emphasis on Canada simply because of my work experience. I assume, however, that various parts of this book will ring true with non-North American practitioners, as museums everywhere share a common body of knowledge, theory and methods, as well as the intricacies, foibles and aspirations of organizational life. When this book doesn't make sense, I am hoping that the dissonance arising from the reader's unique experiences will provoke both comparison and assessment. Indeed, there may also be a sense of relief, or even privilege, for the non-North American reader as the difficulties confronting New World museums are examined. This is not meant to imply that New World museums are uncommonly weak or incompetent – I simply know more about them. The lack of a truly global perspective in this book reflects the limitations of the author and not the vibrancy and depth of the international museum community.

Where possible and appropriate, I will call upon the international museological literature and I concede at the outset that even this effort will be incomplete. There is important and innovative work under way in Europe and Latin America, for example, although of necessity I have focused on the English language literature.[4] In the final analysis, none of us can do more than write from our experience. 'My work is best,' wrote Wendell Berry, the American farmer, essayist and conservationist, '... when I talk as a person who's not an authority on anything but his own experience.'[5] The same is true of the observations in this book.

Sobering assumptions

As knowledge and experience are always laden with assumptions, it is best to make mine explicit now. My first assumption is that we, as human beings, are co-creators of our lives and our organizations if we accept the responsibility to do this. By extension, outside experts and consultants do not necessarily know the answers that an organization needs to solve its problems and improve.[6] A museum's board, staff and supporters are potentially the real experts on the organization and what is needed – the challenge is to unlock their tacit knowledge and put it to use. There is also an essential role for both unorthodox and non-museum perspectives and this is a valuable contribution that consultants can make. The tendency among museums, however, is to engage consultants to deal with demanding operational tasks, such as planning and organizational dysfunction, rather than as sources of new ideas and catalysts for change.

The reluctance to use consultants and knowledgeable outsiders to tap different, and perhaps contradictory, perspectives to stimulate internal rethinking may be the result of professional conceit or insecurity among senior staff, but the consequences are the same – the loss of untapped internal knowledge and creativity with which to build institutional renewal. The museum consulting business is flourishing, nonetheless, as evidenced by the 90 pages of text on the internet devoted to museum consulting in 2008. A significant portion of the current consulting work is devoted to the recent vanity architecture movement among museums, predicated on the resurrected axiom, 'If you build it, he will come.'[7] This critical topic will be discussed later, but I note here that the museum community may have overlooked some important wisdom in its haste to embrace the edifice complex. With apologies to Yogi Berra for recasting his baseball philosophy, 'if people don't want to come to your museum, you can't make them.'[8]

Museums are privileged

My second assumption is that museums and galleries are potentially the most free and creative work environments on the planet – but note the word 'potentially'. Having been challenged by colleagues because of the undisguised idealism of this

15

claim, I now qualify my enthusiasm. Nevertheless, the scope for creativity and initiative should be just about limitless in a well-run museum. There are very few other workplaces which offer more opportunities for thinking, choosing and acting in ways that can blend personal satisfaction and growth with organizational goals. These opportunities constitute the true privilege of museum work, and it is up to each museum worker to seize them.

Unlike the private sector, museums do not have production or sales quotas, although the current imposition of quantitative measures is certainly moving museums in that direction. Nonetheless, they are still relatively immune to the tyranny of production that marks the private sector. In contrast to the public sector, museums are not forced to administer unpopular government policies. In fact, some museums are now being called upon by government to implement progressive social policies, such as in the United Kingdom, where publicly funded museums, galleries and archives are expected to play a part in the combating of social exclusion.[9] In short, museums have led a privileged existence as agenda-free and respected custodians of mainstream cultural values – not ever truly wealthy, but mostly comfortable, and certainly not beholden to the incessant demands of the so-called real world. Not until recently, that is – the pressure is mounting.

Most importantly, museums are privileged because they are organizations whose purpose is their meaning.[10] This elegant observation suggests that any activity unaligned with organizational purpose could jeopardize the meaning. A growing lack of alignment is now creating enduring difficulties for many museums, whether or not they are aware of them. In particular, the failure to ask 'why' museums do what they do discourages self-critical reflection, which is a prerequisite to heightened awareness, organizational alignment and social relevance. Instead, in the absence of 'why', the focus is largely on the 'how', or the clichéd processes of collecting, preserving and earning revenue – the latter being the cause of much of the organizational drifting characteristic of many contemporary museums.

If an exhibit gallery closes during public hours in order to accommodate a private wedding and increase earned revenue, is this museum adrift without a home port? Recalling Fuller's vignette in the Prologue, the admirals on the board of directors may all agree on this course, but what or who is steering the ship? All of which brings me back to the qualifier underlying my second assumption – the museum's 'potential' to be the most free and creative work environment on the planet. This potential will remain unfulfilled as long as mission statements fail to answer the question of 'why', and museums continue to accept the host of unnecessary and self-inflicted challenges which are the subject of the next chapter.

Learning means questioning

My third assumption reflects the widespread assertion in our so-called knowledge economy that learning is essential to intelligent and caring change. Much of this appears to be rhetoric, as corporations outsource jobs to sweatshop labour and universities favour techno-scientific initiatives at the expense of those less glamorous disciplines that are committed to critical thinking – the liberal arts, for example. Sweatshops and techno-science are obviously mainstays of hyper-capitalism, but one is hard pressed to see them as commitments to intelligent foresight since they are firmly anchored in the status quo.

More to the point, and one which apparently escapes many who tout its importance, is that learning requires that we ask difficult and uncomfortable questions of ourselves and others. The unwillingness or inability to ask these questions is characteristic of individuals and organizations with a vested interest in the status quo – an obvious explanation for the lack of self-critical and innovative leadership on the part of big business, government and universities. Are any of these massive organizations actually leading the way to a sustainable future, once the magazine advertisements and the election speeches are unmasked? My assumption about learning is grounded in the idea of self-critical and reflective thought, a task which has become an essential survival skill for those organizations and individuals who wish to learn.[11] I will ask a variety of uncomfortable, perhaps annoying, questions throughout this book, along with critical observations on all manner of things related to museums. I will be dismayed if the reader sees these as only gratuitous attacks, and heartened if they are seen as invitations for learning and reflection.

The future is not knowable

My fourth assumption requires a brief foray into the future, still a rare topic for museums to contemplate. This is understandable for institutions whose focus is on the past, but it is also slightly schizophrenic, as museums rush to install the latest technological wizardry or attach whimsical architectural appendages to their buildings. Nonetheless, the future requires some serious reflection precisely because it is not knowable. Irrespective of all the futurists and the pundits, the future is not knowable because the links between cause and effect in organizations are complex and mostly lost in the detail of what actually happens in between.[12] Interestingly, examining the consequences of this insight unlocks the possibilities of the future, for one simple reason. If museum staff and boards cannot know where their museums are going because the future is unknowable, then they should not all believe in the same things. They should question everything, and generate new perspectives through discussion, debate and dialogue.

I am not claiming that there is no disagreement within museums, or that staff and boards are in accord on most issues. The conflict between museum staff and their boards is alive and well, and the anecdotes are always fresh and encyclopaedic. I note, however, that tradition and orthodoxy still prevail and that innovation is at a premium in the museum world. It is only through confronting convention that museums will be able to create, invent and discover their futures as they go – the true hallmarks of an innovative organization.[13]

Museums cannot be replaced

I must acknowledge Neil Postman, the iconoclastic academic and essayist, for the substance of my fifth and final assumption, which is that the purpose of all competent museums is to provide answers to a fundamental question, 'What does it mean to be a human being?'[14] At their very best, museums present the richness and diversity of life, and keep reflection and dialogue alive for their visitors. Governments are not equipped to do this, business is committed to homogenization and efficiency in the name of profit, and most universities are still grappling with their real and perceived separation from their communities.

Churches should not be dismissed as a possibility, but it is increasingly difficult to grasp how a commitment to contemporary monotheism will allow the tolerance and understanding that social cohesion and cooperation require. In fact, Christian fundamentalists in the United States claim that they are engaged in the latest, perhaps the last, instalment of the Crusades in the Middle East, which will see total victory over the Muslims.[15] In combination with other causes championed by organized religion, such as anti-abortion, homophobia and the exclusion of women, the ideology of mainstream religions casts serious doubt on their capacity to steward the tolerance and intercultural understanding demanded by the complex difficulties of the contemporary world.

This leaves museums with the obligation to probe our humanness and, in assuming this responsibility, museums are unique and valuable social institutions that have no suitable replacement. In short, museums are dissimilar to all of the institutions noted above and therein lies their great worth. My idealism ends here, however, as the presentation of diversity and the nurturing of reflection are unrealized opportunities for most museums. Instead, museums are using existing mental maps while they drift onto the shoals of unthinking imitation, repetition and excess. An alternative view might see museums as all about empowerment, trying to enable people to participate in making decisions in our so-called participatory democracy.[16]

This is a radical alternative, indeed, but one that merits close scrutiny at a time when our collective passivity seems to be at an all-time high, whether it is low voter turnout in Canada or the amount of television viewing in the United States. Recent research reveals that the television is on for a total of 6 hours and 47 minutes per day in the average US home, with two-thirds of those households having three or more television sets.[17] Garrison Keillor, the American radio personality, expressed his disdain by noting that 'You can learn more about life drinking gin straight from the bottle, than you can by watching T.V.'[18] One of my colleagues noted that she likes to drink gin while watching TV and she asked me if that makes her a lost cause. I don't think so, but there are definitely alternatives to watching television.

To conclude this discussion of my assumptions about the value and meaning of museums, I will risk repeating a large, but useful, generalization – that is, the world can be divided into two types of people, the performer and the learner.[19] Performers are unwilling to attempt to accomplish anything that might fail, and thus limit their experience of growing beyond their current capacities. This might be the museum director with 20 years of experience: the same year repeated 20 times. Learners, on the other hand, develop the capacity to grow beyond their present abilities. To learners, perfect performance is not an issue, the final results are. It has been said that 'if something is worth doing, it's worth doing poorly until you can do it well.'[20] Learners take risks and use moments of failure and disappointment to become more competent. It is difficult to imagine a greater contrast with the contemporary museum mindset, as museums are inveterate performers.

It is also too early to tell if museums are able or willing to become learners on a sufficient scale to avoid irrelevance or decline, and embrace renewal. With permanent exhibits requiring years to complete, an obsessive fear of deaccessioning collections, and the absence of research and development funding in museum budgets for nurturing experimentation and risk-taking, it is difficult to be sanguine about a bright future replete with museum learners. There are untold possibilities, as well as abundant rewards, but learning to learn requires both a change of heart and expanded consciousness. Museums, irrespective of their size or subject matter, have the freedom and opportunity to reflect on their habitual performance, and to consider other options that have more to do with change and growth in a nonmaterial sense.

Uncertainty, elitism and myopia

In exploring the best and worst of contemporary museum practice, I have no intention of judging the conduct or commitment of individual museum workers. I ask the reader to recognize that there is an underlying paradox at work here, and resist the urge to dismiss many of my observations as judgemental. The paradox I am referring to is the widespread disconnection between individuals who work in a museum and the manner in which the museum functions as an organization. Individual staff members can be insightful and innovative, yet these qualities may never be translated into institutional reality. With this in mind, my purpose is not to challenge the commitment of any museum worker, especially in light of the multifarious and often contradictory requirements of museum work. These challenges include notoriously low salaries, high professional standards, and governing authorities who lack relevant expertise, not to mention fickle funding agencies that encourage mission drift through their insistence upon short-term, project funding.

Although my assessment of museums is both reasonable and rational from my perspective, the reader may see this as an attack on well-intentioned and accomplished individuals and organizations. I concede that my perspective is controversial and that there are those who would dismiss my concerns out of hand. There are also those who share these worries, yet are bound to traditional practices. There are also those who share these concerns, but who vigorously dispute how they should be addressed. My intention is not to dismiss the past or present contributions of museum workers and their museums, as reality in the museum world is complex.

I hope to respect this complexity with discretion and thoroughness, and contribute to a better understanding of the challenges confronting the museum community, rather than be seen to be condemning that community. That is not my purpose, and there is nothing to be gained by criticizing traditional museum practices without offering some constructive alternatives. Doing this requires a certain amount of idealism, grounded in the belief that if individuals do not have any ideal of a better world, then they have lost something and humanity is a diminished species.[21] Anecdotes and examples are key ingredients throughout this book, but in situations which might prove to be embarrassing or regrettable, the salient identifiers have been eliminated to protect both the innocent and the guilty.

Uncertainty

Even a brief exploration of contemporary museum practice reveals a range of issues and topics that can bewilder, and even stun, the most seasoned museum workers, causing them to wonder if things are out of control, what will be next, and how they can cope with all of this. The status quo has indeed become challenging, and it is double-edged. At the same time that the status quo allows the bulk of museums to remain immune from the pressing issues of our day – avoiding involvement in the guise of moral and intellectual neutrality – it has also created a highly stressful work environment driven by numbers and measured by consumption. Neither of these realities point the way to long-term sustainability, and I am compelled to challenge the dualistic and reductive thinking that underlies both of these conditions. The result is a widespread myopia, shared by practitioners, academics, professional organizations and government alike, that is undermining the real and potential value of museum work.

Museums have inadvertently arrived at a metaphorical watershed where it is now imperative to ask broader questions about why museums do what they do, to confront a variety of admittedly unruly issues, and to forge some new choices. This metaphorical watershed is not unlike Peter Drucker's concept of a 'divide.' In his words, 'Within a few short decades society rearranges itself – its worldview; its basic values; its social and political structure; its arts; its key institutions. Fifty years later, there is a new world.'[22] Drucker notes that we are currently living through the transformation to a post-capitalist society, with knowledge being the real and controlling resource, not capital, land or labour.

Thinking about what this post-capitalist, societal transformation might mean for museums, as knowledge-based institutions, may be seen as navel-gazing, that popular and ambiguous accusation which emerges at all kinds of museum gatherings, be they small staff meetings or national conferences. Levelling this criticism among museum workers is usually sufficient to quell any further reflection, irrespective of whether the speaker is considering change or stasis. The message is clear – 'Let's not talk about this, we don't have time;' 'It's time to get on with the work.' Or, 'We know what to do; what's the sense in talking about it.' Many of us have felt the sharp edge of this peer pressure, which is not unlike the manipulation found among codependent families and partners who deny an illness or addiction. It is immaterial if the symbolic watershed mentioned above is navel-gazing or not, as its value lies in the opportunity it presents to reflect, grow and act.

Nor have I set out to support or disclaim a particular theory, as the meaning of social engagement for museums is not only deep, varied and untested but it is also too unwieldy to be subsumed under a particular intellectual model. This potential variability is akin to the concept of the biosphere, where the diversity of life is the key to ecological health. So should it be with museums, where individual and organizational approaches to social relevance can be as diverse as the communities which spawned the museums themselves. Although this book lacks a theoretical stance, I have drawn on various theoretical perspectives as both stimuli and counterpoints to my own thinking, including modernism, postmodernism, positivism and materialism. While theory plays an important role in any well-reasoned proposition, my bias is toward practicality. I will be grateful if the same is said of this book.

If the thesis of this book can be said to reflect any particular aspect of modern thought, it would be in the realm of the civil society, or the so-called public sphere. Simply put, the civil society is that part of society lying between the private sphere of the family and the official sphere of the state, and refers to the array of voluntary and civic associations, such as trade unions, religious organizations, cultural and educational bodies, that are to be found in modern, liberal societies. Museums belong in this sphere, yet have received little or no attention as fundamental agents in advancing the collective good, other than in the realms of education and entertainment.[23]

Elitism

I note that there has been some recognition of museums as civil society organizations, but the recent use of the concept is limited in its vision. In a recent paper by Gail Lord, co-founder of Lord Cultural Resources (the world's largest museum consulting firm), civil society is defined as 'an idea of community in which citizens enjoy equal opportunity to participate in public life and culture.'[24] This definition is a useful starting point, but its generality obscures the responsibility of civil society organizations to purposefully craft missions that enable participation in public life, well beyond the passive cultural consumption of architectural space. Rather, the onus is on museums to assist in creating the idea of community that will enable citizen participation. I agree that Lord's definition of civil society is useful in promoting the construction of new museum buildings but, ironically, it is a matter of record that museums know little or nothing about equal access or opportunity. The majority of the world's museums still cater to society's elite – the most educated and most well-off of our citizenry – an obstinate characteristic of museums that continues, albeit unfairly at times, to undermine the public perception and value of museums.[25]

This reputation for elitism unavoidably leads to further speculation about the role of museums in our increasingly stratified society. It is a matter of record that governments, notably in the West, are increasingly influenced by a small and powerful corporate elite (multinational oil corporations, pharmaceutical companies, the arms industry, industrial food conglomerates and so forth) with a vested interest in defining and maintaining the status quo.[26] These corporations use ostensibly benign instruments such as the North American Free Trade Agreement and the World Trade Organization to garner privilege, while espousing the superiority of so-called free-market capitalism. It is also common knowledge that museums acquire support from these corporations – giving them both public profile and credibility in the process. Indeed, the success of raising corporate sponsorships is now a path to distinction for many museum executives and creates enormous bragging rights for the successful. What's more, the high salaries commanded by fundraising and marketing executives are continuing to distort museum salary grids, while further stressing beleaguered budgets.

Myopia

It is no longer sensible simply to ignore the web of these relationships by claiming some sort of benighted status for museums as innocent beneficiaries. Can we not expect more deliberate reflection from museums about their societal role – as organizations that pride themselves on their historical acuity and their objective frame of reference? Is it sufficient to accept that raising money is now the *sine qua non* of museum leadership, and that all else must assume lesser importance? I will argue throughout this book that, although fundraising must remain a core responsibility of any competent museum, it is maladaptive to do so unless the effort is accompanied by a heightened awareness of its implications for museums as civil society organizations. There is also no doubt that the time and energy spent in relentlessly seeking more money from the denizens of economic privilege could be more profitably spent in designing a sustainable future for museums.

I recall speaking at a museum conference in Grenoble, France in 1994 on new approaches to museum management, where I listened to an afternoon discussion on the implications of corporate funding for museums. I silently derided the collective anxiety about accepting corporate funding, as I had already embraced the purported largesse of the private sector in the face of declining government support for Canadian museums. I was both directed and assisted by our corporate board members, all of whom were quick to note that less government is better government. I, like so many other directors, eventually grew weary and despondent with the unrelenting focus on the financial bottom line. I willingly concede that I learned much in the process, although I remain embarrassed by my unthinking reaction to those uncommonly prescient deliberations in France.

In short, the discussion of museums as true agents of the civil society must be deepened, in a manner which transcends vanity architecture, attendance and consumption. Museums have the opportunity to honour the trust and respect that the public affords them, in part by engaging in the interests and aspirations of their communities – irrespective of how seemingly remote these issues may now appear to museums. There is certain urgency in doing so, as many of the structures and organizations that we have been accustomed to are now altered by the sheer force of the economy in which we live. Whether government, universities, newspapers or social assistance programs, these organizations and institutions are not what they used to be, and there is ambiguity and anxiety about our individual and collective existence. The future of all these organizations is 'obscure', to quote the British historian, Eric Hobsbawm.[27]

It is even more incumbent upon museums, as social institutions, to navigate thought-fully through this madcap realm of hyper-capitalism, globalism and branding, in order to ensure that the best interests of museums and the communities they serve are not subsumed under the mantle of culture as consumption and corporatism. At the same time, new concepts such as social marketing are emerging, which are intended to channel corporate wealth to enhance social good. Despite these initiatives and the good practices to be discussed later, museums must not lose sight of the age-old adage – *caveat emptor.*

Although I have no theory to espouse, other than an abiding interest in social capital and the civil society, I also intend to debunk the imposition of free market ideology on the museum sector. I will do so by interpreting a collection of empirical observations and data based on my professional experience, the literature, and my belief that it is incumbent upon us to question ourselves about where the future is leading – all in an effort to demonstrate that museums have far greater value than is currently being realized. My approach most closely resembles the pattern model of explanation.[28] Explanation, within the structure of this model, consists of establishing or discovering relations. In seeking these patterns and relationships, I will venture beyond the dialectic, where social forces and concepts are seen to be in opposition – i.e. earned revenues are good; museum research is bad. Again, the complex reality of museum practice is simply immune to this sort of facile thinking. Perhaps a more useful synthesis can be forged from the collision of traditional museum practices and those museum initiatives that have gone beyond the safety of the status quo.

Uncertainty again

In an attempt to make some sense of the complex and changing world of museum practice, I will also be engaging in an activity which has remained unnamed for me until recently – 'intellectual activism'. This is defined in *The Independent Scholar's Handbook* as activities which do not necessarily create new knowledge, but make existing knowledge more accessible, understandable and useful to others.[29] Perhaps most importantly, intellectual activism creates the conditions for fresh discoveries through the conjunction of challenging ideas, or stimulates others to discover. These activities can range from speaking to audiences other than one's peers, to applying knowledge through consulting, or to bringing scholarly work to a wider public.

In distilling this book to its essentials, there is nothing particularly original about it. I note this with composure, as I believe that there is much to be done with what we already know, rather than striving for originality for its own sake. If this book has any value, it is in the attempt to identify and examine seemingly peripheral issues and insights with the purpose of raising the consciousness of individual museum practitioners and their organizations. Although the collective perspective of the museum community is dangerously narrow at this point in history, many of these limitations are self-imposed, as some institutions have already discovered.

Having left the organizational life of museums nearly a decade ago to make my way as an independent consultant, editor and volunteer, I am not as institutionalized as I once was. In the words of Hazel Henderson, the evolutionary economist, I am now 'unschooled and unchurched.'[30] The lack of the filtering devices that normally color the perceptions of people who work in organizations is a distinct advantage and an opportunity to address the unmet potential of museums. I am also mindful of the words of Karen Kaiser Clark. She noted, with forceful and atypical brevity for a politician, that 'life is change; growth is optional; choose wisely.' Yet, even if some degree of greater understanding is achieved in the course of this book, the task will never be finished. The American author, the late Frank Conroy, said it best when he noted that understanding does not always mean resolution. He wrote that 'in our intellectual lives, our creative lives, it is perhaps those problems that we will never resolve that rightly claim the lion's share of our energies.'[31]

This book, then, is both a work in progress and a goad to action, which begins with a fanciful prologue and an initial inquiry into the presumed irrelevance of museums, guided by some troubling questions and my own assumptions as a museum worker. This sets the stage for the next chapter – a summary look at our increasingly dysfunctional world, with an emphasis on selected issues that mirror both the civic responsibilities and intellectual legacy of most museums. In addition to these societal and global issues, museums have created a host of internal challenges that serve to forestall or inhibit active engagement beyond conventional practices. The most powerful of these self-inflicted challenges are identified and examined in an effort to refute their putative value.

One unique challenge (which is both internal and external) is the rise of marketplace ideology and museum corporatism, whose uncritical acceptance by museum practitioners has created a Frankensteinian phenomenon that is unravelling or enfeebling a host of otherwise competent museums. The scope of this trend and its implications for the museum community require their own chapter. Lest the reader lose all interest or hope in the eye of this gathering storm, the next chapter attends to those museums and projects that demonstrate the true meaning of social responsibility and civic engagement – to wit, relevance matched with inspiration. Innovation and creativity are rife in these examples, but only in a relative sense, as these stellar examples stray far, and often radically, from mainstream museum practice.

This means that the museum enterprise has an inordinate amount of rethinking to do, and the penultimate chapter of this book is devoted to the characteristics of a new kind of museum – the mindful museum. This hypothetical museum is offered as an alternative to the declining era of museum privilege. By privilege I mean that paradoxical mixture of societal respect and indifference which has allowed museums to stand sedately on the sidelines in the service of their own self-interests or societal elites. The decline in privilege is inevitable for the unprecedented reason that various social, economic and environmental issues have now transformed into a critical mass that can no longer be ignored by government, corporatists and citizens. In comparison, no such urgency attaches to the purpose and goals of the vast majority of museums, despite the fact that the status quo for museums is arguably even more brittle and beleaguered than it is for society at large.

It is puzzling that the slippery slope of irrelevance remains unacknowledged by all but a handful of practitioners and critics. Concealed in this admittedly gloomy scenario, however, are opportunities with the potential to actually enhance or secure long-term sustainability for museums. Breaking the mould of societal privilege will require exploration, experimentation and innovation – initiatives that are seen by most museums, if at all, as the purview of scientific agencies, business and the universities. One need only look at the conference programs of most museum associations, with their continual reiteration of the familiar, to confirm that it is largely business as usual. Appealing to the diverse range of member institutions is the standard rationalization for this lack of discernment, which is akin to saying that the lowest common denominator is sufficient justification for a professional organization. In short, the future for museums is going to have to be invented, with courage and with difficulty.

An ecology of museums

This book is more about the forest than the trees, although a variety of individual species of museums will be examined for the lessons and clues they provide for moving beyond the familiar. An ecological metaphor is useful here, as ecology is about the relationships between organisms and their environments – dependent, independent and interdependent relationships. Museums have predicated their survival on being both dependent (for all forms of sustenance) and independent, as exemplified by commonplace comments such as 'give us the money; we know what to do' or 'how dare you measure our performance.' In the process of overlooking the meaning of interdependence, museums have contributed greatly to their own marginalization. It is time to forge an ecology of museums that recognizes that a broad web of societal relationships is the bedrock of successful adaptation in a complex, and increasingly severe, world. The Willow Lake hunters, described in the Prologue, are modern exemplars of this knowledge, having prospered for millennia in one of the world's harshest regions.

The lack of interdependent relationships among most museums is an increasing liability, and being valued for ancillary educational offerings and often ersatz entertainment is no longer sufficient to ensure intelligent sustainability. There are alternatives to the familiar, and the search is well under way by a coterie of individuals and museums who are not taking the future for granted. The last chapter will consider the implications of the failure to act, including the possibilities of increasing irrelevance and possible collapse. Six fundamental reasons are also offered for why museums can, and must, transform.

As some of the most conservative institutions in contemporary society, many museums will be unwilling or unable to grasp the import and necessity of rethinking their current successes and failures. This is not a bad thing, for the disappearance of myopic museums may well be beneficial, as the public and private resources allocated to museums diminish. There may, in fact, be too many museums, even now. However, this is not about the survival of the fittest, but about choosing renewal over decline. It is hoped that this book might help point the way.

2

A troubled world

The absence of stewardship

It is common knowledge that the planet earth and global civilization now confront a constellation of issues that threatens the very existence of both. These issues range from climate change to the inevitability of depleted fossil fuels, not to mention the bewildering array of local concerns pertaining to the health and well-being of myriad communities the world over. There is nothing new about these challenges and there is a burgeoning literature which offers dire warnings and solutions for their resolution.[1] Surprisingly, museums are rarely, if ever, discussed in these books, causing me to conclude that the irrelevance of museums as social institutions is a matter of record.

Accounting for the origin and meaning of this seeming irrelevance requires a consideration of the larger social and environmental contexts. The challenge is to do this with both economy and depth, as a multitude of facts, figures, warnings and alarmism confronts us daily. Indeed, to be unaware of the current threats to our future as a species would be a singular achievement in denial, although, admittedly, none of us would survive without tuning out the lion's share of this relentless barrage. Persistent denial obviously has some short-term adaptive value, but it now threatens our collective future. In combination with the superficiality of market-driven journalism, the steady release of alarming scientific assessments on the state of the world, and the 700 to 3,000 advertisements the average person must confront every day – it is miraculous that there is any motivation at all for self-reflection and appropriate action.[2] From all indications, there is a lack of both in the world of museums.

Of necessity, I will not attempt to catalogue the world's woes but will focus instead on the need for heightened stewardship in several selected areas. Stewardship has been the *sine qua non* of the museum enterprise from its inception, and this commitment to stewardship lies at the heart of every permanent collection. There is no doubt that museums have excelled at this form of stewardship, and no one would dispute that there would be little or no material record of our mortal existence without the custodianship of museums. The idea of stewardship should provide a clear and comfortable resonance with museum workers, although its contemporary expression must move beyond the museum's preoccupation with its permanent collection. Stewardship has

Figure 3 Hiker at the Great Divide in the Rocky Mountains, Alberta, Canada, 2007.

Photo: courtesy of Robert R. Janes

a profoundly broader meaning which, for a variety of reasons that will be examined in this book, seems to have escaped the attention of mainstream museums.

For the purposes of this book, stewardship means to assume personal and organizational responsibility for the long-term care of public resources. Underlying my particular choice of words is Eric Hoffer's observation that 'the test of a civilization is in its capacity for maintenance.'[3] Most succinctly, stewardship means 'simply the care of something that doesn't belong to you.'[4] Care, maintenance, individual and collective responsibility are interchangeable from this perspective, and all of them constitute stewardship. The salient question for museums is whether they can transcend their commitment to the stewardship of collections and embrace broader societal issues?

The idea of stewardship is not without controversy. On one side, various humanists, spiritualists and environmentalists assume that they are the superior species in a Great Chain of Being, with stewardship over lower life forms and the earth itself. Deep ecologists, by contrast, do not make such value judgements.[5] In effect, deep ecology rejects the view that people should assume stewardship over other life forms and the earth, and prefers to let nature take its course. Although I make no claim for the superiority of our species, that's where my understanding of deep ecology begins and ends. Superior or not, *Homo sapiens* has now jeopardized the biosphere to the extent that we must now mitigate our very presence by assuming more responsibility for our individual and collective behaviour. To embrace the critique of deep ecology – that there is no basis for environmental policy because humans are the result of the accidental draw of the genetic lottery – imposes an irresponsible passivity that serves neither our species nor the planet.

The need for heightened stewardship is imperative, as most of us tacitly know, and museums are a unique and essential resource in this undertaking. Where there is no obvious relationship between museums and the broader societal issues concerning stewardship, perhaps it is time for museums to consider 'how the specialists will interact with citizens, and whether the performance can be imbued with wisdom, courage and vision.'[6] Before considering the specialists, the citizens and the performance, however, it is time to consider that much abused world we live in – beyond the walls of the museum.

A troubled world

It is useful to begin with a bird's-eye view of our global predicament, as the generality of this overview will ease the reader into a more compelling look at the assault on stewardship that pervades both our individual and organizational lives. To introduce this predicament, I can do no better than turn to Ronald Wright, the Canadian novelist and historian, who wrote with reference to our civilization that 'The vessel we are now aboard is not merely the biggest of all time; it is also the only one left. The future of everything we have accomplished since our intelligence evolved will depend on the wisdom of our actions over the next few years.'[7]

A litany of stressors

Thomas Homer-Dixon, the Canadian author and political scientist, has looked broadly and deeply at our civilization, as well as the medium of our journey – the earth – and has identified various global pressures that he calls the 'five tectonic stresses that are accumulating deep underneath the surface of our societies.'[8] He has organized them into five broad categories, including:

1   Population stress arising from differences in the population growth rates between rich and poor societies, and from the spiralling growth of mega-cities in poor countries;
2   Energy stress – above all, from the increasing scarcity of conventional oil;
3   Environmental stress from worsening damage to our land, water, forests and fisheries;
4   Climate stress from changes in the makeup of our atmosphere;
5   Economic stress resulting from instabilities in the global economic system and ever-widening income gaps between the rich and the poor.

Another view of global reality, created by the Copenhagen Consensus Center (CCC), offers more detail on our global afflictions, including a pragmatic dimension. The idea behind the formation of the CCC (under the auspices of the Copenhagen Business School) was to improve the prioritization of the numerous problems the world faces by gathering together renowned economists to assess some of the biggest challenges. There is a certain irony in this approach, recognizing that traditional economics, with its fixation on growth and no cost accounting, is one of society's biggest obstacles to rethinking the status quo. This will be discussed later, but I will reinforce this sentiment now by noting that economics has been called a pseudoscience and a form of brain damage.[9]

Nonetheless, the CCC uses expert panels, not only to rank the opportunities that would address the global challenges but also to produce a prioritized list of the opportunities to meet the biggest challenges. In short, the CCC analyses the world's greatest challenges and identifies cost efficient solutions by establishing a framework in which solutions to problems are prioritized according to efficiency based on economics and scientific analysis. In 2007, the CCC did another global ranking, which is summarized below in an effort to provide the reader with a more detailed view of the world's woes to complement Homer-Dixon's five tectonic stresses.[10]

The Copenhagen Consensus Center's Global Ranking

THE TOP THREE PROBLEMS

1   Unsafe water and a lack of sanitation
2   Hunger and malnutrition
3   Lack of education

OTHER PROBLEMS

4   Diseases
5   Corruption
6   Deforestation
7   Conflicts
8   Land degradation
9   Subsidies and trade barriers
10 Air pollution
11 Population: migration
12 Vulnerability to natural disasters
13 Terrorism
14 Financial instability
15 Climate change
16 Living conditions of women
17 Living conditions of children
18 Loss of biodiversity
19 Arms proliferation
20 Money laundering

THE BOTTOM THREE PROBLEMS

21 Drugs
22 Lack of people of working age
23 Lack of intellectual property rights

As mentioned above, the CCC approach is based on the assumption that when financial resources are limited, the work must be prioritized. Further, the CCC contends that instead of being based on facts, science and calculations, decisions are often made for political motives or the possibility of media coverage. Alternatively, the CCC commissions expert papers and presentations on the challenges and opportunities for action, which are then examined and ordered into rankings. The CCC ranking is somewhat surprising, and far less integrative than Homer-Dixon's broad sweep of the issues noted above. In contrast to Homer-Dixon's overview, the CCC ranks climate change as #15, while population stress does not make the top ten, and energy stress resulting from the increasing scarcity of conventional oil does not even appear on the CCC's list. It is difficult to understand this latter omission, as the price of oil exceeded US$140 per barrel at the time of writing.

Retreat to the temple

In the end, these distinctions make little difference, however, as most of these problems are ultimately interrelated and many of them are a result of our troubled and failing relationship with nature. But where is one to begin in arguing for the potential relevance of museums, given this maelstrom of issues, challenges and human suffering that stultifies our good intentions and our will to act? Many of these issues are germane to museums; others are not, and one must concede that hunger, sanitation, arms proliferation and money laundering are beyond the mandates and capabilities of museums as we know them. There is no doubt, however, that museums are capable of raising awareness about these issues. Recognizing that it is impossible for museums to address these particular issues directly, as well as many others, it is tempting to dismiss all of these problems as irrelevant or immune to the museum's *Weltanschauung*.

This temptation has proven to be irresistible, as the majority of museums have apparently elected to remain remote from the disorder and demands of daily life on this planet, despite their privileged position in society. I attribute this aloofness to an unexamined or unwitting adherence to the museum as 'temple, not forum' – that misunderstood duality first articulated in a seminal paper by the late Duncan Cameron, the noted Canadian museologist.[11] In 1971, Cameron wrote that museums were in desperate need of psychotherapy, as they were unable to resolve their problems of role definition. In clear and compelling language, Cameron called for the creation of forums for confrontation, experimentation and debate, in contrast to the temple or traditional museum. These forums are related to the traditional museum, which he also valued, but different. Although he debated whether or not the forum and the museum should be housed in the same structure, there was no ambiguity in his understanding of the need for the forum. Cameron wrote:

At the same time, and with a sense of urgency, the forums must be created, unfettered by convention and established values. The objective here is neither to neutralize nor to contain that which questions the established order. It is to ensure that the new and challenging perceptions of reality – the new values and their expressions – can be seen and heard by all. To ignore or suppress the innovation or the proposal for change is as mindless as to accept that which is new because it is novel.[12]

It appears that we have done a disservice to Cameron's prescient wake-up call, as he was clearly calling for the creation of socially relevant institutions alongside, and in conjunction with, the temple or traditional museum. Instead, we have indulged our predilection for either/or thinking, whether by design or disinterest, and perpetuated a dichotomy where practitioners choose the forum or the temple. Despite the rhetoric about engaging the community, and with few exceptions, museums have resoundingly chosen the temple and enshrouded themselves in the comfortable weight of tradition. In reality, the temple and the forum are two sides of the same coin, and quietly ignoring the importance of the forum is an invitation to irrelevance.

The individual and the organization

We have a preponderance of temples in the West – collecting, exhibiting and interpreting in keeping with their process-driven mission statements – but very few forums. There is no doubt that each of the societal issues outlined above is potentially crippling or overwhelming in its own right, which might help to explain why we have not only grown accustomed to the temple, but have also done so in the absence of any professional discussion to the contrary. While museum workers may have some interest in these issues, or have been impacted by them, this awareness rarely transcends the boundary between one's personal life and the life of the organization. This disconnection between the individual and the organization is a growing liability as societal stressors cascade, causing one to question how much longer these two solitudes can persist. Happily, more and more museums are becoming aware of the undeniable linkage between the private person and the museum worker, as evidenced by the growing popularity of identifying values as part of strategic planning.

Values are essential and enduring beliefs that articulate how a museum will conduct itself, as well as how it wants to be treated and how it will treat others. These values can range from teamwork and collaboration, to freedom and responsibility, to environmental stewardship, and everything in between. In short, the greater the congruence between individual and organizational values, the stronger the organization. As Gareth Morgan, the management scholar, noted, 'Organizations end up being what they think and say, as their ideas and visions realize themselves.'[13] Perhaps a more accurate observation is that 'museums end up being what they do *not* think or say.' Given a healthy congruence between individual and institutional values, there would be little need to ponder the relevance of museums. In fact, the congruence between individual and organizational values remains elusive in the museum world.

Whether one synthesizes the collective challenges, in the manner of Homer-Dixon, or segregates them as the CCC does, there are numerous issues that can no longer be ignored by museums as social institutions. In making the case for socially responsible museums, I now want to examine consumption, biodiversity and the plight of indigenous peoples, all of which are directly relatable to the privileged purview of museums. The earlier bird's-eye view of our global condition will now assume a finer focus, albeit in summary form, given the breadth and depth of each of these topics. My intention is to provide a glimpse of the enormity of these challenges as an incentive to contemplate the possible roles and responsibilities of mainstream museums.

Our lethal footprint

Every day, the world's population is witness to the worsening damage to our land, water and forests (the #3 tectonic stress in the Homer-Dixon list above), the consequences of which have been researched and packaged into an elegant, albeit dire, indicator known as the Ecological Footprint (EF). Incidentally, there is a powerful and parallel lesson for the global museum community in this, for the EF stands in stark contrast to our collective failure to develop a consensus on qualitative indicators of museum performance and value. By default, the measures of museum performance are now largely quantitative and market-driven.

Invented in Canada by a graduate student and a professor in the School of Community and Regional Planning at the University of British Columbia, the Ecological Footprint of a population is estimated by calculating how much land and water are required on a continuous basis to produce all the goods consumed, and to assimilate all the wastes generated by that population.[14] According to the authors, 'the strength of the EF analysis is its ability to communicate simply and graphically the general nature and magnitude of the biophysical connectedness between humankind and the ecosphere.' In short, the EF captures the essence of this relationship as manifested through consumption, something that none of us can escape. Incidentally, did you know that half the dogs in America received Christmas presents in 2006?[15]

Just how consumptive we have become merits some discussion, especially in a book about museums whose very purpose is preserving the panoply of our material culture. In 1998, the Pulitzer Prize-winning biologist, Edward O. Wilson, noted that the Ecological Footprint for each European, using existing technology, was 3.5 hectares (a hectare is 2.47 acres), for each American 5.0 hectares, and for each Canadian 4.3 hectares.[16] In most developing countries, the footprint is less than half a hectare per person. According to Wilson, to raise the whole world to the US level of consumption, with existing technology, would require two more planet Earths. If we fast-forward to 2007, there has been significant change, but the trend is decidedly in the wrong direction. On average, a Canadian's Ecological Footprint is now 7.6 hectares or approximately the size of 15 football fields. Only the United States and Australia have larger footprints at 10.3 and 9.0 hectares respectively.[17]

By comparison, the average person in India has a footprint of 0.8 hectares, almost 90 percent smaller than the average Canadian footprint. In the United Kingdom and Germany, average footprints are 5.2 and 5.3 hectares respectively, or about 32 percent smaller than ours. Overall, Europeans use about half as much energy per capita as Americans do and produce far less carbon.[18] In 2003, humanity's footprint exceeded the earth's biological capacity by over 25 percent, with analysts having estimated that our fair share of the earth's resources amounts to 2 hectares per person, or a footprint that is 75 percent smaller than the average Canadian Ecological Footprint.[19] It has also been noted that the more you work, the larger your EF, because you are spending more money and consuming more, rather than having the time to do less consumptive things like cooking at home.[20]

Uncontrollable consumption

It is useful to have a look at our voracious consumption in terms of objects, not only because this makes the Ecological Footprint less abstract, but also because objects are the encapsulation of meaning for museums. Bill McKibben, the farsighted American environmentalist, who wrote the first book on climate change for a general audience (it has been compared to Rachel Carson's *Silent Spring*), also has a deep-seated interest in consumption.[21] According to McKibben, our consumption finds its most complete expression in the *SkyMall* catalogue, available in the seatback pocket of every aircraft in North America. He concludes that we now have solutions to problems we never knew we had, as exemplified by the trouser rack that keeps twenty pairs neatly hung; the giant-capacity mailbox that holds up to two weeks of mail (catalogues, presumably); the ultraviolet toothbrush cleaner, and my hands-down favourite – the automatic watch-winder.[22] This device is for those who have a lot of watches, and it mimics the action of the human wrist, with intermittent timers and directional controls, to keep all of them fully wound at all times. Yes, seriously. McKibben's conclusion – we now have even run out of things that we might plausibly desire.[23] He suggests that insecticide-impregnated bed nets, to stop the spread of malaria, would be a more sensible purchase at five dollars each.

In light of this growing cornucopia of useless objects, one might wonder if the collecting of contemporary material culture is destined to implode. How does one assess the significance of an object in a culture that has managed to transform our adaptive genius as toolmakers into the unbridled production and consumption of unnecessary and increasingly ridiculous things? This curatorial challenge is better guided by a well-informed and critical perspective than by postmodern concepts of relativism in which the objective evaluation of competing points of view is impossible since all points of view are thought to be biased by race, gender and culture.[24] That these biases exist is no doubt true, but the danger in adopting a postmodern perspective in the museum world is the risk of eroding or rejecting values and critical thought in the name of relativism. Postmodernism has been called the culture of no resistance, and the intelligent stewardship of collections and communities demands resistance.[25] So does our biosphere.

The humour provided by McKibben's absurd objects rapidly dissipates when consumption is viewed globally, and in comparative terms, as illustrated in the following summary:[26]

Global consumption	*US$ billions*
Cosmetics in the United States	8
Ice cream in Europe	11
Perfumes in Europe and the United States	12
Pet foods in Europe and the United States	17
Business entertainment in Japan	35
Cigarettes in Europe	50
Alcoholic drinks in Europe	105
Narcotic drugs in the world	400
Military spending in the world	780

Global priorities	*US$ billions*
Basic education for all	6
Water and sanitation for all	9
Reproductive health for all women	12
Basic health and nutrition	13

A virtual impression

Clearly, these global priorities fall outside the purview of museums as social institutions, and nothing is to be gained by thinking that museums are accountable for either these startling expenditures or the unmet needs. Consumption occurs at many levels, however, including the individual, the family, the organization and the nation, and we do have control over our own consumption and that of our workplace. With this in mind, it is instructive to examine the role of the Ecological Footprint in the strategic thinking and organizational makeup of an unscientific sample of some mainstream museums. To do this, I surveyed eight of Canada's flagship institutions on the internet, including the four National Museums and four provincial museums that include both human and natural history in their mandates. I selected these government-owned institutions because they are the largest and best funded of Canadian museums, and are presumably capable of paying attention to issues which transcend immediate operational concerns. The results of my virtual tour are instructive and, although the sample is not representative or statistically valid, it does provide a glimpse of current thinking about socio-environmental issues in a slice of the Canadian museum community.

The National Museums

Starting with Canada's National Museums, I note that the Canadian Museum of Civilization (CMC), with its monumental architecture and record-setting attendance, makes no mention of the environment or sustainability in its strategic issues or guiding principles.[27] Nor is there any mention of the environment in their Risk Assessment. This is perhaps understandable, recognizing that 41 percent of the CMC's 2007/2008 operating budget is spent on building and accommodation costs.[28] Interestingly, this museum opened in 1989 and would not normally be considered an aging building, although it is claimed to be one in the CMC's *Summary of the Corporate Plan, 2007/2011*.[29] Reducing the Ecological Footprint of such a consumptive structure might be akin to the mouth-to-mouth resuscitation of a blue whale – the method is proven but the scale is overwhelming.

The National Gallery of Canada, 'one of the world's most respected art institutions, renowned for its exceptional collections, revered for its scholarship, and applauded for its unique ability to engage audiences'(according to their website), has no identifiable reference to the environment or sustainability in its 'Distinct Values', 'Key Objectives' or its 'Environmental Scan'.[30] The proverbial visitor from another planet, confined to the websites of these two prominent museums, would remain oblivious to the many socio-environmental issues that are currently besetting the nation. One might argue that this is as it should be, for what business does a human history museum and an art gallery have discussing our maladaptative species? More on this later, but I note that this compartmentalized thinking does nothing but nurture the mounting irrelevance of museums.

The Canada Science and Technology Museum (CSTM) is charting a different course, although it required some searching to become familiar with their plans and activities. In the CSTM's *Summary of the Corporate Plan, 2007/2011*, there is no mention of environmental sustainability or consumption in their Strategic Framework (also called the Pillars of Success), or in their Environmental Scan. The latter recognizes changing demographics, increasing cultural diversity and the pace of change driven by technology, but the relationship to the biosphere is missing.[31] I was ready to move on when I came upon their Contemporary Issues Research Program, apparently a new initiative which mentions 'socio-political preoccupations', such as food safety and climate change. This program is slated to unfold over the next five years, which reminded me that this lack of urgency is both a typical museum characteristic and an unacknowledged threat to the museum community at large.

The overall impression of these three National Museums, based on a review of the documents available on their websites, is one of preoccupation with internal concerns such as operating budgets, buildings, collections, staffing, and programs – in no order of priority. The exception was the fourth National Museum, the Canadian Museum of Nature (CMN), which happens to be immersed in a massive and escalating capital project to renovate the historic building where their exhibitions and public programs are housed. This renovation is not an indulgence in vanity architecture, however, but rather the massive facelift of an aged building which opened its doors in 1912.

Figure 4 A Canadian Museum of Nature botanist shares his knowledge of arctic plants with a participant in the 2008 'Students on Ice' Arctic Expedition. This museum collaboration motivates students to debate, discuss and understand the challenging world we live in.

Photo: courtesy of Lee Narraway, 'Students on Ice'

In keeping with the CMN's mandate for the natural world, three of their seven organizational objectives are centred on the environment, coupled with a clear awareness that they are in the service of society and don't have all the answers themselves. By this I mean that their strategic objectives talk about 'making access-ible to the public relevant information about the environment and our place in it;' 'providing vehicles to encourage public engagement in natural history issues and to contribute to informed public policy on those issues;' and 'building the capacity of Canadian natural history museums to respond effectively to natural history issues of relevance to Canadians.'[32] Although these are not radical commitments, they stand out for the simple reason that none of the other National Museums have sought to articulate their role in the bigger scheme of things, beyond the confines of conven-tional museum activities.

It is difficult to attribute this passivity to a lack of intelligence or resources; it is more likely the result of a widespread and taken-for-granted introversion that is typical of museums – resulting in the museum taking its own counsel to define what is important. At the same time, conventional wisdom among museum prac-titioners, and supported by the museum literature, indicates that there has been a paradigmatic shift from collection-driven institutions to visitor-centred museums.[33] Although there is some truth in this assertion, there is no compelling evidence to support a fundamental change in approach and assumptions among mainstream museums. Collections continue to be a primary occupation, or perhaps rationalization, for museums, notwithstanding their growing inability to house and care for them. Nonetheless, if the visitor experience is now paramount, as museum practitioners and academics suggest, greater reflection on the potential scope and meaning of visitor-centred engagement is required. Will museums be confined to an ever-increasing reliance on consumption, entertainment and pedagogy, or will they engage in more substantive issues and interests? Some museums, discussed later in this book, have started to ask and answer this question, and the results are salutary. The majority of museums, however, remain content with the familiar, a pattern that was visible as I continued my web-based tour of four of Canada's distinguished provincial museums.

Four provincial museums

The Royal BC Museum (RBCM), located in Victoria, British Columbia, is known for its excellent exhibits, pioneering research on flora and fauna, and innovative community outreach, yet provided no mention of sustainability and consumption in its institutional goals.[34] As a provincial corporation, the RBCM does align its work with the provincial government's strategic plan, and one of the latter's goals is to 'lead the world in sustainable environmental management.' To that end, the RBCM's role is to investigate climate change, identify rare and endangered species, and educate visitors about environmental changes through collections, exhibitions and programs. Oddly, none of these government-directed tasks appears in any of the RBCM's institutional goals, although some valuable work is under way. The RBCM, through its 'Climate Change Exhibit' and new 'Climate Change' film strives to illustrate the benefits of environmental awareness to its visitors. Many stations throughout the exhibit allow visitors to access the most current information regarding climate change, and what each person can do around their own home that will help them with the impending changes. I also note that one of their organizational values is 'environmental responsibility' but no further details are provided. In their assessment of 'Risk Factors,' the environment is absent, as it is in their 'Vision of the Future.' This is a good start, but one wonders how to explain the gap between institutional priorities and the deteriorating condition of the biosphere. Institutional oversight or reluctance do not prevent individual staff members from speaking up, however, and the reader is referred to an excellent piece on museums, climate change and sustainability written by an RBCM curator.[35]

Moving east across Canada in my search for explicit recognition of current socio-environmental issues, I stopped at the website of the Manitoba Museum in Winnipeg, Manitoba – the province's largest heritage facility. Although the website states that 'environmental preservation and education factor significantly in museum research,' and 'museum publications are critical to our understanding of the natural world,' there were no specifics and no mention of the global imperatives we now confront.[36]

Figure 5 The Michael Lee-Chin Crystal at the Royal Ontario Museum, Toronto, Canada, 2008.

Photo: courtesy of Douglas Worts

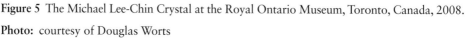

The next stop was the Royal Ontario Museum (ROM) in Toronto, Ontario, an encyclopedic museum which is 'one of the world's greatest museums' (according to their website). The ROM is abuzz these days, having recently opened the Michael Lee-Chin Crystal – a massive architectural renovation which 'marks the beginning of a new age for the ROM, as the country's premier cultural and social destination.'[37] The ROM also sports a new logo balanced graphically with the words 'World Cultures' and 'Natural History', an obvious incentive to continue my search. But the trail was cold. Although the mission cites 'the conservation of cultural and natural diversity,' no further details were provided.[38] Instead, ROM describes itself as the new agora, or marketplace, as well as an agent of 'social integration' and a 'social and knowledge destination.'

To what extent this museum has embraced the substance of Cameron's definition of the forum, as in challenging the established order, is not clear. It is doubtful, as the ROM's focus appears to be heavy on consumption, with repeated reference to great shops and excellent dining, in combination with the 'hey, look at me; I'm the biggest and best' grandiloquence that is commonplace among museum websites these days. One unnamed Canadian museum, for example, calls itself 'one of the foremost cultural institutions in the world.' I suppose this could be true, but there are no criteria for establishing and assessing this claim, which is consistent with the museum community's persistent failure to develop qualitative measures with which to assess value and performance. What can be better than simply stating what you wish – perhaps it will come to pass? This widespread, self-congratulatory rhetoric is undoubtedly attributable to the uncritical adoption of corporate marketing and branding, where hype and hyperbole are requirements of the business model. More on this later, when the marketplace is examined.

My virtual tour concluded on Canada's east coast, stopping at the Nova Scotia Museum of Natural History (NSNH) in Halifax, part of the Nova Scotia Museum (NSM). NSM is the corporate name for the most decentralized museum in Canada, consisting of 27 museums across the province, with over 200 historic buildings, living history sites, marine vessels, specialized museums, and close to a million artifacts and specimens. These resources are managed either directly or through a unique system of cooperative agreements with societies and local boards. Although the NSM does natural history research (including a research associate who is working on the long-range transport of air pollutants), and has hosted a special exhibition on climate change, their website yielded nothing about their mission or values, nor any sense of the socio-environmental issues beyond the walls of their decidedly progressive network.[39]

The tyranny of convention

What can one conclude from this virtual glimpse of eight of Canada's more significant museums? Only the Canadian Museum of Nature demonstrates an explicit concern for promoting public engagement and a deeper understanding of environmental issues in its institutional goals, despite the fact that four of the other museums have natural history mandates and, with the exception of the National Gallery, are multidisciplinary institutions. Achieving a multidisciplinary or interdisciplinary focus is admittedly a challenge, both in theory and in application, especially for all those museums that have adopted a corporate organizational model, based as it is on internal territoriality and procedures which act as toll-booths to open communication. Organizational design alone, however, is not sufficient to exempt museums from their responsibilities as knowledge-based organizations. To continue to engage in dualistic thinking, as exemplified by museums that reveal no connection between the natural and cultural worlds in their work, is to nullify the very reason for keeping multidisciplinary collections in the first place. Clearly, this limited thinking is not the property of museums per se, as it is also characteristic of most universities which continue to struggle with the rigidity of discipline-based departments. Homage is paid to interdisciplinary work, but it is commonly more show than substance. Can not museums, with their disciplinary complexity and enviable autonomy, not break away from the pack?

In summary, as a gauge of museum sensitivity to contemporary socio-environmental issues, my virtual tour was disappointing. In fairness, the notable lack of environmental awareness could actually be an artifact of the websites themselves – meaning that they are out-of-date, or poorly designed, or do not reflect the current scope and depth of the museum's work. This is also noteworthy, as we live in an increasingly web-based world, where recent research reveals that museum visitors are incorporating digital museum resources into their lives, as well as being interested in creating relationships where museums, museum websites and museum information resources feature prominently in their daily lives.[40] Whether or not a poor website is disguising a museum's values and commitments, the result is the same – a growing perception that mainstream museums are not paying attention to the economic, environmental and social issues that are now commonplace. In this respect, counter to the proclaimed sensitivity of museums, they are no different than any other traditionally-minded organization or industry, handcuffed by conventional thinking and seemingly unable or unwilling to embrace new ways of thinking and acting.

Thinking that there may be greater foresight to be had in the intersection between museums and the private sector, I consulted an article by Amy Kaufman, the Managing Director of the US office for Lord Cultural Resources. In an article entitled 'Ten Steps to Successful Reinvention', change in museums is discussed in terms of exhibits, branding, building, organizational structure, financial models, technology and so forth.[41] Although the need to adapt buildings to meet 'green standards' was noted, no mention was made of the importance of asking 'why' things are done in an organization as part of the reinvention process. Nor was any mention made of the need for heightened consciousness, the implications of socio-environmental issues, and the importance of community engagement. Although concerns about values and global issues are qualitatively distinct from the imperatives of audience development and revenues, I found their absence in this article to be a confirmation of the widespread museum myopia mentioned earlier. Paradoxically, I note that the tag line of this premier consulting firm is 'planning and preparing museums for the 21st century.'

Thinking and acting

The preoccupation with what museums are already doing well is commonplace, as compared to a broader awareness of what needs attention. I know of one museum that has adopted the goal of reducing its Ecological Footprint as part of its strategic plan – the Western Development Museum (WDM) in Saskatoon, Saskatchewan, Canada.[42] Although hardly revolutionary, this is an uncommon and thoughtful undertaking in the museum world, and will hopefully become a trendsetter. The WDM's commitment to reduce its consumption has nothing to do with proselytizing, but rather a sense of collective responsibility, coupled with a pragmatic need to reduce water and energy costs. The staff have made the simple choice to consider the environment and consumption in their daily activities. If they end up becoming a community leader in environmental consciousness, that will be an unanticipated bonus. The Imperial War Museum in London is also leading the way, with its new *Sustainable Development Policy Statement* (2008).[43] This policy commits the Trustees of the Museum and the Senior Management Team to reducing the impact of the organization's operations on the environment, reducing its carbon footprint and reducing the effects of climate

Figure 6 Rendering of the wind turbine installation at the Western Development Museum, Saskatoon, Saskatchewan, Canada, 2008.

Photo: courtesy of Brian Newman, Western Development Museum

change. Most importantly, their annual report and website will include details of environmental performance.

All museums are capable of similar thinking and action, whether it is reducing, reusing or recycling. How many museums and galleries recycle their de-installed exhibit materials? How many donate these materials to smaller institutions for reuse and keep them out of the landfill? How many museums and galleries have formal programs for buying recycled materials and products? How many museums have done an energy audit in an effort to reduce their consumption of utilities? Is it even necessary to ask these questions in the twenty-first century?

It is puzzling that reducing consumption is not as fashionable as enhancing the visitor experience, especially as climate change, unbridled consumption and environmental degradation directly affect all people. Are museums unwittingly becoming agents of distraction rather than opinion leaders? The tacit authority and respect enjoyed by most museums could be put to very good use by challenging the excessive consumption that motivates contemporary society and contributes to several of the 'tectonic stresses' mentioned earlier. How long will society wait for mainstream museums to recognize this, and employ their varied resources to provide, at minimum, a diachronic perspective of our feckless behaviour? Perhaps it is not the museum's responsibility, a popular disclaimer heard throughout museums, as well as at professional meetings and in board rooms. This reluctance might be arguable, if only the museum community recognized this responsibility as an issue worthy of serious consideration in the first place. The Museums Association (MA) in the United Kingdom is a notable exception to this silence, having recently prepared a discussion paper for its membership entitled 'Sustainability and Museums.'[44] This will be discussed in more detail in Chapter 5. Other museum associations would do well to model the MA's leadership by examining this important topic with their memberships. And selling carbon off-sets for jet travel in advance of museum conferences is no substitute for substantive engagement in these issues.

Killing our relatives – close and distant

There is also a much darker side to human consumption, with the practice of killing our fellow human beings continuing with a vengeance, and becoming a growth industry. There were 42 armed conflicts under way throughout the world in 2008, with 75 percent of those killed or wounded being non-combatants.[45] Global military expenditures and the arms trade form the largest spending in the world, at over one trillion dollars annually and rising in recent years.[46] As appalling as these facts are, it is obviously not within the power of museums to intervene in this global business. Equally alarming is the destruction of other sentient beings, including the winged, four-legged, and crawling. A case in point is how we treat our closest living relatives – the primates, the order of mammals which includes humans, apes and monkeys. Within the next five decades, such well-known animals as chimpanzees, primates with which humans share 98 percent of their DNA (the nucleic acids that are the molecular basis of heredity), may be extinct in the wild. In short, 114 of the world's 394 primate species are classified as threatened with extinction.[47] Our greatest impact on these animals is our practice of taking over their habitat for our own use, in addition to the fact that we are the only primates, with the exception of chimpanzees, who deliberately hunt other primates.

Destroying biological diversity

With respect to habitat loss, this negative trend continues to accelerate and has become a major global issue. Primates aside, the conversion, degradation and fragmentation of ecosystems continue apace around the world. In many countries, more than half of the original territory has been converted from natural habitat to other uses, much of it irreversibly.[48] As a result, nearly one in four mammal species is in serious decline, largely because of human activities. This is the complex and pressing realm of biological diversity or biodiversity, which refers to the variety of life forms including the different plants, animals and microorganisms, the genes they contain, and the ecosystems they form. Despite the scientific formality of its name, biodiversity is as essential to our well-being as clean air and clean water. In fact, biodiversity provides us with clean air and water through 'a self-regulating bubble that sustains us indefinitely without any thought or contrivance on our own.'[49] This living wealth is the product of hundreds of millions of years of evolutionary history; and the three different levels of biological diversity – genetic diversity, species diversity and ecosystem diversity – are now all under siege.[50]

Biodiversity is important simply because it is the basis of a diverse and more productive ecosystem that can better prevent and recover from a variety of disasters, in which every species has a role to play. This is in stark contrast to the agricultural monocultures created by the industrial food corporations, where resilience has been replaced by fragility and dependence on chemical fertilizers and pesticides. Healthy biodiversity provides yeoman's service for all of the creatures on the planet, including soil formation and protection, nutrient storage and recycling, pollution breakdown and absorption, enhanced climate stability, the maintenance of ecosystems and recovery from unpredictable events.

Equally importantly, biodiversity provides food, medicinal resources, pharmaceutical drugs, breeding stocks, diversity in genes, species and ecosystems, population reservoirs, all manner of wood products, not to mention all of these resources in the future.[51] For example, more than 40 percent of medicines dispensed by pharmacies are substances originally extracted from plants, animals, fungi and microorganisms. In addition, recreation, tourism and many of our cultural values owe their existence to a flourishing flora and fauna. With biodiversity serving, in effect, as our life support system, its overall health is obviously of overriding importance to all of us. But because biodiversity is inextricably linked to our consumptive habits, it will come as no surprise that our self-destructive behaviour is inflicting enormous damage on the biosphere. A brief overview will suffice.

It is difficult to estimate the overall rate of extinction, but biologists generally agree that on the land, at least, species are vanishing at a rate one hundred to a thousand times faster than before the arrival of *Homo sapiens*.[52] Others note that the current extinction rate is now approaching 1,000 times the background rate (the standard rate of extinction before humans became a primary contributor to extinctions), and may climb to 10,000 times the background rate during this century, if the present trend continues. This would mean that one-third to two-thirds of all species of plants, animals and other organisms would be lost during the second half of the twenty-first century – a loss that would equal those of past extinctions.[53] To put this in perspective, evolution required about 10 million years to restore the levels of diversity lost in the previous 350 million years of extinctions. As E.O. Wilson notes, 'Faced with a waiting time that long, and aware that we inflicted so much damage in a single lifetime, our descendants are going to be – how best to say it? – peeved.'[54]

Our declining biodiversity goes far beyond the world's fauna, with freshwater ecosystems being even more pressed than forests and grasslands. It is in freshwater ecosystems where the largest portion of the earth's biodiversity occurs, including 10,000 of the 25,000 known fish species. As a sober counterpoint to China's much-celebrated economic growth, 80 percent of China's 50,000 kilometres of major river systems no longer support fish of any kind because of pollution.[55] To put a finer point on the status of water in our biosphere, fresh water is only 2.5 percent of all the earth's water and the bulk of that is contained in the polar ice caps. We are rapidly drawing down the aquifers (permeable rock that holds or transmits water) around the world, in part to support such things as golf courses in the deserts of Arizona and Nevada. By 2025, some 40 percent of the world's population could be living in countries with chronic water scarcity.[56]

Enter museums

The continued loss of biodiversity confirms that we have enormous challenges ahead, given that the pace of destruction persists unabated. Unabated is not entirely accurate, however, as the preservation of biodiversity has become a focus for some natural history museums, and it is here that we get a glimpse of heightened consciousness in the museum world. This resurgence of interest in the natural world is welcome news indeed, as taxonomy, the principal occupation of museum scientists, has suffered because of declining budgets and waning interest in traditional taxonomic research on whole plants and animals. A sort of renaissance is now in the making, as exemplified by several pioneering initiatives.

The Buffon Declaration

The first of these is a groundbreaking and largely unheralded document known as *The Buffon Declaration: Natural History Institutions and the Environmental Crisis.*[57] Representatives of 93 natural history institutions (natural history museums, research institutes, botanic gardens and zoos) from 36 counties from all continents met in Paris in 2007. The occasion was the tercentenary of the birth of the French naturalist Georges Louis Marie Leclerc, Comte de Buffon – one of the founding fathers of the scientific study of biodiversity. The *Declaration* notes that science is critical for the sustainable management of biodiversity, ecosystems and the survival of human populations on this planet, and that natural history institutions make vital contributions as repositories of specimens, as leading-edge researchers and in developing partnerships and programs throughout the world to address environmental challenges.

Most exciting is the signatories' claim to be 'a forum for direct engagement with the civil society, which is indispensable for helping bring about the changes of behaviour on which our common future and the future of nature depend.' 'Changes in behaviour' – could there be a more explicit statement of the role of museums in serving the collective good? In fact, the *Declaration* goes on to make an even stronger case for the role of museums, by noting that 'today natural history institutions have particular responsibilities because global diversity is collapsing ... and current approaches are inadequate in the face of this challenge.' The 93 institutions reaffirm their commitment to work together and to develop new and integrated approaches to understand and address the environmental crisis, and to communicate the issues to the public, policymakers and a broad range of stakeholders. Note the inclusion of policymakers – there is an explicit interest here in trying to make a difference.

The *Buffon Declaration* is exemplary in its collaborative commitment to maintain and restore the ecosystems upon which civilization depends, in conjunction with scientists, policymakers and the civil society. In so doing, the signatories to this *Declaration* have gone beyond institutional self-interest to reaffirm their societal relevance and value. As such, the *Buffon Declaration* is a model that would serve any museum collective that is seeking to broaden its perspective and enhance its value to society. Sentiment must be translated into action, however, and it will be important to keep an eye on the outcome of this collaboration.

The Encyclopedia of Life

There is another initiative well under way that also underscores the essential role of museums in addressing the steady decline of the world's biodiversity. This is the *Encyclopaedia of Life* (EOL), a free, online collaborative encyclopaedia intended to document all of the 1.8 million species of living organisms known to science.[58] In keeping with the time-honoured museum tradition of nurturing amateurs, this encyclopedia is being compiled from existing databases and from contributions by experts and non-experts throughout the world. The project began with a US$50 million commitment from two American foundations and its steering committee includes the Field Museum and the Smithsonian Institution. It would be tempting to dismiss this initiative as the purview of large museums only, with their large scientific staffs and resources, but bigness is not a prerequisite for innovation and commitment.

The Alliance of Natural History Museums in Canada is a case in point, consisting of a diverse range of national, provincial and territorial museums. The members came together to create a network of equal and independent museum partners that will each be initiators, co-coordinators and facilitators to pursue a common goal – connecting people with nature. This Alliance is the harbinger of a more conscious future for Canadian museums where, perhaps, history and anthropology museums could also adopt a similar approach and work together to inventory pre-fossil fuel technology to assess what was adaptive and what is relevant to today's challenges. If the price of oil continues its ascent (it is US$144 per barrel as I write), it will be essential to access this dormant knowledge and consider ways of reducing consumption with alternate tools and technology from our past. In a rather chilling glimpse of a post-apocalyptic world, the writer James Kunstler asks, 'If the social and economic platform fails, how long before the knowledge base dissolves? Two hundred years from now, will anyone know how to build or even repair a 1962 Chrysler slant-six engine? Not to mention a Nordex 1500 kW wind turbine?'[59] Museums have always claimed to be the custodians of our collective memory and knowledge, and there is now a compelling role for this birthright.

The message is old but plainly obvious – the total is more effective than the sum of the parts. Yet museums, with few exceptions, have great difficulty in acting collectively and cooperatively. It is going to be impossible to address the loss of biodiversity, and enhance our commitment to stewardship, without the concerted involvement of the world's museums, as their collections, expertise and public face are essential to addressing these environmental issues. As Charles Handy, Britain's management guru, noted, 'If we wait around for someone to tell us what to do, we shall wait a long time.'[60] The trouble with waiting around is that our passivity will have created what E.O. Wilson calls the Eremozoic Era – the Age of Loneliness. This will mark the sixth mass extinction on earth, following the meteoric demise of the dinosaurs 65 million years ago. Unlike any of the earth's previous five great disturbances and the loss of biodiversity, 'we will have done it all on our own, and conscious of what was happening.'[61] Museums included.

Homogenizing the ethnosphere

I do not mean to imply that only encyclopedic natural history museums have a role to play in our troubled world, as they are far outnumbered by the many other kinds of museums whose focus is solely on our species. These museums include history museums of all shapes and sizes, art museums, and anthropology museums, not to mention the Sulabh International Museum of Toilets in New Delhi and the Museum of Sex in New York City. Wade Davis, the explorer-in-residence at the National Geographic Society, has called the phantasmagorical realm of human diversity the 'ethnosphere' and, it too, seems to be going the way of biodiversity.[62] My entry into the museum world was kindled by a formative experience among a culture far different than my own, and recounting the nub of this experience will set the stage for a brief look at the current assault on cultural diversity.

Apprenticing with hunters

As a novice graduate student in archaeology, I participated in various field projects in the early 1970s, which led me into the far reaches of the Mackenzie River Valley, located in Canada's western subarctic. I was unaware that the Mackenzie River rivals the Mississippi River, winding its way 4,300 kilometres from Great Slave Lake to the Arctic Ocean. I knew nothing of this vast wilderness – the size of the subcontinent of India with a population of fewer than 55,000 people. I had read and heard about the inhabitants of this region, the Dene, one of the world's greatest hunting cultures, and I was eager to meet them. But this was not to be, as the local and traditional knowledge of indigenous peoples was not part of archaeological research in the 1970s. I struggled to ignore my dismay with this arrogance as we travelled the length of the river, observing the Dene going about their lives while we remained secure in our positivist bubble.

The wrongfulness of this approach culminated later that fall when I assisted another graduate student with a survey of several interior lakes, not far from the Arctic Circle.

Figure 7 Willow Lake women (Charlotte Menacho, Stella Baton, Elizabeth Yakaleya, Alina Baton, Alice Bernarde, and Rosa Bernarde) attend a feast at the Willow Lake hunting camp, Northwest Territories, Canada, 1974.

Photo: courtesy of Robert R. Janes

We worked until late in October, when every night was below freezing and the snow came and stayed. We travelled fast – on foot, by canoe and by prearranged float-equipped aircraft. We travelled light – sleeping bag, tent and axe – and lived primarily on rice and pemmican made of meat, fat and saskatoon berries. In this way, we covered a lot of territory and visited Dene hunting camps in our search for archaeological sites. On one lake, several families of hunters were busy netting whitefish and lake trout, stocking up for the winter in the bush. We landed close to their camp, with no explanation of who we were or why we were in their homeland. My self-consciousness was acute until that evening, when we visited their camp to introduce ourselves and our work. Several adults listened politely (some of them speak three languages – Athapaskan, English and French), followed by a male elder, who advised us that winter was approaching and that sensible shelter was a canvas wall tent with an airtight wood stove. They gave us both for the duration of our stay, without any ridicule of our unheated nylon tent or incriminating questions about what we were doing there. This polite act of unconditional generosity led to a six-month stay among the Dene of Willow Lake two years later – the hunters described in the Prologue.

Living with these seven families in the northern boreal forest, my wife, Priscilla, and I were humbled daily by the ease with which they navigated intricate drainage systems (no maps, no GPS), endured the cold of an all-night beaver hunt, created beautiful beadwork, and instructed their children in the intricate challenges of life in the bush – by example. We departed with a profound respect for the cultural diversity embodied in the Dene way of life, having been given an intimate glimpse of their masterly adaptation to one of the most severe environments in the world. Yet the Willow Lake Dene are not pristine hunters frozen in time – they are individuals and families who are playing out their lives in the midst of profound cultural and environmental change. They are no different than many other cultural minorities throughout the world, many of whom are the begetters of the world's most highly-prized museum collections. The question of how these diverse cultural groupings are faring is not commonly discussed in the museum world – a conspicuous irony when you consider the role that indigenous peoples and their patrimony have played in the genesis of museums.

Assaulting cultural diversity

There are some 300 million indigenous peoples in the world today, defined as any ethnic group which has historically belonged to a particular region or country, before its colonization or transformation into a nation state. Although this number is roughly 5 percent of the global population, these cultures account for 60 percent of the world's languages and collectively represent over half of the intellectual legacy of humanity.[63] Many of these peoples are as beleaguered as the biosphere, and the loss of their languages is a startling indicator. It has been estimated that between 10,000 and 15,000 languages once existed simultaneously in the world.[64] Today, only about 6,000 languages survive, and only about half of these are being learned by children. As a result, about half of these languages are likely to become extinct within the next century. Of the 175 aboriginal languages in the US, for example, 55 of them are spoken by fewer than 10 individuals. Only Navajo is spoken by more than one hundred thousand people.[65] In addition, some 80 percent of the world's electronically-stored information is in English.

The overall situation is much more desperate than language loss, as the people themselves are disappearing. Wade Davis notes, for example, that indigenous societies in Brazil have disappeared at the rate of one per year throughout this century.[66] Genocide and ethnic cleansing are taking their toll, whether for political or cultural reasons. It also seems that global capitalism, the same phenomenon that underlies our relentless consumption and the collateral wreckage of the biosphere, is hard at work homogenizing the world's cultural diversity. Anthropologist Richard Robbins writes that the toleration of cultural diversity is not a strong point of the culture of capitalism, for a variety of reasons.[67] Indigenous societies often hold property in common, are kinship-based and lack the need for individual autonomy so characteristic of capitalist societies, as well as being more egalitarian which reduces the need for individuals to assert their status by owning things. Perhaps most importantly, indigenous societies control land, mineral rights and intellectual resources that capitalists want. As a result, they are disappearing through violent suppression, modernization, economic development and assimilation. The pressures on indigenous

Figure 8 Home of the headman of the nomadic Manaseer tribe, near the ancient city of Meroe, Sudan, Africa, 1971.

Photo: courtesy of Priscilla B. Janes

peoples have become so severe that Survival International now has supporters in 82 countries. This organization works for indigenous rights through education and advocacy, and their mission is a brutal reminder of the continued oppression of tribal peoples around the world.[68]

I was aware of the disappearance of hunting societies in the early 1970s, as I searched for ethnographic information to help strengthen my understanding of the archaeological record in the boreal forest. Although the role of the so-called free market in the homogenization of world cultures was only dimly apparent to me then, I recall the words of anthropologist, Allen Johnson, who wrote that 'if no one bothers to amass comprehensive descriptions of those ways of life within the next few decades, the truths they tell about human experience will be forever forgotten.'[69] Nearly 40 years later, and well into the twenty-first century, is amassing ethnographic descriptions enough? Is curating permanent collections of the world's exotic patrimony an adequate response to the increasing loss of cultural diversity? Should museums be content with celebrating lost diversity, or should they be advocates and defenders of its preservation? In short, what constitutes museum stewardship for those peoples on the margins of the modern world? According to the International Forum on Globalization, the plight of indigenous peoples is severe:

Today, they face the challenges of extinction or survival and renewal in a globalized world. The impact of globalization is strongest on these populations, perhaps more than any other, because these communities have no voice and are therefore easily swept aside by the invisible hand of the market and its proponents. Globalization is not merely a question of marginalization for indigenous peoples; it is a multi-pronged attack on the very foundation of their existence and livelihoods.[70]

Museums and the ethnosphere

Fittingly, some museums are grappling with these questions and the following examples demonstrate both the value of stewarding the ethnosphere and the daunting enormity of the task. The Imperial War Museum in London provides a noteworthy example of heightened consciousness with its exhibition entitled 'Crimes against Humanity: An Exploration of Genocide and Ethnic Violence.'[71] A specially-commissioned 30-minute film is the central element of this exhibition, which examines the theme of genocide and ethnic conflict, and looks at some of the common features shared by the horrendous bloodshed in Armenia, Nazi-occupied Europe, Cambodia, East Timor, Bosnia, Rwanda and elsewhere. The film runs continuously and contains harrowing elements – it is not recommended for children under 16. A small interactive learning centre within the exhibition space offers the opportunity to explore the histories of particular instances of mass murder.

A bold and innovative initiative is also under way at The Kelvingrove Art Gallery and Museum (part of Glasgow Museums, UK), with an exhibition and project called 'Survival: People and Their Land'. The exhibition tells the stories of some of the world's indigenous peoples who are fighting to keep their ancient cultures alive within the modern world.[72] Visitors can also speak directly to the people whose stories are told in the display by using interactive links to various indigenous peoples, including the Cofan of the Ecuadorian Amazon (South America), who have united to defend their rainforest home. Drilling by oil companies has polluted their land and destroyed their livelihood.

Perhaps the most explicit commitment to cultural stewardship is embodied in the International Coalition of Sites of Conscience (ICSC).[73] There are currently 23 of these museums around the world which deal directly with issues ranging from child soldiers to genocide and to sweat shops. These museums and sites are dedicated to remembering past struggles for justice and addressing their contemporary legacies, and they employ a variety of traditional and non-traditional museum approaches in doing so. Members must commit to engaging in programs that stimulate dialogue on pressing social issues, promoting humanitarian and democratic values, and sharing opportunities for public involvement in these issues.

In Canada, there has been continuous tension between First Nations (also called Native or Aboriginal peoples) and the dominant culture since Euro-Canadians arrived in the New World. This tension also permeates relationships between museums and

First Nations, despite various efforts at amelioration. The most concerted of these attempts was the Canadian Museums Association and the Assembly of First Nations Task Force on Museums and First Peoples – a national forum for discussing and finding resolutions to issues concerning First Nations and museums.[74] The Task Force (1989–92) sought to define more equitable relationships among First Nations and Canada's museums, and addressed such issues as representation on governing boards, training and the interpretation of First Nations cultures, as well as access to collections and repatriation. The ensuing recommendations have no legal status and are not binding, and there has been no systematic follow-up to determine the extent to which museums have implemented these recommendations.

As a result, the relationships between First Nations and Canadian museums range from ugly to enlightened, and many issues remain to be solved. In the United States, where federal legislation exists to protect the interests of aboriginal peoples vis-à-vis museums, the relationships remain problematical. Museologists Elizabeth Scott and Edward Luby note that, while indigenous groups have come a long way in the past 20 years, 'it does seem possible that relationships between museums and Native groups could stall and never reach their full potential.'[75] The antidote to this eventuality, in their view, is for museums to formalize their relationships with indigenous groups, and develop close working partnerships based on a mutual long-term vision and plan. Amen.

As these examples indicate, various museums around the world are contributing to the stewardship of the ethnosphere in new and valuable ways, although with less critical mass than the biodiversity initiatives under way in natural history museums. These examples of caring for the biosphere and ethnosphere are clear signals of an evolving consciousness among museums, but there are simply not enough museums involved in this work, recognizing the unique resources and the trusted status of museums in contemporary society. This potential is also blocked by the manner in which museums separate the human and natural worlds with traditional disciplinary boundaries. There are museums that include both human and natural history, but internal organizational boundaries regularly obstruct or disrupt productive and creative collaboration.

Most indigenous peoples, on the other hand, have complex relationships with the land, water, animals and plants, and all of these relationships have spiritual, economic, social, protective and recreational significance. These peoples are not only living self-sufficiently but they also educate their children in relationship to the land. Indigenous communities are, in fact, concrete examples of sustainable societies, as they have evolved in diverse ecosystems over millennia. In short, there is a deeply intimate connection between the conservation of biological diversity and the conservation of indigenous cultural identities. Are any organizations better suited to affirm this vital connection than museums, especially considering their potential for multi-disciplinary collaboration?

If museums are one of society's principal repositories of collective knowledge and wisdom, as they claim to be, how can they continue to downplay or ignore their role in addressing the grim litany of cultural and environmental destruction? The role of museums is even more important when one considers our inability to solve the

Figure 9 Blacksmith and his wares at the Kabushiya market, Sudan, Africa, 1971.

Photo: courtesy of Priscilla B. Janes

problems we are creating, as described by Homer-Dixon.[76] He notes that 'an increasingly homogenized, transnational super elite is at work, earning an ever-larger slice of the economic product.' These elite must obviously play a key role in supplying the ingenuity required, but according to Homer-Dixon, 'they are separated from reality, isolated in a land of human construction and human ideas, where reality and illusion are intermingled.' Biodiversity and indigenous societies are the antitheses of the super elite's reality and illusion, and society is simply in need of better institutions to help overcome the unreality and illusion that currently besets the world.

Blockbuster shows and high attendance figures aren't really the point when one considers the urgent need for ingenuity and leadership. Ideas and solutions are needed to address a host of technical, social and environmental issues stemming from the tectonic stresses discussed earlier. Museums of all shapes and sizes are untapped and untested sources of ideas, knowledge and information, and are ideally placed to foster individual and community participation in the quest for greater awareness and workable solutions. What incentives are required to shake loose museums from the bounds of convention so that they may fulfil their unique and latent potential, and become one of the world custodians of extant biological and cultural richness?

Diagnosing the assault on stewardship

The erosion of stewardship, in both the natural and cultural worlds, enjoys our collective denial because there is no individual, organization or conspiracy to blame. The problem is actually much deeper and more difficult, because the problem is all of us. Many of us, including organizations, have entered that perplexing realm of being in conflict with our own sense of values and principles, and we are uncertain about what to do. Limitless economic growth, for example, is creating genuine and profound dilemmas, including damage to the natural environment and a growing disillusionment with buying 'stuff' as the key to happiness.

One of the most prominent factors in our confused thinking is the propensity for reductionism. We come by this habit honestly, as reductionism was one of the Enlightenment's gifts to the development of science. At its best, reductionist thinking is the cutting edge of science – 'the search strategy employed to find points of entry into otherwise impenetrably complex systems.'[77] At its worst, reductionism is over-simplification, grounded in the belief that 'complex wholes and their properties are less real than their constituents, and that the simplest part of something is the most real.' Put another way, 'the whole is *not* greater than the sum of its parts.'[78] This in turn leads to fragmented thinking and the assumption that things are understandable in isolation from their contexts. The persistent loss of habitat, in the name of economic growth, is reductionist thinking run amok.

Dualism

Another liability that underlies failed stewardship is best described as dualism – the belief that 'alternatives to thought and endeavour are polarized, and guided by the law of the excluded middle.'[79] This is also a variation of 'either/or' thinking, mentioned earlier. More specifically, this kind of thinking finds expression in the view that nature exists to serve the interests of human beings, and that we as humans, have dominion over the plants and animals. In the end, all aspects of our lives are embedded in nature, and to think that we can somehow separate ourselves, or opt out, is simply not possible without the dire consequences we are now experiencing. Museums, being knowledge-based, are duty-bound to distance themselves from what will be seen as one of the greatest fallacies of our time – the idea that we can get along without natural resources, an idea that is now apparently widespread in rich countries.[80] Equally importantly, it must be recognized that nature does not belong to us – it is not 'our' natural environment, and contrary to conventional wisdom, nature is not infrastructure standing by to accommodate us.[81] Rather, it is its own entity – people are but one part of it and it is imperative that we embrace this unfamiliar reality.

Indivisible benefits

In addition to the threats posed by reductionist and dualistic thinking, there is also the matter of divisible and indivisible benefits. I am indebted to the brilliant physicist and humanist, Ursula Franklin, for her clear thinking on this contemporary affliction.[82] In short, divisible benefits are those which accrue to an individual or organization because they earned them or created them. Indivisible benefits, on the other hand, are concerned with the 'common good' and include such things as justice and peace, clean air, drinkable water, and so forth. Indivisible benefits belong to everyone. All of us give up our autonomy and a great deal of money in the form of taxes in order to ensure that governments protect and advance the common good. As the discussion of the erosion of stewardship indicates, there appears to be a marked deterioration among all levels of government, around the world, in safeguarding indivisible benefits.

Whether it is clear-cut logging or the contamination of ground water from industrial meat production, it is clear that all levels of government are key partners in eroding society's indivisible benefits – rationalized in the name of economic growth. It is essential that all levels of government be accountable for safeguarding the world's indivisible benefits, as multinational corporations (second only to governments in their influence on public policy) have clearly demonstrated time and again their inability to separate the common good from their private gain. Museums have always existed in the realm of indivisible benefits, as public institutions owned by no one and materially supported by everyone. The time has come for museums to fulfil this privileged role and add their voice to the conservation of indivisible benefits. Museums are experts in the fiduciary care of collections for posterity and the vision of what is relevant must now embrace the biosphere – on whatever scale and with whatever means are appropriate for a particular museum.

The curse of neo-classical economists

I'll conclude these comments on the underlying reasons for the assault on stewardship with some observations on economists. The erosion of stewardship, ranging from language loss to the demise of non-human primates, is largely a result of an economic world-view based on the belief that continuous economic growth is essential to a healthy society. As noted earlier, museums are not immune to this belief, and there is a growing preoccupation among museums with the marketplace. Museum performance is now judged primarily by consumption – attendance figures, shop sales, earned revenues and so on, and money is now the primary measure of worth for most museums and their governing authorities. Museums, unwittingly or not, are now consumed by the values of relentless consumption and limitless economic growth that underlie many of our planetary difficulties.

We are faced with a poverty of thought and action in this regard, and professional economists are one of the greatest obstacles to achieving some degree of understanding and realism.[83] Based on the insular nature of neo-classical economic theory, economists

largely ignore human behaviour and the environment in their analyses and pronounce-
ments. Most importantly, they do not use full-cost accounting, which means that they
fail, for example, to recognize the depletion of natural resources as a cost. The general
failure of this academic discipline to acknowledge the real world has not gone unnoticed, and a new school of ecological economics has been steadily developing.

In 1997 a group of these progressive economists published a paper in which they set
a value on 'ecosystem services' such as pollination and decomposition.[84] They estimated all these services to be US$33 trillion, although all of them have always been
counted as free. Ecological economists are also attempting to replace or supplement
the gross national product as the measure of societal success, with a more realistic
assessment of economic activity that includes both expenditures and costs, such as
pollution and disease. Regrettably, such innovation has had little effect, as these
thoughtful economists have failed to get the attention of key policymakers. Despite
the growing public awareness of the madness of traditional economics, the health of
the economy still trumps the health of the biosphere.

The snare of instrumental reason

Underlying all of these considerations, from mass consumerism to environmental
destruction to the myopia of economists, is what political scientist Charles Taylor
calls 'the primacy of instrumental reason.' Taylor defines instrumental reason as the
rationality we use to calculate the most economical application of means to a given
end – maximum efficiency and the best cost–output ratio become the measure of
success.[85] There are two obvious consequences of instrumental reason, the first being
the prestige and value that is granted to technology. Many people believe that the
development of appropriate technology will combat global warming when, in fact,
something very different is called for – a fundamental change in how we conduct our
lives. In addition, the primacy of instrumental reason helps to explain our attitude
to life on this planet.

In contrast to the Great Council of All Animals in the Prologue, where all living
things occupy a sacred niche in the scheme of things, instrumental reason permits us
to use what we wish as raw materials or objects for our own projects. Instrumental
reason, with its focus on the cost–benefit, is so ingrained in current thinking that it is
difficult to imagine a world without it. Yet it is this thinking that has created many
of the current challenges, including the homogenization of our lives in the name of
global economics. Lessening the role of instrumental reason will require both individual commitment and institutional leadership, with a much greater emphasis on
what should be the 'ends,' or purpose, rather than the means to the end. Stewarding
the biosphere is only one such end, and museums, with their demonstrated ability to
honour and empower their communities, are key institutions in lessening the dominance of instrumental reason.

This discussion of the troubled world provides an overview of the context in which
museums find themselves in the first decade of the twenty-first century. Various

linkages between some of these issues and the unique capabilities of museums are also identified, in an effort to broaden the understanding of what constitutes appropriate museum activity. Some museums, as discussed in this chapter, have already broadened their scope and embraced forward-looking and vitally relevant work. For the majority of the world's museums, however, it is business as usual, based in large measure on traditional practices and an introverted sensibility of what constitutes collective good – locally and globally. For museums, the idea of collective good must also go beyond the socio-environmental issues discussed in this chapter to embrace the challenges of a dramatically aging population in the Western world, as well as the need to more fully engage people with disabilities – to mention only two societal concerns. More on this later when examples of innovative museum practice are discussed.

The next chapter will explore museums from the inside out, and consider various characteristics of museums that are hindering their evolution as more conscious, empathetic and self-critical organizations. I hope to make explicit various traditions and practices that are taken for granted, along with their underlying assumptions. In doing this, I cannot pretend to be an impartial anthropologist doing ethnography. Having left organizational life in museums a decade ago, however, I lay claim to an 'outsider's' perspective.

3

It's a jungle in here: Museums and their self-inflicted challenges

The three agendas

In reflecting on the low profile of mainstream museums in issues of natural and cultural stewardship, it won't do to attribute this passivity to the much-vaunted view that museums must remain protective of their authority and respect by remaining aloof from activities that entail competing views and values. As discussed earlier, this in itself is a commitment to the status quo and its deprivations, including the presumption of unlimited economic growth and the tacit support of the governments and corporations who are committed to this ideology. Nor is it sufficient to use the inertia of museum tradition as a rationalization, for such practices are not immutable, as the examples of progressive practice in the previous chapter testify. There are simply too many museums submerged in a miasma of sacred cows, unquestioned assumptions, groupthink and habitual behaviours.

The purpose of this chapter is to identify and discuss some of the more potent of these habits, all of which museums have wittingly or unwittingly imposed upon themselves, and all of which can be overcome by awareness and will. I contend that these challenges have hindered many museums from moving beyond the temple to embrace a deeper consciousness and a broader outlook. There is good reason to believe that these internal hindrances, in combination with the spread of marketplace ideology, are not only enfeebling otherwise competent museums but are also serving to divert museums from realizing their unique strengths and opportunities as stewards, not spectators.

Museums are highly complex organizations – housing multiple professional allegiances, competing values and interests, and a range of diverse activities that would give pause to the most seasoned executive. In distilling this complexity, I am indebted to museum and business consultant, Will Phillips, and his concept of the 'Three Agendas.'[1] This concept is useful for distinguishing between the complex activities that characterize museums as organizations, and in identifying various internal issues which confront museums. The first agenda focuses on the work and content of the museum, including the mission, exhibitions and programs, collections, conservation, marketing, audience development and so forth. This is where boards of directors and staff normally focus, as well as the vast majority of professional conference programs.

The second agenda is about how things are organized – the people and resources required to do the work, including strategic plans, organizational structure, delegation, staffing, training, systems for communication, methods for resource allocation, coordination and control, reward and recognition systems and so on. In short, the second agenda is the all-pervasive culture of the organization, and the automatic pilot that keeps the museum moving along in its old and familiar track, even when changes are being made in the first agenda. Phillips notes that only 1 to 2 percent of typical industry conferences focus on the second agenda.[2]

Although there are no statistics available for museum conferences, 32 years of attending conferences has also convinced me that the time and energy devoted to the second agenda are negligible. These topics are largely the private purview of museums, and suffer from neglect and disregard. One doesn't learn much about innovative organizational designs or how to improve internal communication at museum conferences. Whether or not a museum's organizational culture is healthy or dysfunctional is generally not the subject of public discussion or analysis – it is mostly the stuff of innuendo, rumour and staff conversations at all levels of the organization. A willingness to be vulnerable is a prerequisite to the exploration of the second agenda, and vulnerability, like innovation, does not come easily to any kind of organization.

The third agenda is concerned with change, and with a focus on the mental and emotional constructs in individuals that set the stage for how they interact within the organization.[3] This agenda is about individual development, learning and transformation, all of which museums must address if they are to answer the crucial question of 'why' they do what they do. Phillips notes that many businesses and museums are 'stalled out' because of unresolved third agenda issues. There is no doubt that these issues are daunting, unacknowledged or intractable for many museums, which explains why they are not the subject of professional discussions and public forums. The idea of the third agenda is essential to the purpose of this book, as the change required by museums has much to do with third agenda issues – rethinking the role and responsibilities of museums and museum workers at a time of unprecedented global challenges.

It is obvious why the museum community's attention is on the first and second agendas, recognizing both their importance and the difficulties inherent in transforming individuals and organizations. I mentioned earlier the widespread disconnection between an individual's values and perspective, and the actual behaviour of the organization. The third agenda is the watershed or minefield, where individuals and organizations can come together for mutual growth and transformation, or not. Although this book is ultimately a journey into the third agenda, many of the obstacles along the way originate in the first two agendas. They are numerous and formidable, and must be addressed if the capacity for museum renewal is to be realized.

Before launching into this discussion, I should note that the larger the museum, the greater the potential to suffer from the self-inflicted challenges catalogued in this chapter. This doesn't mean that small museums have mastered the three agendas, as they can be as bogged down with these complexities as large museums. I hope that the reader from a small museum resists the temptation to dismiss these challenges as belonging to bigness, as smaller museums are no less immune to the tyranny of tradition. While one size does not fit all, I must, of necessity, generalize about museums as organizations in the following discussion. Generally speaking, small museums have more effective internal communication simply because they are smaller, and can be more nimble and flexible as a result. This does not mean, however, that these advantages are necessarily seized upon.

The fallacy of authoritative neutrality

With so many museums joining the perpetual round of entertainment, with borrowed exhibitions and impressive restaurants, one must ask what is hindering a more expansive understanding of their role in society. One explanation lies in an uncritical commitment to what I have labelled 'the fallacy of authoritative neutrality.' This is the widely held belief among boards and museum staff that museums must protect their neutrality, lest they fall prey to bias, trendiness and special interest groups. Authoritative neutrality has taken on new meaning over the past decade, as museums have increased their reliance on corporate, foundation and private funding, and business people occupy more seats at the board table. Perhaps the pervasive, albeit discreet, argument is that museums cannot risk doing anything that might alienate a private sector sponsor, real or potential.

The simple truth, apparently unrecognized by the proponents of authoritative neutrality, is that corporations and the business community are themselves special interest groups, marked by a rigid tribalism grounded in marketplace ideology. And make no mistake that this is an ideology – a set of ideas, beliefs, values and passions that justify and mask a specific set of interests.[4] There is no doubt that moving beyond authoritative neutrality requires judgement and risk-taking, and the potential for both enhancing the collective good, or abusing it, lie dormant in every opportunity.[5] The following little-known examples from the museum world are salutary case studies of both extremes.

Museum eugenics

The Hall of Human Biology and Evolution at the American Museum of Natural History (AMNH) in New York City is the next iteration of the Hall of the Age of Man (closed in 1984), first mounted by Henry Fairfield Osborn, the museum's Director of Vertebrate Palaeontology and its President from 1908 to 1933. Osborn was the child of one of the most prestigious families in the city, and felt called upon to provide moral and intellectual leadership in confronting the problems of a rapidly industrializing society due to massive immigration and the mixing of racial and ethnic groups.[6] He feared that the human species was becoming diluted and weakened, and the subtle message in the Hall of the Age of Man was the need to preserve natural and racial purity.

Osborn also chose to preside over the Second International Eugenics Congress in 1921, which coincided with the opening of the Hall of the Age of Man. Equally harmfully, the Congress was financed by J. Pierpont Morgan, the American banker and financier, who also served as president of the Metropolitan Museum of Art in New York. A series of temporary exhibits, one floor below the Hall of the Age of Man, promoted the value of eugenics – breeding superior people and preventing those deemed inferior from reproducing – the essence of Nazism and ethnic cleansing. In short, the AMNH had become the site of a 'powerful constellation of economic and political interests ... bent on exercising social control, with the aim of preserving the priceless gene pool that supposedly had made America great.'[7] Osborn's work is a clear case of advocacy run amok, but the potential for wrong-doing persists, albeit with far greater subtlety in contemporary museums. Are museums, with their commitment to authoritative neutrality, being sufficiently self-reflective and appropriately critical about the real interests at play in their exhibitions, programs and governance, and who they actually represent? Museum scholar Kevin Coffee has asked this question and concluded that no museum can 'effect broad accessibility if it does not intend to confront, at least episodically, the social forces that underlie or overlay its existence.'[8]

MoMA and the Nazis

In the fall of 1940, an exhibition proposal entitled 'For Us, the Living' (codenamed 'Exhibition X' in the museum files) was submitted to the Museum of Modern Art's (MoMA) Executive Committee in New York.[9] Conceived in response to the Nazi occupation of Paris in June of that year, the proposal was developed by the Librarian of Congress, Archibald MacLeish, MoMA's Director, Alfred H. Barr, Jr., the historian and critic, Lewis Mumford, and the Director of the Baltimore Museum of Art, Leslie Cheek. It is doubtful that a more blue ribbon museum team has ever been assembled, and I can do no better than to quote directly from their proposal:

> The magnitude of America's task in confronting the immediate threat of world domination by Hitler and Stalin has expanded the task of the show itself. What began as a mere exhibition has become a dramatic initiation into the spirit and purpose of American life.[10]

This exhibit was to use every means available, including pictures, 'written legends', three-dimensional figures, the human voice and music, as well as a new building. The building was required to house this unprecedented initiative, erected on MoMA's garden plot. The proponents of 'For Us, the Living' also noted that this show is 'our American reply to the many grandiose, if empty, exhibitions that Mussolini, Hitler and Stalin have put on during the last decade,' and that 'millions of people will take part in it; millions will be influenced by it.'[11] MoMA's Executive Committee voted to cancel the proposed exhibition, citing the US$750,000 budget and expressing doubts about its effectiveness. Ironically, the AMNH succeeded, while MoMA failed, and even with the passage of time, the relevance of MoMA's s proposed exhibition is defensible, irrespective of the timidity of the governing authority. Both of these examples attest to the risks inherent in taking a position.

A critical museum executive speaks up:

'We can't possibly take a stand, or advocate for a particular position, perspective or issue. The world is too complicated, and truth and opinions come and go in this postmodern world of ours. We might get caught with our pants down – unprepared to deal with the complexities. Besides, it's too risky; we might risk alienating a donor, sponsor or supporter. Taking on an issue is none of our business – our museum has to be seen to be fair and impartial.'

And I say:

'That sort of thinking is akin to the slippery slope argument, so ubiquitous in museums. Museum boards and staff who subscribe to this way of thinking maintain that they cannot move a centimetre from their position without sliding into oblivion, or worse. Unfortunately, the slippery slope argument is not useful, simply because the abuse of something does not bar its use.[12] Experience, intelligence and prudence all require that one assess each situation, compare the advantages and disadvantages of various courses of action, and then choose the one that best fits the purpose and circumstances. If that prescription for moving beyond one's institutional neutrality is too commonsensical, there may be a greater stimulus in what the museum-going public is currently thinking. For example, the results of a 2003 survey of 2,400 Canadians indicate that 60 percent of the respondents believe that 'museums can play a more significant role in Canadian society,' although this role was not defined. For those respondents who visited museums most often, this view rose to 82 percent.'[13]

Fiona Cameron's recent museological research in Australia confirms this expectation, and she notes that 'bringing important, challenging and controversial points of view in a democratic, free-thinking society was seen as a key role for museums by many.'[14] Granted, presenting controversial points of view is not the same as committing to a particular perspective, but it is a giant step along the continuum of social responsibility. Similar sentiments are also emerging from the United States. Twenty-nine percent of respondents to a summative visitor study of the American Museum of Natural History's 1992 exhibition entitled 'Global Warming: Understanding the Forecast' said that it 'was superficial, and that it should go deeper into the issues, touch on more topics or take a stronger stand.'[15] And this was in 1992! Needless to say, the museum was surprised by the responses. If museums can be thought of as mirrors of social belief, then it is reasonable to assume that they have an obligation to give back what their communities put in front of them.[16] Are museum staff listening, reading and reflecting, or are they on autopilot, unaware that those they serve are considering a new destination?

The lone museum director

There are basically two organizational traditions in the Western world.[17] The first of these is the hierarchical tradition which places one person in charge as the lone chief at the top of the organizational chart. With few exceptions, all of our institutions, including government, corporations, churches, universities and museums, see no other way than to hold one person responsible. There is another organizational tradition, rarely identified or discussed, which originated in Roman times, known as *primus inter pares*. In this leadership tradition, the principal leader is the *primus inter pares*, or the first among equals. The *primus* is the leader, but not the chief or the boss, and must prove and test his or her leadership among a group of peers. Radical, indeed, especially for inherently conservative organizations like museums that have embraced the hierarchical model with great enthusiasm. I have written about this elsewhere, but feel compelled to reintroduce the Roman model again as an alternative, with the belief that the lone museum director is an increasing liability in these complex times.[18] I have chosen to use the outmoded title of museum director in this discussion, as opposed to the fashionable title of chief executive officer, simply to draw attention to the unnecessary imposition of business terminology on museums.

A flawed model

There are so many flaws in the lone director model that it is difficult to know where to start. The difficulties are present from the beginning, when the director leaves and the search begins for a replacement. Although succession and transition planning are still uncommon in the museum world, they have been recognized as a duty by at least one museum director.[19] In this instance, the incumbent gave sufficient notice of his departure to plan for an orderly transition, including a two week overlap with the new director in order to provide an 'open, reflective and candid' briefing – ranging from donor issues to staff talents to organizational history. In the absence of a transition plan, there is commonly a disruption of varying severity when the incumbent leaves, irrespective of whether there happens to be an internal replacement for the interim. Interestingly, research indicates that the appointment of internal candidates as interim museum directors significantly alters the social ecology of the museum.[20]

In the absence of succession and transition plans, most museums inevitably enter a period of organizational drift, as a result of the incumbent leaving on short notice either because he or she was dismissed, or because there was no adequate notice period required in the employment contract. A minimum of six months allows for an intelligent transition, and far outweighs the disadvantage of the lame duck syndrome. In any event, the museum goes on hold, with the acting director in a custodial mode, postponing the substantive decisions for the new director. And everyone else waits with great anticipation for the mythical leader – sometimes idealized as 'the 18-year-old who has fought in both world wars.'

Impaired judgement

Once on the job, the remaining flaws of the lone museum director model emerge, and persist with a vengeance. Cut off from the grapevine of internal rumour and intelligence, the lone director is soon isolated – a person with subordinates, not colleagues. The pyramidal structure erodes information links and destroys channels of honest reaction and feedback.[21] Perhaps this is why there is so much unthinking and unnecessary change when a new director arrives, as this isolation seems to create a certain all-knowing quality in the new director, cut off as he or she is from genuine and critical interaction with peers. I should note here that the museum CEO in the Prologue is only partly fictional.

The result is impaired judgement, and there are too many examples where the new director pays little or no heed to the evolution and qualities of the museum as he finds it, and begins changing the museum in accordance with what he or she knows to be true, or has experienced elsewhere, however limited or inappropriate that may be. This is particularly common when a museum director comes from a considerably smaller museum, or has no museum experience at all. In the *primus inter pares* model, any attempt at arbitrary change would have to be fully scrutinized by one's senior peers, which would do much to prevent the squandering of resources and morale resulting from the omniscient, but disadvantaged, lone director.

Loneliness

The human dimension of this inordinate amount of authority is, of course, loneliness for the director. The loneliness of the museum director and the business CEO has achieved a level of hackneyed empathy among incumbents, causing one to wonder why something hasn't been done about it. In fact, some remedial attempts are under way, most notably the directors' roundtables, as well as self-organized meetings of museum directors such as Museums Anonymous in Canada. The Museum Directors' Roundtables in the United States, founded and facilitated by the Qm2 museum consulting company, consist of small groups of museum directors who meet together every four months to help one another solve problems and improve their museums.[22] Informal discussions with other directors help clarify issues and transform concerns into practical action. An experienced facilitator chairs the sessions to produce the maximum benefit for each participant. As an early participant in one of these Qm2 Roundtables I can attest to their unique value, but they are no substitute for the *primus* model, as roundtables occur outside of the workplace. The sustained interaction required to move beyond the lone director model must occur within the museum, among senior colleagues.

Overburdened

It is also apparent that the lone director is hopelessly overburdened. Depending upon one's appetite for long hours and prodigious work, these demands destroy, debilitate, or severely discourage lone directors on an ongoing basis. More to the point, these excessive workloads replace or erode the lone director's creativity at a time when the leader's growth, awareness, communication and sensitivity are critical to the institution.[23] This diminishment of time and creativity, as more and more work converges on the lone director, results in a number of conventional, yet decidedly dysfunctional practices. I am thinking of how often the lone director must resort to briefings from staff, like the typical politician, and have others write his or her correspondence and reports. As these positions are currently structured, there is little choice, but surely this must diminish thought and creativity.

As the Editor-in-chief of *Museum Management and Curatorship* (MMC), an international, peer-reviewed journal, I see the woeful lack of practitioner contributions every day. I attribute this absence directly to the overburdened lone director, not to mention the overburdened museum staff. For example, the past 14 issues of *MMC* (volumes 20 to 23 – March 2005 through June 2008) contained a total of 62 full-length, peer-reviewed articles. A total of 14 of these articles were authored by museum practitioners – individuals who actually work in museums. That is only 22.6 percent of the articles, with all the others being written by academic museologists, consultants and students. Recognizing the amount of experience and knowledge residing in the world's lone directors, their absence in the museum literature is nothing less than alarming. What's more, this absence of practitioners contributes to the isolation of both academics and practitioners, as academic research and writing are far less likely to make their way into actual practice, and the academics, in turn, are deprived of the practitioner's knowledge, wisdom and experience.

The loser is the museum community itself, where the need for new knowledge, method and theory is essential to critical reflection, growth and renewal.[24] My attempts to encourage practitioner contributions are mostly met with polite rejections, tinged with genuine incredulity. It is hardly necessary to even pose the question these days, as I approach the harried lone director. The answer emerges almost telepathically – 'How in the world do you think that I possibly have time to read and write?' Acknowledging the tyranny of the hierarchical leadership model, I understand perfectly. Is it time for museum leaders to pay attention to other leadership models and unburden themselves?

Contrast all the flaws of the lone director model – isolation, omniscience, loneliness and overwork – with the inherent advantages of the *primus inter pares* model. To begin with, the *primus* model embodies a collective approach to work and learning that all museums require continuously in order to integrate the work of a variety of specialists. This leadership model exemplifies this multifunctional approach in a highly visible way, while at the same time offering unprecedented opportunities for executives to test their ability to rise above the particular interests of their own work unit. The *primus* model, based as it is on collective and shared executive authority, is a prerequisite to moving beyond territoriality in the interests of the organization.

It is also an arena for collective inquiry into complex issues, which in turn builds depth in the leadership of the museum. And in the process, leaders are built and nurtured, who then constitute the intellectual and practical capital that any competent museum must have in the twenty-first century.

With this depth, the departure of the *primus* does not occasion the trauma and the handwringing that stem from the departure of the lone director, simply because the leadership is not stalled while waiting for the arrival of the new director. They know what they are doing because they are already fully engaged on behalf of the whole museum, not just their own bailiwick. This promise of relative calm is in itself an organizational sigh of relief, especially for the governing authority. Finally, I contend that the *primus* model would, in fact, mitigate the workload for each member, because the *primus* is not expected to handle things alone – there is no concentration of power to stunt a person's growth, as happens with the lone director. In summary, I turn to the words of Robert Greenleaf, the most articulate advocate of the *primus* model, who noted:

> Finally, the prevalence of the lone chief places a burden on the whole society because … It nourishes the notion among able people that one must be the boss to be effective. And it sanctions, in a conspicuous way, a pernicious and petty status striving that corrupts everyone.[25]

Having started and finished my museum career as a museum director, I concur. With 24 years as a director in both flat and hierarchical museums, including one experimental attempt at the *primus* model, there is no doubt that effective leadership is less the property of a person than the property of a group. Put another way, the 'real strength of a leader is the ability to elicit the strength of the group.'[26]

A dubious deputy director speaks up:

> 'We already have an executive team. We meet regularly and work out what we have to do. We don't need such a far out approach to leadership – it would never get anywhere with our board – they have to have someone to blame if things go wrong. You can't blame a group. Besides, if we did it, we would all have to have similar salaries and benefits, because we would all be sharing in the responsibility of running the whole museum, not just our divisions. Our lone director is making $125,000 right now anyway, and she won't take lightly the democratization of her salary. Things would be looking up for me, on the other hand, as I am making $100,000 as deputy director. I am also worried that, even with the *primus* model, my colleagues would continue to jockey for power and influence, which they are always doing when they meet privately with the director. How do you deal with that?'

And I say:

> 'Thanks for your candour, but the *primus* model is not as radical as you might assume – its low profile is characteristic of its very nature. No one knows who is

in charge of Switzerland, because there are seven people on the Chief Executive who run the country and serve for limited terms. How many people accuse the Swiss of bad management? Jockeying for power and influence is an executive pastime, and it's well known that tensions and conflicts which originate at the executive level (and most of them do) find expression throughout the organization – it's only a matter of time. The rapidity with which these conflicts spread is directly related to the severity of the disagreements among senior people, and their willingness or unwillingness to deal openly with these difficulties.

The *primus* model also provides the context to nurture collective action, in a more deliberate and demanding manner than the traditional management team – afflicted as it is by the underlying one-on-one meetings with the lone director and the attendant psycho-politics of complex and cross-functional turf wars. I agree that we always have to contend with colleagues who do not want to look bad, who like to lay blame and cannot stand disagreement. So, I have a proposition for you. You and your management team should prepare a proposal for your board, wherein you request that they delegate the management of your museum to your group, based on the *primus inter pares* model. You divide up the work according to your abilities, and ask for an annual payment, from which you will each draw your salaries, based on mutual agreement about what each of you is to be paid. That should help even out some of the growing salary disparities plaguing your museum. The *primus* will report to the board on behalf of the group and, other than that, the senior managers will be running the show – as a group.'

To sum up this rather lengthy look at the tired museum leadership model and what can be done to improve it – 'none of us are perfect by ourselves.'[27]

Management myopia

Much has been written about the differences and similarities between leadership and management, and it is not necessary to review this work for the task at hand, other than to note that they are best described as two sides of the same coin. Management is about coping with complexity, while leadership is about coping with change. The challenge is to combine them, and use each to balance the other.[28] The management myopia which plagues museums, and underlies their inability or unwillingness to embrace socially relevant missions beyond education and entertainment, is essentially a lack of foresight – a seeming inability to anticipate future events that have little or nothing to do with current activities and commitments. This short-sightedness is not restricted to museums, however, as the following observation by psychologist and former CEO, Richard Farson, indicates:

The difficulty for all of us is that our absorption with what we do well may blind us to what will enable us to do even better. The particular challenge for managers is to remain mindful that organizations can set themselves up for trouble when they rely solely on the things they are already doing well and fail to see what they *really* need to do.[29]

Confronting this myopia is particularly important, because it erodes the museum's untapped potential 'to envision how the community's ongoing and/or emerging needs in all their dimensions – physical, psychological, economic and social – might be served by the museum's particular competencies,' to quote the late Stephen Weil.[30] Management myopia has been identified in the business world, and is amenable to both analysis and remediation, once one is aware of its underlying principles or beliefs. It is useful to reiterate these principles here, as they are rarely, if ever, questioned or challenged – either in the private sector or within museums.

Myopic principles

There are four principles or beliefs which give rise to management myopia, and all of them are alive and well in the museum world. I am indebted to Ralph Stacey, the management specialist, for his insightful analysis of these complexities.[31] The first principle underlying museum myopia is that the museum should have a visionary director who determines the future destination of the museum and guides it to that point (recall the earlier discussion on the lone director). The assumption is that the lone director, along with the less celebrated management team, are in control of their museum and its journey. The second belief is that the museum must have a common and unified culture, sharing a single vision and committed to the same rules. The third belief, once the sole concern of business and now the preoccupation of countless museums, is the focus on the balance sheet and the financial bottom line. This is the direct outcome of the belief in continuous economic growth as essential to societal well-being, resulting in the ever-increasing primacy of economic interests in institutional decision-making. The fourth root cause of management myopia is the belief that the museum should determine what it is good at, give people what they want and adapt to the market environment.[32]

All of these principles or beliefs are familiar and sensible in terms of our individual and organizational experiences, but they are based on an erroneous and, ultimately, dangerous assumption – that the internal and external worlds are stable and marked by regularity, predictability and adaptation. In short, 'we're in control; we know where we're going, and we don't want any surprises.' Implicit in these perspectives is the assumption that the future is knowable, and that it is possible to know enough about what is going to happen.[33] The result, as noted earlier, is museums getting better and better at doing more of the same. This may be the foundation for current success, but the earlier overview of socio-environmental issues demonstrates that the natural and cultural worlds are not in stable equilibrium. In fact, we are bombarded daily with the instability of it all, ranging from the rising price of oil to the continued loss of biodiversity, not to mention the increasingly evident consequences of climate change.

It borders on hubris for any museum to assume that it is business as usual when both the biosphere and ethnosphere are on such perilous trajectories. Stable management is, of course, essential for all healthy museums, but this is not the issue. The issue is one of heightened consciousness, and the need for museums to create new mental maps, new mindsets, new perspectives and new ways of working that will allow them to meet the challenges of our troubled world, with empathy and commitment to the communities they serve. Doing away with the hollowness of authoritative neutrality and the lone director model are an excellent beginning, in combination with replacing the four myopic principles with a new sense of how people can work more effectively in museums. There are various practical and achievable antidotes to management myopia that do not require wholesale changes in organizational dynamics and outlook, however, as outlined below.

Research and development

There is an obvious need for risk capital in museums, just as there is in the private sector, where it is called venture capital. Venture capital is money provided by outside investors to high-potential companies, in the interests of preparing a company to issue its common stock to the public for the first time. The museum's need and the entrepreneur's need correspond in an important way – the need for money to finance the necessary research and development to bring an idea or product to fruition. In the business world, companies and entrepreneurs must raise sufficient capital to see them through research, product development and marketing, until there is a return on investment.

In contrast, museums are expected, and required, to develop new programs and services on a balanced budget, as they have no risk capital with which to experiment and try new things. The notable exception to this is the current spate of vanity architecture projects, where deficit spending is apparently assumed. Instead, what seems to matter in these building projects, according to author, James Kunstler, is 'that the city was blessed with a fashionable object created by a celebrity shaman. Alas, nothing is more subject to losing value by going out of date than something that is valued solely for being up-to-date.'[34]

The risk capital that museums require would not be spent on new buildings and vanity renovations; nor would it be a stabilization fund, which is intended to introduce stability and discipline into organizations that are on the edge of collapse. The purpose of the research and development fund proposed here is to finance the challenging of traditional practices in order to create new possibilities, designed to enhance relevance, value and meaningful renewal. As mentioned repeatedly, museums are not known for innovation, and such funding would provide both a stimulus and the means to move beyond this impasse. A public/private funding partnership would be a sensible approach to establishing a research and development fund, ideally as an endowment – the income from which would be distributed to multi-year projects based on merit. The funding could be made available in a variety of ways, including grants and loans, with or without interest charges. It is essential that the funding be multi-year to allow sufficient planning and follow-through.

The current preference of many governments and foundations for one-off project funding is creating no end of stress for a host of museums and other non-profits, including the debilitating phenomenon known as mission drift.[35] As organizations scramble to obtain operating money through short-term project grants, they begin to forget why they exist in the first place. Assembling and administering a museum venture fund would be a valuable role for a collective of museum associations to assume, and potentially much more effective than the popular strategy of lobbying government for museum funding. Accountability would be essential, but so would a wide tolerance for mistakes and failures, as these are unavoidable in any attempt to develop new mental maps and new ways of working.

Research and development possibilities

The research and development possibilities for stimulating innovation are only limited by the imagination of the museum community, and they could include:

1   *An Annual Think Leak* – This would be an annual forum of museum 'insiders' intended to share the successes and failures of the research and development program with the museum community at large. The purpose here is collective learning and it should be thought of as a think 'leak', rather than a think tank, as the emphasis would be on evaluating and disseminating new ideas, approaches and improvements to current practice, as well as those that failed.

2   *Creativity Forums* – These forums would involve recognized museum thinkers and experts, as well as non-museum innovators, in a think-tank context. It appears that museum conferences are becoming increasingly diluted, partly because of the need to appeal to a broad and diverse membership. The result is a dearth of new and creative ideas for practitioners, and regular creative forums that engage the very best minds in pursuit of better museums would be a great boon to the profession. In short, there is no such thing as too many ideas. These forums should also include citizens who have a particular interest in mobilizing the unique qualities of museums to address community issues.

3   *Local and Regional Heritage Federations* – These could be pilot projects to explore the value of creating federations of like-minded museums, for the purpose of developing shared strategic visions, including the sharing of organizational costs and revenues. In a time of increasingly scarce resources, many museums continue to dissipate their fragile budgets by publishing separate periodicals, developing their own information systems, purchasing materials and supplies in low volumes, and so forth. Although such collaboration runs counter to conventional practice, the research and development fund could provide an opportunity to explore the potential advantages of less insularity.

Reaching out

Collaboration must also include non-museum organizations, since broadly-based coalitions of unrelated but like-minded partners can be very powerful.[36] There is little doubt that both governments and citizens pay serious attention to cross-sectoral approaches, and museums are sadly out of date when it comes to this level of collaboration. There are numerous examples of museums partnering with university faculties, for example, but this is only the beginning. Where are the collaborations and partnerships with environmental organizations, health care providers, community development agencies and humanitarian organizations? Although the world is full of vibrant and intelligent non-governmental organizations espousing values and concerns compatible with those of museums, collaboration with museums is virtually non-existent.

Although difficult for museums to acknowledge, there is untold expertise, experience and commitment residing outside of museums, all of which are essential for forging new mental maps. The understanding and scope of what constitutes collaboration in the museum world require deliberate experimentation and enormous expansion, and the venture funds would permit this. Surprisingly few museums have considered the organizational design options inherent in mergers, alliances and joint ventures, according to a recent article on intelligent organizational design. Collaboration and consolidation are obvious strategies for enhanced sustainability, and doing so requires careful design and a disciplined process of decision-making containing a number of distinct steps.[37]

A thoughtful middle manager speaks up:

> 'I don't see how we could possibly do away with the four causes of management myopia. First of all, it would mean rethinking the role of our all-powerful director who, for example, allows no one else to attend board meetings. In fact, we don't see him much, as he is the only one here with an international travel budget. Not only that, but we've done a lot of work around here to make everyone think alike, and that would have been for nothing. We've spent a great deal of time developing a uniform set of procedures, practices and policies to protect our organization from making mistakes. Personally, I was opposed to this, as these sorts of regulations are designed with the least competent person in mind, and end up forcing everyone to perform at the lowest level of competence.

> 'When it comes to the bottom line, that's the name of the game here, and it comes directly from the board and the director. I'm hoping that someday we can get the board membership back into balance, and replace some of the corporate and business people with a more accurate reflection of our diverse community, including some different cultural groups, some community organizations, and youth. I also believe that there are limits to revenues and growth, and the board and managers need to think a lot more strategically about what constitutes long-term sustainability – it's not just money – it's about being valued by your community.

'As for giving people want they want, we never really ask them what they want. We got into blockbusters to increase revenues and pay off our renovation, and that's about all we do now. Personally, I think it's destroying our brand, as most people only visit when we have a borrowed show – they don't seem to care much about our collection, our knowledge and the unique qualities of our staff. We're on a treadmill now, doing more of the same, and adapting to the market doesn't leave us much time to do anything else.'

And I say:

'Amen.'

The consequences of hierarchy: Learning from hunters

I have a sustained interest in how people are organized to do their work, a topic that has received remarkably little attention in the museum literature.[38] Although it is a subject of intense and daily discussion for many museum workers, seasoned with much angst and frustration, museum administrators are apparently content with the hierarchical organization imported from elsewhere. There are two experiences in my museum career, however, that regularly remind me that the internal organization of a museum is ill-served by corporate or military convention, and instead requires, imagination, creativity and care.

As a brand new, '20-something' museum director, hired right out of graduate school with no museum experience, I had no choice but to assemble the best group of museum workers I could find, or resign immediately. My new job came with an immediate and compelling focus – build the museum from scratch for a public opening by HRH the Prince of Wales, already confirmed with the Royal Family for three years after my start date. It was to be a professional facility with full environmental controls, in a region where winter temperatures drop to minus 50° Celsius. There was no comparable facility in northern Canada to consult for guidance.

I assembled a core team of five, including a curator, a designer, a technician and an administrative assistant and, together, we solidified our purpose, divided up the tasks, and worked both individually and as a group, as required. We opened the building on time and on budget – fully staffed and programmed. It was long before the tidal wave of teamwork hype, now a management industry in its own right, and none of us had any formal knowledge or training in team dynamics and interpersonal communication. We were self-organized, with each of us having particular kinds of knowledge and skills. We also had an explicit understanding of our collective purpose, and knew, above all, that we had to be respectful of time and money. This early approach to our work served the museum well, as it grew to a staff of 28 in the years to come and became a relatively 'flat' organization – with one or two levels of reporting relationships.

Figure 10 Prince of Wales Northern Heritage Centre, Yellowknife, Northwest Territories, Canada.

Photo: courtesy of the Prince of Wales Northern Heritage Centre

Hierarchy in action

I returned to southern Canada 14 years later to assume the directorship of one of Canada's ten largest museums, complete with 160 staff, an art gallery, the largest non-government archives in Canada and a public research library. Imagine my surprise, on my second day of work, when I was politely admonished by an assistant director for speaking directly to a department head, as I sought information to assist me in my orientation. The Glenbow Museum had 18 departments and four divisions in those days, and the organizational map was byzantine for the uninitiated.[39] I told my colleague that I was in search of some particular information and I had gone directly to the source. He patiently noted that that department head reported to him, and that information flows in prescribed directions at Glenbow. In the future, he suggested, it would be best to speak to the vice-presidents and avoid any confusion.

I knew, at that moment, that the future would require some redefinition, as the brittleness of strict reporting lines is an inevitable liability. I later installed a management principle, as part of our strategic planning, which stated that any person, in any part and at any level of the museum, is encouraged to go directly to any other person in the museum for information or assistance needed to perform his or her job. This, however, was not enough, and the next three years would see a dramatic alteration, wherein Glenbow's 18 departments and four divisions were collapsed into six multi-disciplinary work units, each headed by a director. This transformation produced anxiety and trauma, along with change and results, and has been documented in excruciating detail elsewhere.[40]

Hunters

In keeping with the museological interest in understanding the origin of things, it is useful to note that, of the two million or so years that our species has been on earth, over 99 percent of this time has been lived as hunter-gatherers. It is only in the last 10,000 years that we have domesticated plants and animals and harnessed energy sources other than the human body. In short, 'the hunting way of life has been the most successful and persistent adaptation that man has ever achieved.'[41] As anthropologists Richard Lee and Irven Devore note, if we fail to survive our current socio-environmental challenges, 'interplanetary archaeologists of the future will classify our planet as one in which a very long and stable period of small-scale hunting and gathering was followed by an apparently instantaneous efflorescence of technology and society leading rapidly to extinction.'[42] I have not yet read a more succinct and sober foretelling of the consequences of our current dilemma – leave it to anthropologists to elegantly objectify our collective peril.

Because our hunting adaptation has strongly affected both our biological and cultural evolution, including our social, psychological and behavioral characteristics as human beings, it is a mystery why we don't pay more attention to the organizational dynamics of this way of life, irrespective of the fact that there are few, if any, traditional hunting cultures still intact. The hunting way of life is, in fact, the progenitor of self-organization and flexible work design. This is the legacy of the Willow Lakers in the Prologue and the precursor to every effort to work in teams, and it is time that this hard-won wisdom and practice be recognized for its relevance and value. Leaders and managers, including the management consulting industry, are only dimly aware, if at all, of this ancient legacy. It seems that management consultants, in particular, behave as if everything is new and it is their invention. Their lack of familiarity with indigenous hunting traditions is regrettable in light of the vigorous body of anthropological knowledge devoted to this subject.

Self-organization

The stereotypical band is egalitarian, mobile, adaptive and responsive to individual and collective needs, and leaders emerge according to the skills required for the task at hand.[43] The link between the lives of hunting bands and the idea of self-organization in museums lies in the fact that much of the work in museums is done in small groups. It is in the small group that 'most habits become shared, modified, rejected, etc; and it is here that the individual adjusts not only to small groups but to larger

Figure 11 Willow Lake hunters, Paul Baton and Maurice Mendo, butchering a woodland caribou, Northwest Territories, Canada, 1974.

Photo: courtesy of Robert R. Janes

groups as well.'[44] We do not have to reinvent the fundamentals of small group culture for organizational life – we just have to pay attention to our origins as hunters.

Self-organization is a ready alternative for those museums seeking solutions to the self-imposed rigidity inherent in hierarchical organization. Senior managers will have to lighten up, however, as seeking to maintain control over this particular work design is abundantly stressful and ultimately self-defeating. It is preferable to get comfortable with the observation that 'if you know about everything that is going on in your museum, there isn't enough going on.' I've used these words many times and they help to bolster managerial self-respect, as the fruits of self-organized work begin to roll out. But what is the potential fit between an organizational model that is millennia old and the contemporary museum?

Having spent close to 35 years in and around museums in a variety of capacities, I cannot recall the number of times I have been approached by concerned museum workers about their lack of control over their work, the indecisiveness or insensitivity of their supervisors, the consequences of undefined expectations, inadequate communication – the list goes on. Granted, there are always multiple sides to these conflicts, but there is definitely a pattern here, and it has to do with the systemic obstacles to freedom and creativity that are inherent in hierarchical organizations of any size or description. This is especially onerous in museums, which have a large number of highly trained and highly motivated individuals who are committed to the work itself. Museums are not alone, however, in producing disgruntled employees. Despite all the efforts of organizations and management consultants to understand employees and to manage them more effectively, many employees remain stressed, poorly managed and generally dissatisfied. According to the World Health Organization (WHO), stress, anxiety and depression will become the leading causes of disability in the workplace over the next 20 years.[45]

Hierarchical structures are prime contributors to this unhappiness, and it is in the best interests of museum executives to pause and consider if there might be a better way to organize work, if for no other reason than to head off the WHO's predictions. Most leaders and executives know, based on their own substantive experiences, that both authority and responsibility for one's work are essential for effectiveness, efficiency and satisfaction. Shouldn't this realization be returned in kind to the staff? For those museum workers who do not wish to assume authority and responsibility for their work, and insist upon being told what to do, the sun is setting. Waiting around to be told what to do is incompatible with the need to develop proactive, socially responsible missions. Besides, this kind of passivity squanders the potential freedom inherent in all museums – perhaps a manufacturing assembly line would be a better choice for those who are more comfortable with compliance and passivity.

Collective intelligence

Promoting the growth, development and self-respect of museum workers requires abandoning, or at least minimizing, hierarchical structures, and many small museums have known this all along. Hierarchy can be replaced with self-organization, a group phenomenon that occurs spontaneously when members of a group produce coherent behaviour in the absence of formal hierarchy within the group, or authority imposed from outside it.[46] Decisions are made at the most local level in the organization where they can be made well, and this requires that managers respect and nurture the so-called informal leaders – those individuals who exercise influence and authority by virtue of their competence and commitment, and not because of any formal position in the hierarchy. Informal leaders exist at all levels in all museums, and are essential ingredients in effective self-organization by fostering interaction and interdependence.

This description of a self-organized work unit is strikingly similar to the task group of the Willow Lakers, described in the Prologue. The task group comes together for a specific purpose (fishing, for example), is of limited duration and stresses individual autonomy, egalitarianism, decision-making by consensus and limitations on the exercise of power. An informal leader may not even be required in a task group, if the outcome is clear and the necessary skills are present in the group. In summary, there are ancient lessons to be learned that can inform and inspire the organization of contemporary museum work, as well as guide it into the future.

Individuals, in organizations, may choose to learn new things rather than persisting with the familiar. To make the transition to a more conscious and engaged museum will require substantive internal changes that both allow and nurture the autonomy required to continually develop ideas, experiment and evaluate. Hierarchical structures are simply too restrictive to allow the unfettered interplay of the 'what, how and why.' The key point is for management to focus on results, rather than insist upon any particular process or means for achieving the results. David Bohm, the physicist, writes that human beings have an innate capacity for collective intelligence, based on dialogue.[47] Dialogue does not require that people agree with one another, but rather allows people to participate in a pool of shared meaning that can lead to aligned action. Simply put, hierarchical structures get in the way of collective thinking, as staff attempt to navigate across and between organizational boundaries, be they departments, divisions or the manager's office. Organizational structures can be replaced with multifunctional work groups, while individual tasks co-occur. They have to, as there is no substitute for the individual work that underlies group work.

Autonomy works

Of particular importance to museums is the use of multidisciplinary, multifunctional and cross-departmental teams which may include educators, marketers and security staff, as well as curatorial and exhibition staff. In some instances, these teams also include individuals from outside the museum, who are given both the authority and responsibility for decision-making, in partnership with museum staff.[48] It is increasingly recognized that multifunctional teams are essential in cross-fertilizing the rich storehouse of knowledge, skills and experience inherent in museums, not only to develop programs, exhibitions and services but also to enhance the general level of creativity and innovation by bringing in non-museum perspectives from the community. This will be absolutely essential as museums reach out to their communities in search of solutions to both local and global issues. Giving up top-down authority and control is not easy, but an organizational design that permits autonomy at the working level is now a prerequisite for an engaged museum.

This need not be as disturbing as it sounds – something I learned when I first became aware of the Glenbow Museum School, several months after it had been conceived and designed. The first of its kind in Canada, it is based on one-week visits by school classes with custom programs designed by the teacher and involving up to 20 or more museum staff during the one-week sessions.[49] The museum school had been developed before I knew anything about it, yet I could only feel grateful to have staff with such initiative and confidence. When asked by a colleague why I didn't know about the school from the beginning, I could only say, 'If I knew about everything that is going on in this museum, there isn't enough going on.' Zen master Suzuki Roshi has another way of expressing this approach to work design: 'to control your cow, give it a bigger pasture.'[50]

A seasoned curator speaks up:

> I've got several big concerns about self-organized groups, because they are based primarily on the idea of teamwork, and that has a bad name around here. It starts with the fact that everyone on the team thinks that they know how to do your job. There's a lot of second guessing and interference in my view. I also don't like the fact that the vice-president has control over our group's budget and has to authorize all of the expenditures. We need to be able to get on with the work. I also can't spend all my time in meetings – if I can't get my individual work done, there won't be any contribution to the group. I don't think that working in groups, and self-organizing is genetic – it's more like learned behaviour. The individual is everything in our society, and that is how we have been socialized and educated. Working together, in close quarters, is not as easy as you might think. And we also have individuals who just won't cooperate or produce and there is nothing we can do. But, you know, when the team is working well and the project is getting done, there's absolutely no better way to pool the creativity and energy around here – there aren't any organizational barriers to decision-making and getting things done.

And I say:

> I understand and appreciate everything you're saying. Teams are not, in fact, the best way to approach every task, as there's still a lot of museum work that is routine and predictable and that requires individual effort, like accounting, collections management and public inquiries. There is also solitary work, like research and writing. You have to use your judgement, based on the desired outcome, to determine when you need a self-organized group. Each member of the group also needs to be respectful of everyone else's knowledge and experience. Just because a curator isn't in charge of the group doesn't mean that everyone else can be the curator. Each group consists of people with particular expertise and they have to be respected and used appropriately. That doesn't prevent open dialogue and examination, however, because that is a distinct advantage of a cohesive group.

> As far as the money goes, if you don't have control over the budget, then you don't have authority and responsibility, which means that it is impossible to be accountable. It doesn't work that way, and the sooner the senior managers understand the need for budgetary control at the working level, the better. It won't be easy, however, as self-organized work groups are difficult for upper management because power and authority are dispersed. The senior managers also have to appreciate that group work isn't genetic, as you noted, and funds have to be available for ongoing training in project management, interpersonal

communication, conflict resolution and so forth. Probably one of the biggest criticisms of group work is the amount of time taken up in meetings. Personally, I wouldn't even attend a meeting without an agenda and defined outcomes presented in advance of the meeting. As for those individuals who are incapable or unwilling to work in a group, they will eventually be passed over. That will be their loss, for the potential to unlock individual talents and contributions in self-organized groups is enormous.

Museum exhibitions: Ploughing old ground

None of the previous challenges – claiming neutrality, the omniscient director, short-sighted management and unsuitable hierarchy – is the focus of concerted analysis or much discussion in the museum community or in the museum literature. Thus, my criticisms of these challenges may be buffered by a certain amount of disinterest on the part of the reader. Not so with the next topic of discussion – museum exhibitions – the mainstay and one of the defining features of all museums. All museum workers are involved in this enterprise in one way or another and all museums struggle daily with producing exhibitions and marketing them. This means that there are a lot of experts out there, from curators to designers to marketers, which makes it all the more surprising that museums continue to use methods, techniques and mental models that have remained unchanged for centuries. It is for this reason that exhibitions are included on my list of intractable habits that require rethinking and reinvention. I first expressed my concern about the future of museum exhibitions over a decade ago, and my unease has not abated.[51] The current approach to exhibitions is yet another internal obstacle to achieving relevance and meaning for many museums.

More and more of the same

These concerns have been reinforced and heightened in an excellent article by exhibit planner, designer and developer, Kathleen McLean.[52] McLean read the entire first volume of *Curator: The Museum Journal* (published in 1958) and compared the 'musings, expectations, and best practices of today with those voiced by our colleagues 50 years ago.' This diachronic approach alone is a treat; the results of her inquiry are even more instructive. McLean's observations are many and rich, but what sticks in my mind is her comment that 'I detected a disconcerting similarity between much of what was written those many years ago and what is still being debated today.'[53] McLean worries that museums haven't evolved much over the past 50 years. She then goes on to describe her visits to three mainstream museums and galleries, in preparation for a conference presentation, and concludes that museum exhibitions might be an obsolete medium, 'out on a dying evolutionary limb' and unadapted to the rapidly changing environment.

She attributes the obsolescence of the museum exhibit to various factors, including a lack of imagination about what exhibitions could be in our complex world, as well as the traditional ways in which exhibitions are developed – requiring huge amounts of time, people and money. Nonetheless, the museum community is generally accepting of all these limitations and continues to produce more and more of the same, often at tremendous cost. An important Canadian museum with modest means, for example, recently opened a permanent exhibit at a cost of CA\$12 million – an undertaking whose expense is rivalled only by the outmoded thinking that led to its development. Big and expensive exhibits are what museum people like to do, and this is not an isolated example. Nor will be the benign neglect of this exhibition – no renewal, refreshing or replacement for decades – as staff deal with scarce resources and the imperative of driving admissions to appease the marketplace.

Both the lack of imagination and the complex production requirements are key factors in what McLean calls the 'stultifying sameness' in museum exhibitions, and there are several other causes which also merit attention.[54] The first of these can be attributed to a tacit presumption on the part of museum workers – that linear constructions of glass and wood, incorporating massive amounts of two-dimensional text in conjunction with objects that can be only visually examined, is the most effective means of providing meaning and value to visitors. The museum exhibition, as traditionally conceived and currently presented, is essentially a book, without any of the advantages of book technology, such as portability and ease of way-finding. These exhibitions convey the notion that knowledge and information are timeless, and that is simply disingenuous. Moreover, these exhibitions are the most time-, labour- and capital-intensive work that museums do, and are stubbornly resistant to renovation and upgrading without large amounts of money. Upgrading is seldom, if ever, built into the budget at the outset, with the consequence that these exhibits remain in place from 15 years to a half century, despite the fact that they are clearly dated, shabby, tired and often shockingly irrelevant.

Is it any wonder that visitors react appropriately, noting that 'they saw the exhibits when they visited with a grade 6 field trip.' This is not to imply that there is no place for exhibitions with longevity, as many museums have concepts and information that they wish to convey to all visitors by way of orientation, and durable exhibits are the means to do so. Nor do I wish to imply that only temporary exhibits are appropriate. My concern is that the linear inertia that characterizes most, if not all, of these exhibitions is losing its appeal for many museum visitors, particularly youth. Recall McLean's discouraged comments on her museum visits, which are all the more disturbing, assuming that she is unusually empathetic as a museum worker herself.

A litany of ills

Why don't museums spend more time considering what actually happens in people's private and social lives? Meaning, value and pleasure come from a variety of sources in our lives, including conversations and discussions grounded in memory and experience; the presence of material objects that are valued for their meaning; a variety of multimedia devices ranging from televisions to portable multimedia players (the iPod, for example) and, in many cases, an eclectic collection of printed materials including books, magazines, newspapers and so forth. We use all of these things, alone or in combination, intermittently or constantly, depending upon our changing needs and interests. Do museum exhibitions come close to providing this real-life menu of thinking, doing and aspiring? The answer is sometimes, thanks in part to the advent of the 'discovery centre' as part of some museum exhibitions. These are dedicated spaces, within or adjoining exhibitions, which provide a comfortable setting and resources, ranging from staff to printed materials to objects that can be handled. The focus in these activity areas is most often the family, and the space and its contents are designed to enhance visitor interaction. Nonetheless, the 'discovery centre' is mostly an afterthought, intended to overcome the inertia of traditional exhibitions. It should be obvious by now that all exhibitions should be designed as 'discovery centres' in their own right, from the outset.

The typical exhibition is also plagued by another major omission – the lack of authorship or attribution. It is *de rigueur* to acknowledge sponsors and donors, but rarely does the exhibit make explicit who conceived of the exhibit, who did the research and writing, and why. I don't know what purpose this anonymity serves – is it modesty, adherence to unthinking convention, or the subtle maintenance of assumed authority? Very few books are written anonymously; why should museums persist in this omission? The implication in maintaining this anonymity is that there is one perspective or interpretation, and the museum owns it. As we all know, nothing could be farther from the truth. Although exhibition team members are increasingly being identified, this should be a universal and ethical requirement, along with some explanation of the etiology and motivation for the exhibit. The late Stephen Weil, with his typical clarity, summed up the need to sign exhibitions by noting that,

> In the end, an exhibition is not made by the institution but by the curator or a group of curators who ought to be able to say what they think. The public should know they are dealing with human beings who have opinions … signing exhibits gives the museum the ability to go much further and … make statements that might be troublesome coming from an institution.[55]

Distinctiveness, comfort and usefulness

It is also obvious that the typical museum exhibition does little to contribute to a museum's unique identity. Recall McLean's observation on the 'stultifying sameness' in many of the exhibitions being created today – irrespective of the expensive furniture, media and graphics. At a time when so many different businesses, organizations and issues are clamouring for people's attention, Rob Ferguson, a maverick marketing consultant, has some straightforward advice:

> What do you have to be bold about? If you know something no one else knows, say it! In this noisy, cluttered, over-communicated society, people take pride in associating with people, places, and organizations that stand out and have the appearance of being unique. That, in a nutshell, is knowledge marketing:

it's about packaging your leadership in a way that makes a clear, unequivocal statement that your organization has unique knowledge. It's about being recognized for your high ideas, about carving out a brand for your organization as a thought leader.[56]

Ferguson is a great admirer of the National Geographic Society (NGS), for various reasons that seem to have escaped the attention of museums. While the NGS's mission is 'the increase and diffusion of geographic knowledge' (undoubtedly a yawner for most people), it also happens to be a billion dollar business that is 'pathologically adaptable' in Ferguson's words, and devoted to accomplishing its mission in every possible way. The NGS has moved from photographs, to documentary films, to television, to the internet, while staying true to its reputation and ability to 'use fresh, compelling content to infect ordinary, intelligent people with a sense of wonder about the world.'[57] Although the NGS now has a vast range of knowledge products, they have maintained their original identity.

The forward-thinking NGS provides a useful contrast to the museum community's fixation on the time-honoured exhibition as its flagship knowledge product. If distinctiveness is the goal, and sameness is the result, it appears that some rethinking is required. Objects and collections are not enough; nor are exhibitions and programs that fail to deal with the many issues our society confronts – from global warming to species loss; from war to global epidemic disease. McLean asks if museum exhibits will ever deal with these contemporary issues in a manner that will be 'enlightening, comforting and useful to museum visitors?'[58] Ferguson asks 'if you want people to believe in the capacity of your organization to deliver on its mission, where is the proof of your distinctiveness?'[59] And I ask, where is the reflection required to challenge the tyranny of tradition and complacency embedded in contemporary museum exhibitions?

Asking the right questions

Rethinking the traditional approaches to museum exhibitions requires dialogue, critical thinking and new ideas, and happily, this conversation has started. The Mid-Atlantic Association of Museums (MAAM) hosted its inaugural 'Symposium on Creating Exhibits' in April of 2008 and the conference program was heartening. Although much of it was devoted to sessions that can be found at museum conferences anywhere – technology, labels, exhibit teams and contracts – there were several sessions which demonstrate that critical thought is alive and well at this particular meeting.[60] The first noteworthy session was entitled 'Why Do an Exhibit at All?', with an iconoclastic preface which stated that 'some of the most expensive projects of the past decade have amazingly turned incredibly interesting events, unique collections and stories into completely unenlightened and boring experiences.' Another session, 'Cabinets and Curiosity', asked where the cabinets of curiosities went and wondered if current exhibitions are just too overdone – 'Overly curated, educated, designed, evaluated, and marketed?' The organizers worried that technology and interpretation are not enhancing the experience. A third session, 'Have Our Audiences Left Us Behind?' asked, 'Does the exhibit experience as it is now defined need to reinvent itself to meet the changing experiential expectations of our audiences?'

These are wonderfully important questions and ones that the entire museum community should be asking daily. Perhaps this kind of questioning could lead to some genuine experimentation where, for example, the exhibitions could be designed as a series of family rooms or living rooms; modules or activity areas (call them what you wish), each devoted to the theme or topic the museum wishes to explore.[61] The visitor would be free to engage in the variety of behaviours noted earlier, be it conversing, reading, observing, sitting quietly, using media devices, and so on. The contents of these activity areas could change as required, without excessively expensive demolition and renovation. I am not thinking of a uniform approach, but rather creating the opportunity for visitors to assume much more responsibility for discovering the meaning in their own experiences. As the MAAM sessions indicated, money has nothing to do with the quality of the experience and, may in fact, be a liability. Nor is money doing anything to counter the steady decline, perhaps unravelling, of the value of traditional museum exhibitions. Whether it is corporatism in the museum boardroom, or an honest effort 'to keep up with the Joneses', the resulting imitation and excess are only making obvious the need to replace traditional practices.

The active agora

Museums might consider departing from their preoccupation with exhibitions and replace them, or augment them at least, with a dialogue centre. I don't know where this idea originated (it may be a Canadian invention), but the model I have in mind is the Morris J. Wosk Centre for Dialogue in Vancouver, British Columbia, Canada, part of Simon Fraser University. The Wosk Centre describes itself as 'an intellectual home and an advocate for dialogue.' At the Centre, practitioners, researchers and students of dialogue probe the nature of dialogue—that process of interaction whereby open-minded discussion leads to mutual understanding and positive action—and they nurture it in practice.'[62] The Centre has ergonomic seating for 154 participants and is arranged in concentric rings for maximum interactivity, with each desk equipped with technology to enhance dialogue.

A dialogue centre is also part of the Science Museum in London, and is a stylish, purpose-built venue designed for experimental dialogue and 'blending the best from science, art, performance and multimedia to provoke discussion and real engagement with the key issues of the day.'[63] Activities at the Dana Centre include stand-up comics debunking science myths, updates on radical research, and handling sessions of rarely seen objects from the Science Museum's collection, as well as debates on modern science. State-of-the-art digital facilities link the Dana Centre with anyone who has online connectivity, including mobile phones.

Although much has been written, and much said, about the role of the museum as a forum, or the more fashionable museum as agora, little has been done to consciously nurture the visitor's active participation apart from the passive consumption of museum services – exhibits, shops and restaurants. A dialogue centre is a tangible focus for visitor interaction, and could even be used to explore the future of museum exhibits from the visitors' perspectives. This is an opportunity for the rhetoric about museums as 'forums of public discussion and safe havens for dialogue' to actually assume tangible expression. It is highly unlikely that public space in museums, no matter how monumental it is (and there is more and more of this space every year), will ever produce much more than admiration and fatigue. Visitor interaction, as idealized in the forum/agora aspiration, is not going to happen with people standing around as passive observers. Museums are one of the few public institutions that can assume leadership in nurturing active visitor involvement, and dialogue centres are a means to this end. Dialogue centres are a commitment to the future and one which all museums should seriously consider in their renovation or building plans.

Excruciatingly current

Unlike many of the socio-environmental issues chronicled earlier, the rethinking and reinvention of museum exhibitions is within the grasp of all museums. Time is of the essence, as the current approach has outlived the curve of its effectiveness and is now in decline. Fortunately, there is a small pocket of progressive practitioners who are committed to averting further decline, and they are actively experimenting with new thinking, research and approaches. Kathleen McLean, whose work was mentioned earlier, is among these outliers, and her reasons for doing so are an apt summary of the pressures the entire museum community should now be feeling. In response to an inter-view about how technology may change the museum, McLean cites a report prepared by the Irvine Foundation concerned with critical issues facing the arts in California.[64]

This report indicates that visitors will expect museums to be increasingly technologi-cally literate; they will expect that their experiences will be customized to meet their own particular needs and interests, and that museums will have to be 'excruciatingly current.' Being 'excruciatingly current' has never been an imperative in museums – it still isn't – and the vocabulary may not even be recognizable. And yet, 'excruciating currency' is only one of the ingredients required in the makeover of exhibitions – the museum community's most visible and expensive activity. Ignoring this makeover is an invitation to irrelevance which many museums seem ready to accept.

Collections: Museums as consumption

Alone, and on a fine July day in Canada's western subarctic, I had a salutary encounter with an object. While doing an archaeological survey of a cluster of abandoned cabins deep in the boreal forest, I noticed a small piston rod from an outboard motor, entangled in bearberry on the edge of an overgrown trail. This was a most unusual piston rod, for not only was it broken, the shaft had been repaired – bound with green moose hide to a 'shrink-wrapped' hardness, and then tightly bound in a coiled casing of brass snare wire. The care invested in this repair was obvious; its precision and symmetry a pleasure. The mute meaning of this transformed object was a bold contradiction to my own experience and world-view. Paradoxically, in mainstream society, where technology is so revered that it compels religious adherence, a cracked piston rod is akin to a fatal coronary. Repair requires a specialist, and in the absence of this technical skill the part and the whole have no further value. The hunters who made this repair had no access to service centres and paid mechanics; nor were they privileged to simply buy a new rod or motor.

This was the remote boreal forest, distant as light years from the centres of consumption that define our mainstream lives. Life and death in the boreal forest have always hinged on the appropriate tools, and being able to care for them. Someone had made this repair attuned to this imperative, but it was impossible to tell if the repair had worked and if the injured part had once again served its purpose. It doesn't matter. What matters is the timeless evolution of disparate values, skills and aspirations, bound together forever in an object no bigger than the palm of my hand. This is why we have museums, why people visit them, and why people work in them, but are museum collections contributing to this wonder and mystery – the numinous experience?

A growth industry

I have no intention of dismissing museum collections as irrelevant in contemporary society. After all, collections are the acknowledged raison d'être of all museums and what distinguishes them as unique social institutions. I also accept that many people just really love 'things.'[65] Yet, because I believe that 'our engagement with objects is to understand wider things,' various attitudes and assumptions that underpin museum collections require some scrutiny.[66] McLean's earlier observations about the intractable nature of museum exhibitions bring to mind collections, as they, too, are an obstinate arena in which critical thinking seems perpetually stalled. Change is fugitive and innovation is rare – perhaps because 'museums are organisms that ingest but do not excrete.'[67]

The focus on ingestion has made collections an unbridled area of growth for museums, as the numbers testify. In the United States, Schwarzer notes that the nation's museums house some 750 million specimens, objects, artifacts and works of art. It is estimated that the rate of collection growth in the US is 1 to 5 percent per year, which translates into millions of additional objects annually.[68] While Keene reports that there are 200 million objects in United Kingdom museums, there are no data on museum collections in Canada, according to the Canadian Museums Association (CMA).[69] The lack of statistical information for Canada is puzzling, considering that the deterioration of collections is a major plank in the Canadian Museum Association's national lobby campaign for additional museum funding. It would be beneficial to know the metrics of the crisis.

The absolute number of stored objects in the US and the UK and the steady expansion of collections make it difficult to accept that there has been a paradigmatic shift from collection-driven institutions to visitor-centred museums – a piece of conventional wisdom celebrated among museum practitioners and supported by the museum literature, as noted earlier.[70] My own experience as a director and a consultant is at odds with this purported shift, where thoughts of serious deaccessioning remain largely heretical and scarce resources are lavished upon objects that will never see the light of day. Schwarzer reports that less than 5 percent of US collections can be exhibited at any one time.[71] Collections may no longer be seen to be a museum's primary occupation, but they remain a ready rationalization for maintaining the status quo.

The flagship of arrogance

In light of the continuous growth of collections, perhaps the most important question is whether museum collections are fulfilling their purpose? My consideration of this question will be brief, and I urge the reader to consult the excellent work of Suzanne Keene, who continues her thoughtful and in-depth inquiry into the use of museum collections.[72] It can certainly be argued that collections are fulfilling their purpose, and there is some impressive supporting evidence. For example, museum collections provided the comparative specimens which confirmed that the egg shells of peregrine falcons were thinning due to the introduction of the pesticide DDT, which was moving these birds close to extinction in the 1960s.[73] The problem was rectified with the banning of DDT, thanks to the undeniable testimony of the museum specimens. This is a dramatic example, however, and one that is not easily duplicated in countless collection storerooms. My interest lies not with the sensational, but with the unquestioned assumptions and vulnerabilities inherent in acquisitiveness.

Self-interest is a delicate matter at the best of times, and when it involves museum collections it can create a swamp of political machinations, including real and potential embarrassment for the museum community at large. I am thinking of the current flagship of museum arrogance known as the *Declaration on the Importance and Value of Universal Museums*.[74] This manifesto is the antithesis of the *Buffon Declaration* discussed in the last chapter, and can only be described as an ethnocentric and colonial relic. Signed by such luminaries as the Louvre, the Rijksmuseum and the British Museum, the *Universal Museum Declaration* refuses to consider repatriation claims on the grounds that 'universal museums', with their encyclopaedic collections, are best positioned to act on behalf of the world. By claiming to know what is in the world's best interests, the prestigious signatories have violated a cardinal tenet of anthropology, which is to avoid deciding what is in other people's best interests. Who is advising these omniscient directors in such an undertaking, and what is responsible for their lack of intellectual rigour? The extent to which this *Declaration* is harming public perceptions of the museum community is unknown, and I am surprised when many of my colleagues admit to knowing nothing about it – perhaps another expression of museum insularity. The *Declaration* is of considerable concern in both North America and Europe, however, where various signatories are confronted with repatriation claims.

The implications of the *Universal Museum Declaration* for the Parthenon sculptures have not gone unnoticed by museologists and academics, however, and the

Declaration's flawed logic was recently the subject of a philosophical analysis in the journal *Museum Management and Curatorship*, with revealing results.[75] Interestingly, several of the signatories to the *Declaration* declined to participate in this professional discussion for reasons known only to them. One of the contributors, Anthony Snodgrass, Chair of the British Committee for the Reunification of the Parthenon Marbles, distilled the controversy into three cogent factors.[76] The first of these is the knowledge or ignorance of the case, and Snodgrass argues that the more you know about the historical details, the more likely you are to support returning the sculptures to Athens. The second factor has to do with the role of ideology in this debate, and the fact that ideology is seldom moved by reason or logic – witness the *Declaration*'s violation of the anthropological tenet mentioned earlier. Last, and most interesting, Snodgrass singles out the self-esteem of the British Museum, noting that 'the British Museum is really too grand to bandy words with other institutions.' In support of this observation, Snodgrass writes that the British Museum celebrated its 205th anniversary in 2003 with a program entitled 'Enlightening the British.'[77] I can't help but think that the British Museum deserves a backhanded compliment for this degree of panache in the twenty-first century, no matter how misguided it is. How many museums would even contemplate such a pronouncement?

Formidable challenges

The exercise of self-interest and collections is not always as visible as the *Universal Museum Declaration*, as noted by art museum director, Maxwell Anderson. He writes:

> Perhaps the greatest challenge to the good governance of art museums has to do with the participation of volunteer leadership in the art market. The very individuals who are charged with disinterested oversight of museums are often accomplished collectors, whose influence may be greater than is publicly acknowledged.[78]

He goes on to suggest that safeguards must be put in place to ensure that the decisions about what to collect and what to exhibit are made by scholars for the public benefit – not for the collector's benefit. Anderson is diplomatic in his warning, and does not indicate if actual events in his career gave rise to his concerns. Nonetheless, there are numerous examples of perceived conflicts of interest between private collectors and public institutions, including the Los Angeles County Museum of Art, the Museum of Modern Art and the Boston Museum of Fine Arts.[79]

The dangers that Anderson refers to are not restricted to the art world, however, as the looting of archaeological and ethnological collections is a matter of record, and some of the most prestigious museums have participated.[80] Rarely discussed, the opaque world of museum collecting is a Pandora's Box whose dimensions remain boundless, even now. The meaning is clear, as is the vulnerability – museum collections are not immune from the contamination of self-interest, whether dressed up as civic duty or curatorial authority. Assuming intellectual and moral superiority, as in the *Universal Museum Declaration*, is an unfortunate ruse and only proves that the emperor is without clothes in an alarming number of museums.

There is another dimension of museum collections that receives scant attention from practitioners, although it lies at the very heart of the collecting enterprise. In short, it is essentially impossible for museums to keep pace with the changing meaning of objects. Simon Knell calls this an 'interpretive tension' between the values enshrined in the collection and the requirements of modern society.[81] This tension arises from the fact that any collection is a product of its time, and embodies those particular social aspirations and values. Society is forever in process, however, and these aspirations and values change over time. The complex nature of the curatorial process, including the procedures, the time, the energy and the resources required, creates an internal inertia which few, if any, museums can overcome. This makes it mostly impossible for museum collections to reflect the dynamic nature of the society they purport to represent.

Nonetheless, an unknown number of cultural history museums do have contemporary collecting programs, perhaps the most systematic and impressive being Samdok.[82] Samdok is a voluntary association of about 80 Swedish museums of cultural history devoted to contemporary studies and collecting. Founded in 1977, the members cooperate in working groups known as pools. Each pool collaborates to define the content and direction of their work and, at the conclusion of each project, a new piece is added to the Samdok collection of contemporary studies. Samdok is clearly a forward-looking and creative approach to the daunting challenge of contemporary collecting which, inexplicably, has not been embraced by the museum community at large. Perhaps the degree of cooperation required is simply too daunting for the individualistic character of new world museums.

As mentioned earlier, however, the lone institution is simply too bound by the inertia of curatorial and institutional requirements to keep up with the materiality of a society in process. It is perhaps unrealistic to assume that this is even achievable, which causes one to think that most museums are destined to be time capsules only – forever failing to embrace the continuum of time's arrow they are intended to serve. The role of time capsule is a laudable one, but only if it is recognized for what it is, consciously articulated and acted upon. Instead, we have museums promoting the very latest of everything – exhibits, technology and stuff in the shop, while essentially ignoring the temporality of their collections. At the same time, the collections are continuously touted as the core of the mission. Is this a lack of self-awareness, an unavoidable paradox, tacit hypocrisy, or an excuse to sustain the comfortable introversion at the expense of community engagement? Irrespective of the cause of this disjunction, it is another vulnerability that is apparently below the consciousness threshold of most contemporary museums.

Exit the experts

Along with the threats of self-interest and inertia, museum collections are also suffering from a decline in collections-based expertise. Museum workers say repeatedly that the value and the magic reside in the knowledge about the object, not the object itself. Yet, there is persistent talk of 'the death of the curator,' and they remain a target for staff reductions. Simon Knell writes that collections and their authenticity 'critically depend upon the rigour of disciplinary expertise, something in Britain we have rather forgotten. It is expertise – with all the risks of bias – which breathes life into the corpse-like object, by shaping the labels in drawers, exhibits and heads.'[83]

In Canada, the concern over the erosion of expertise and research led to a national meeting to address the status and future of research within Canada's museums. The overall conclusion was that 'the combination of shifting and often urgent priorities, as well as reduced operating budgets, have had an adverse effect on some traditional core museum functions and professional staff, not the least of which are research, collections and curatorship.'[84] It was further noted that 'After years of this debate among museum professionals in Canada, there is now a common consensus that the situation, specifically the capacity to do research and generate new knowledge, has seriously worsened.'[85] Here is yet another example of protracted museum discussions leading nowhere. Meanwhile, one of the legitimate justifications for amassing collections – knowledge generation – steadily erodes.

The most sacred cow

It is difficult to understand why these persistent paradoxes and vulnerabilities confronting collections have not prompted a more concerted inquiry into the very nature, extent and future of collecting. As mentioned earlier, the work of Suzanne Keene is a notable exception, as is the work of Nick Merriman, who articulates the need for intelligent deaccessioning or disposal, as it is called in the UK. Merriman's research clearly demonstrates that, instead of treating all collections as having equal importance, the ascription of value must become a fundamental part of curatorship.[86] Yet there is still no groundswell of professional interest, despite the world having changed significantly since the world powers made their imperial sweep and gave rise to museums as we know them now.

It's as if the museum community is in an everlasting state of denial – continuing to collect with no heed to the consequences of elite self-interest, the inability to keep pace with the meaning of objects, disappearing expertise, and the enormous cost of keeping collections forever in accordance with rigorous professional standards. This is nothing short of nonsensical, and reflects the unrivalled status of collections as the museum's most sacred cow. This metaphorical beast is the largest and strongest of all those in the museum stable, despite its purported meagre diet as of late, and it continues to assume an authority akin to the sacred cow of Hinduism.

The comparison ends here, however, as Hindus believe that the cow is representative of divine and natural beneficence and should therefore be protected and venerated. For museums, the sacred cow of collecting has become a liability, yet is too highly regarded to be open to criticism or curtailment. Or is it too highly regarded? The current state of museum denial does not actually allow any intelligent discussion. In fact, any talk of change is couched in terms of the 'violation of fiduciary responsibility and the alienation of altruistic donors.' Rhetoric aside, just as surely as there are limits to economic growth, the alarming growth of museum collections is no longer tenable. Where are museums to put all of these collections? Who is to pay for their care and maintenance? It is self-evident that museums must either be given the right to treat objects as their own (meaning control over their disposal), or be given appropriate public support to maintain them.[87] Resolving this corrosive contradiction will require a frank and open conversation among the public, governments and museums themselves and, so far, there is nary a glimmer of interest in the museum community in initiating such a discussion. Museums, with few exceptions, remain passive supplicants to donors who are not even required to provide the means to maintain the donations they make (despite the tax advantages), as well as to governments who invoke the obligations of fiduciary responsibility and consistently fail to provide the funding to do so.

In short, museums are in need of a very large dose of self-determination, and this must start with removing collections from their unwarranted pedestal. To do otherwise is to continue jeopardizing the entire enterprise, not unlike the sailors of the British Royal Navy's Franklin Expedition in search of the Northwest Passage. The two expedition ships were trapped in ice in the Canadian Arctic and abandoned in the spring of 1848, when the men set out in search of the mainland and rescue. They were pulling heavy sledges by hand, encumbered with the best of Victorian material culture – watches, spectacles, tools, books, tin boxes, canvas and silver cutlery.[88] The entire expedition perished before reaching safety, succumbing to scurvy, starvation and exhaustion. Repeat – exhaustion. Museums, with their own heavy sledges and their mounting exhaustion, need not suffer a similar fate if there is sufficient collective will to challenge their own conventional wisdom.

Grading collections

Managing collections intelligently and pragmatically is neither mysterious nor rocket science, and there are a variety of real-life museum experiences that model the thinking required to avoid the pitfalls. In concluding this discussion of the self-inflicted challenges of museum collections, I want to briefly mention three approaches to realistic collections management that may or may not be familiar to the reader. I do so in an effort to leaven my jaundiced view of curatorial and institutional automatism, and to emphasize that there are proven methods, as well as opportunities, that can actually strengthen and sustain any museum with the will to act. The first of these is 'grading the collection', the logical precursor to deaccessioning – the dreaded 'D' word. The very word 'deaccessioning' casts its own spell in the museum world, and simply to say the word provokes both trepidation and intransigence among the vast majority of museum workers, irrespective of rank or speciality. Grading can be seen as a comforting first step, however; an exercise in wielding judgement without any immediate consequences. Grading is about rationalizing the collection, and is intended to reduce costs in the long-term and enhance the potential for future growth of significant material. This, in turn, contributes to the overall value and effectiveness of the collection and the museum.

Any collection, contrary to conventional practice, must be 'periodically reviewed and reshaped to serve better the museum's purpose ... pruning and upgrading are the hallmarks of a sound, dynamic and farsighted approach to collections management.'[89] When the Glenbow Museum in Calgary, Canada, graded its collection in 1998, four grades were developed which included the core collection (significant historical and aesthetic importance requiring full museum standards); the community collection (for use in non-museum environments, but not hands-on); the hands-on collection (for use by staff in hands-on programs), and the Grade 4 collection of poor quality or irrelevant objects destined for deaccessioning. Interestingly, the grading resulted in 53 percent of the permanent collection considered to be core, and 19 percent identified as Grade 4.[90] With most museum workers assuming that their entire permanent collection must be core, these numbers are strikingly counterintuitive and underscore two key benefits of the grading process.

First, it allows the curatorial staff to study the collections in-depth, and to shape their future growth with this knowledge. Is this not the heart of the curatorial mission? Second, the outcome of a realistic assessment is guaranteed to increase the use of the collections by a wider cross-section of the public, be they other museums with less than perfect environmental standards, or long-term care facilities where objects have been used for therapeutic reminiscence.[91] For those who argue that everything must be kept for posterity because we do not have the knowledge to assess future significance, two things must be said. Decisions about importance and value can be made intelligently and responsibly, using in-house, curatorial expertise in combination with external advisors, in order to ensure thoroughness and greater objectivity. More to the point, it must be reiterated that the vast majority of museum collections continue to grow with virtually no self-imposed limits, while simultaneously deteriorating. How does one deal with this blatant incongruity?

The 'D' word

As already anticipated, the second approach to constructive collection management, which follows logically from the grading process, is deaccessioning. In short, deaccessioning is the process of disposing, selling or trading objects from a museum collection. Irrespective of the consternation it provokes, there is a body of literature about deaccessioning, and I will not review this hard-won knowledge and experience here. I assume that my belief in its importance to intelligent museum management is abundantly clear by now. Nor will I attempt to distil the 'do's and 'don't's of deaccessioning (and there are many), as these, too, are available in the chronicles of others' experiences. I simply want to relate some personal experiences in an effort to demythologize some of the purported deaccessioning demons that are invoked to prevent its use.

Despite the published theory and method, most deaccessioning continues to be done privately and quietly, 'under the radar,' so to speak. When the Glenbow Museum began its major deaccessioning in the early 1990s, only two examples of deaccessioning by Canadian museums had been published.[92] This persistent lack of visibility further reinforces the stigma of deaccessioning, and fuels the episodic public suspicion which arises when deaccessioning does become public. A fully visible and transparent process is essential, and it will also demonstrate that pruning, as any good gardener knows, is essential to healthy growth. The same is true of museum collections, and deaccessioning must be seen for precisely what it is – sound collections management and a professional necessity. The only alternative lies in sufficient funding to keep everything forever, which is indefensible, irresponsible and unachievable.

Our experience with deaccessioning at the Glenbow Museum has taught me not to assume how the community at large will react – be it government, colleagues or the public. All of these reactions were unpredictable and, with the exception of the public reaction, reflected the dysfunctional thinking that underlies the resistance to deaccessioning. The most severe reaction came from provincial cultural officials who threatened us with a court injunction to prevent our deaccessioning. At the same time, the provincial government had drastically reduced our operating budget over the preceding years. These officials failed in the end and we persevered, intent upon becoming more responsible about our collection costs as part of an institutional plan to enhance our long-term sustainability.[93] This government hypocrisy must be seen for what it is, as museums cannot continue to uphold an idealized and irrational notion of fiduciary trust as public funding stagnates or diminishes.

The reactions of our professional colleagues, including various professional organizations, were also a surprise and, in retrospect, underscored my naivety. I didn't expect any accolades for our initiative from colleagues, but I also did not expect the polite, but firm, opposition. Again, I had assumed that the reasons for deaccessioning were crystal clear and in keeping with sound collections management. The professional reaction once again invoked the slippery slope – the type of thinking discussed earlier which states that museums cannot move a centimetre from their position without sliding into oblivion. In short, 'If you start deaccessioning now, where will it end?' Remember that the abuse of something does not bar its use, and we had no intention of using the proceeds from deaccessioning to pay staff salaries or repair the roof. Instead, we used the capital from the sale of objects to establish a collections endowment fund, the income from which is dedicated to the care of the collections.

If our museum colleagues were cautious, negative or condemning, the public reaction was refreshing. The press was fair and accurate in its reporting and the overall public sentiment was pragmatic and empathetic – as in, 'if you don't use the stuff and it does not serve your purpose, why do you spend money taking care of it?' I had expected empathy from the government and our colleagues, not the public.

The public is continually held up as the bogeyman that will sink any museum that dares to be thoughtful about its bulging storerooms. In fact, the public appreciates intelligence and prudence, especially when they are used in a manner that befits the purpose and circumstances of a particular museum. It's worth a try – as long as the deaccessioning process is well designed, well managed and transparent. As time marches on, what are the alternatives?

Sharing collections

If grading and deaccessioning are simply too radical to contemplate, there is a third approach to collections management that can help to relieve the burden and, more importantly, empower the institution and its community in the process. I am thinking of a very simple and innovative concept – sharing the collection and its stewardship. What follows is an example of an innovative approach to sharing collections which stands in stark contrast to the traditional museum practice of hoarding – nowhere better expressed than in the remarkably antiquated *Universal Museum Declaration*.

The concept of the Museum of New Zealand Te Papa Tongarewa (Te Papa), located in Wellington, was developed through an extensive national consultative process.[94] Te Papa's conceptual framework recognizes three priority concerns – the earth on which we live, those who belong to the land by right of first discovery, and those who belong to the land by right of treaty. These three concerns underlie Te Papa's mission, which is to serve as a forum for New Zealand 'to present, explore and preserve the heritage of its cultures and the knowledge of the natural environment in order to better understand and treasure the past, enrich the present and meet the challenges of the future.'[95] Their approach is important because it is based on the recognition that museums must increasingly accept that *iwi* (indigenous tribes) must be involved in the interpretation, exhibition, and care of their artifacts, and that this involvement can only be achieved through strong and effective partnerships.

The other aspect of Te Papa's work which is of particular value is their commitment to certain core concepts underlying their partnerships. These concepts are spiritual in nature, and are concerned with *tikanga*, or the correct way of doing things. These rules and customs are based on traditional and customary knowledge, as well as the Maori world-view, and a great deal of *tikanga* that relates to museums is associated with *tapu* and *mana*. If *tapu* can be seen as potential power, *mana* can be regarded as actual power and is also seen as emanating from the gods.[96] It is instructive to note how Te Papa, a mainstream cultural institution, is integrating spiritual values and beliefs into what are normally seen as the secular activities of a museum. Here we have a remarkable example of integrating the artifactual and the ecological, as well as people and place – a radical departure from conventional museum practice. Anything is possible, truly.

In concluding this inquiry into the self-imposed challenges of collecting, we have now come full circle back to the troubled world. Have museums become microcosms of the unbridled consumption that is inexorably unravelling the biosphere? In their celebration of materialism, have museums become the unwitting handmaidens to a value system that is at odds with our survival as a species? With unlimited collections growth and declining resources for collections care, coupled with an increasing emphasis on marketplace initiatives, are museums losing their way? At minimum, doesn't the current trajectory require critical reflection and serious adjustment? At a time of unprecedented challenges, are museums modelling the kind of behaviour incumbent upon social institutions and required by succeeding generations? I think not. Is it time to ponder some of the paradoxes, perils and hypocrisy embedded in museum collections and address these issues forthrightly? Museums themselves must decide the future role of collections; it is their collective responsibility. Or are collections the unacknowledged means to sustain comfortable introversion while ignoring a broader engagement?

The answers to all of these questions will vary, depending upon the museum. We do know that various museums are becoming increasingly conscious, but there are so many museums, with so many redundant collections, demanding so many resources. For those museums that are content with the status quo, the material and psychic burden of collections may ultimately be their undoing as societal pressures magnify. I recall a recent bumper sticker, popular in Canada and the US, which reads, 'The one who dies with the most toys wins.' I have always associated that thinking with people who have lots of money but no brains – never with museums.

4

Debunking the marketplace

There is no doubt that museums and galleries worldwide are struggling to maintain their stability in response to the complex challenges facing the non-profit world. These challenges range from declining attendance for most and over-attendance for some, to finding the appropriate balance between public funding and earned revenues, and none of them are easily overcome. Many of these challenges are inescapably economic, and originate in the belief that unlimited economic growth and unconstrained consumption are essential to our well-being. Indeed, capitalism and the lure of the marketplace have become inescapable for all of us, including organizations. As philosopher Mark Kingwell notes, 'every moment of waking and sleeping life is shot through with commitment to the goods and services of the global economy. We are capitalism made flesh.'[1] The dominant ideology of capitalism and the decline of public funding for museums have coupled to produce a harmful offspring – a preoccupation with the marketplace and commerce, characterized by the primacy of economic interests in institutional decision-making.

As noted in Chapter 1, many museums now see no other way but to consume their way to survival or prosperity, failing to recognize that this is increasing their vulnerability as social institutions. The fundamental purpose of this book is to consider some alternatives. The other face of marketplace ideology is corporatism – based on 'our adoration of self-interest and our denial of public good,' to quote the Canadian essayist, John Ralston Saul.[2] He notes that corporatism also results in individual passivity, conformity and silence, because the corporatist system depends upon the citizen's desire for inner comfort. Instead, Ralston Saul argues that our individual and collective responsibilities in a democracy hinge upon participation and the psychic discomfort which inevitably accompanies active engagement in the public sphere. In his view, 'the acceptance of psychic discomfort is the acceptance of consciousness.'[3]

Corporatism has arrived

Like many individuals in our complacent society, many museums are in the grip of passivity and conformity, tacitly rejecting the discomfort that accompanies the uncertain search for relevance. The growing influence of corporatist values in museums is puzzling, however, considering the critical thinking that should accompany the self-proclaimed role of museums as knowledge-based institutions. The marketplace and corporatism are admittedly potent forces, as governments are now 'imbued with a theological belief in the supremacy of free markets', to quote the historian Eric Hobsbawm.[4]

This trend, in combination with the free-market worship of the consumer's supreme power, has made things very difficult for museums. This is all the more reason why museum boards, directors, senior managers and staff must exercise both reflection and caution, and seriously ponder a critically important distinction. That is, while we can acknowledge that the market is the key element in economics and in wealth creation, we are not bound to accept a free-market society, where everything is to be achieved through the pursuit of private interest.[5] It is patently obvious that the marketplace is incapable of addressing the collective good, while museums are potentially key agents in doing so. Corporations, both national and multinational, are second only to governments in their influence on public policy and, as noted earlier, have clearly demonstrated time and again that the common good can be an inexhaustible arena for private gain. It is essential that museums become more conscious of the market forces they are embracing, in an effort to avoid the consequences described in this chapter.

Understandably, criticism of the reigning economic model is considered to be gratuitous by museum boards and executives, who are responsible for the fiscal health of their museums in the face of declining or stagnant public funding, apathetic audiences, competitive fundraising, and the abundance of entertaining distractions for the populace at large. Some museum directors point out that they would not be pursuing a marketplace agenda if they were not forced to by financial circumstances. Recognizing the very real fiscal pressures confronting museums, this chapter is devoted to a critique of the marketplace and corporatism, and their deleterious effects on museums. Both the marketplace and corporatism must be seen for what they are, as they continue to enfeeble otherwise competent museums and divert them from their core values and strengths as social institutions. Moreover, it will be argued that corporatism, the values implicit in the free market, and the strict application of business models are actually obstacles to achieving accountability and long-term sustainability. There are alternatives, but they are not to be found in conformity and unthinking consumption.

Back to the beginning

As the reader might well question my qualifications for undertaking this critique of corporatism and the free market, I must begin by relating some formative experiences that have led me to my current perspective, and which are also the foundation of my current bias against the preoccupation with money as the measure of worth. When I took my first job as the founding director of the Prince of Wales Northern Heritage Centre in Canada's remote Northwest Territories, there were no concerns about money. It was a 100 percent government project, complete with both

Figure 12 Jose Kusugak and the author en route by snowmobile to a museum meeting with Inuit elders in Canada's Central Arctic, 1986.

Photo: courtesy of Robert R. Janes

capital and operating budgets. Unpredictable budget reductions and increases were common, and we never received all the funding that we requested, but admission was free, fundraising was not required, and there was no need to generate earned revenues. In fact, fundraising and earned revenues were never discussed during my 10-year tenure as Director (1976–1986), because the government and the taxpayer assumed the full responsibility. Furthermore, as a line department of government, the museum did not have a board of directors and accountability was to a government minister only.

Our mission was to serve 65 remote communities in the region by providing professional services – ranging from travelling exhibits to archaeological research. This experience was the antithesis of the corporatist imperative and, in retrospect, lacked the discipline and empathy that come from a greater sensitivity to audience needs and aspirations. Actually, I was so naïve and presumptuous that I refused to allow the wife of the government leader to host a tea for dignitaries in our public lounge, claiming that social functions were not the museum's responsibility. She accepted my refusal, as did the government, a tribute to their empathy for my self-serving lack of imagination.

My perspective matured when I left that position and became the founding director of the Science Institute of the Northwest Territories (SINT) in 1986, an arm's-length agency devoted to bridging the gap between mainstream scientific work and the needs and aspirations of northern residents. Beginning a century earlier, the peoples of the Northwest Territories (NT), who include Euro-Canadians, Dene, Inuit and Metis, were the subjects of countless scientific investigations conducted by an international cadre of academics and graduate students. Few, if any, of these researchers ever shared the results or the implications of their work with their research subjects. This was particularly exasperating for the NT's indigenous peoples (the Dene, Inuit and Metis), who constituted two-thirds of the population at that time. They were not opposed to research; they simply wanted to know how they could benefit, individually or collectively, from the ongoing generation of knowledge in their homeland. Although not labelled as such, this was an early call for science in the public interest. Northerners have always had a practical bent – it's a survival skill in a severe land. A group of citizens and scientists eventually decided that this intellectual colonialism must cease, and they envisioned the Science Institute of the Northwest Territories as the mechanism for democratization.

With a culturally diverse board of northern citizens and barely sufficient core funding from the government, the Science Institute was obliged to reach out and define its relevance amidst the volatile politics of remote northern communities, as well as to establish its credibility in the world of mainstream science and grantsmanship. This was done, with programs ranging from the licensing of researchers (to ensure follow-up), to youth programs based on traditional knowledge, to the operation of remote research facilities to assist mainstream scientists and resident researchers in their investigations. The learning was clear – service and accountability to northern communities and the scientific establishment required grassroots support stemming from real and perceived relevance. In retrospect, this was the best fiscal model of all – a governing body of diverse citizens, reliable (albeit modest) core funding, external monetary support from diverse sources for innovation and growth, and the autonomy to act in the best interests of organizational and community aspirations. With my next position, the balance between public funding and earned revenues was destined to change, with the fiscal pendulum careening into the marketplace.

Shortly after I became the CEO of the Glenbow Museum in 1989, I was advised by the Chair of the Board of Governors that the museum's funding agreement with the province of Alberta had expired and no new arrangements had been negotiated. None of this had been discussed during the interviews and selection process, an unfortunate or intentional oversight familiar to many new museum directors. This oversight was the harbinger of a fateful future, as Glenbow had been receiving between 80 and 90 percent of its annual operating budget from the province until I arrived. The year was 1992 and a conservative estimate of income and expenditures revealed a shocking projection – a cumulative deficit of CA$7.7 million by 1997. In short, if we continued at our current rate of expenditures, in the face of declining government support, we would be bankrupt and closed within five years. Thus began a massive organizational change process which led to the redesign and renewal of the museum based on six strategies, all of which has been chronicled elsewhere.[6]

One of these strategies was devoted to developing commercial alliances and business ventures for the sole purpose of increasing earned revenues, and thus began my immersion in the marketplace. We designed and developed Glenbow Enterprises, a for-profit business unit, and engaged in a variety of commercial activities including consulting services, art rentals, facility rentals and the design and construction of collection storage facilities and exhibitions for corporate offices in Calgary. All of these earned revenues were allocated to Glenbow's operating expenses. Federal tax officials had no problem with this initiative, as long as we engaged in activities that were directly related to our mandate as a non-profit organization. As the CEO, I was also given a revenue line in the annual operating budget and was expected to meet it with consulting and public speaking fees. This I did. To shorten a long and arduous story, when I left my position in 2000 after 10 weary years of relentless budget balancing (deficit spending was a cause for dismissal), Glenbow was getting 23 percent of its funding from the province and 10 percent from the City of Calgary. The remainder of the CA$11 million budget, or 67 percent, came from investment income (an endowment invested in stocks, bonds and cash), fundraising, commercial activities, admissions and memberships.[7]

This degree of financial self-sufficiency continued with my successor, with Glenbow reporting a budget of CA$13 million for 2006–2007, made up of 37 percent of public funding and 63 percent coming from fundraising, investment income, commercial activities, admissions and membership.[8] Although Glenbow has been the most self-sufficient of Canada's ten largest museums for well over a decade, this distinction has come with a significant cost, and has meant a preoccupation with attendance numbers, borrowed blockbuster exhibitions and fundraising. To what extent this has hindered more innovative community engagement is difficult to say, but a preoccupation with the bottom line is precisely that. This has also prompted the Glenbow's board to chase the allure of corporate partnerships, a cautionary tale which will be discussed later in this chapter.

The circle is now complete, and my thinking has returned to where I began as a novice director, only this time with an understanding of what is required. With the benefit of having engaged in the three most typical operating models used by museums, I can only conclude that the domination of the earned-income imperative is debilitating, inappropriate and unnecessary. The totally dependent Northern Heritage Centre is also unacceptable, as the introversion afforded by complete government funding impairs or prevents true accountability. This model is a twentieth-century relic – nice if you can get it, but ultimately untenable. In short, over-reliance on public funding can be as insidious as the market model. Nor is the severe economic self-sufficiency of Glenbow realistic, as it is oblivious to the purpose and values of museums, as well as being dangerously consumptive of staff energy and commitment. Long-term sustainability lies in a diversified and reasonable balance of public money and earned income, similar to that of the Science Institute.

As noted earlier, however, there has never been any concerted discussion within the museum community about what the mixture of public funding and earned revenues should be. Unfortunately, in this age of hyper-capitalism, maximum self-sufficiency based on earned income has become the grail of many museum boards, subjecting all concerned to myriad complexities and pressures that have nothing to do with the inherent purpose of museums. But if health care, prisons, public transportation, the quality of food, the availability of water, media concentration, and so on, are all amenable to the profit motives of the marketplace, why should museums be exempt from the imposition of marketplace ideology, especially when public funding is inadequate to keep them afloat?

They aren't, nor should they be, as business literacy and efficiency are essential in a competent museum. More on this later. For museums, however, financial self-sufficiency is a myth that permits museums and their boards to pursue growth and consumption as the keys to the future, thus avoiding any substantive consideration of what sustainability might look like in the long term. Sustainability could actually mean a smaller core staff, or a smaller building, or starting afresh with a new mission and values, or merging with like-minded organizations, or even deaccessioning or mothballing a portion of the collection. Boards and staff might even consider asking the two essential questions posed in Chapter 1 – 'If museums did not exist, would we reinvent them and what would they look like?' And, 'If the museum were to be reinvented, what would be the public's role in the reinvented institution?' These are the conversations that are really required, because to ignore them is both chimerical and dangerous, as global issues mount and the unique world of museums inevitably chills. It might be helpful to bear in mind that 'the crucial dimensions of scarcity in human life are not economic, but existential. They are related to our needs for leisure and contemplation, peace of mind, love, community and self-realization.'[9]

A clash of values

The marketplace is now the 'elephant in the room' for a host of museums, and the danger lies in both the size and the nature of the beast. This elephant can no longer be ignored because it has created a conflict in values, which has nothing to do with the use of sound business practices in museums. The inappropriateness of unthinking adherence to the marketplace lies in the complexity of museums as institutions, because every museum, in the language of the marketplace, is a mixed portfolio. Some museum work is clearly subject to market forces, such as restaurants, shops and product development, while other activities such as collections care, scientific research and community engagement are not. The latter bear no relation to the market economy and, in fact, require a safe distance from marketplace and corporatist fallout.

Market ideology and corporatism have failed to demonstrate any real ability to deal with the complexities of a competent museum and are, instead, homogenizing the complex portfolio with a stultifying adherence to financial considerations – at the expense of most everything else. The tyranny of quantitative measures, such as attendance numbers and shop revenues, is a clear indication of this reality. I am curious about how a bottom line mentality would cope with the complexities inherent in the following fictionalized glimpse of a museum director's meeting schedule, the details of which are all based in fact.

Figure 13 The Royal Ontario Museum's paleontological excavations at the Burgess Shale, Yoho National Park, British Columbia, Canada, 1999. The Burgess Shale fossils are unique because they are 500 million years old, exquisitely preserved and reveal important clues to the nature of evolution.

Photo: courtesy of Priscilla B. Janes

The museum director's datebook

Tuesday, 4 January

Meeting with conservation and curatorial staff concerning the storage of a sacred medicine bundle.

Reality check   It has come to the attention of the curatorial staff that the elders of the First Nation who borrowed this medicine bundle for ceremonial use consider it to be the equivalent of a living child. Professional conservation standards require that the bundle be placed in a freezer to prevent any infestation of the existing collections when the bundle is returned to storage after the loan.

Thursday, 11 January

Meeting with the Director of Development concerning the raffle results at the annual fundraising event.

Reality check   A donated motorcycle was raffled off at the annual signature fundraising event, but the winner, a prominent citizen, does not want the motorcycle and wishes to donate it back to the museum for a tax receipt.

Tuesday, 15 January

Meeting with the Investment Oversight Committee of the Board of Directors concerning the underperformance of the endowment.

Reality check   The endowment is currently managed by two investment firms that have different investment philosophies to ensure a balanced approach. Both firms have underperformed for three consecutive quarters and a change in approach has been recommended by a board member who owns a wealth management company.

Friday, 4 February

Meeting with government protocol staff concerning the upcoming visit of senior elected leaders.

Reality check   The government wishes to host a large reception for foreign delegates to an international trade meeting, which will require the closure of several public galleries for a full day. The reception happens to be on a Saturday, which is a free admission day to encourage attendance by underprivileged families, the costs of which are underwritten by a family foundation.

Monday, 14 February

Meeting with the Senior Vice-President of Community Affairs for a multinational corporation

Reality check   Three years ago this corporation signed a five year funding agreement to underwrite 75 percent of the costs of an innovative education program devoted to children with learning disabilities. Senior personnel have changed, along with corporate interests and priorities, and the corporation now wants to reduce their financial commitment by half within 30 days.

Tuesday, 22 February

Special meeting of the Senior Management Group and the Executive of the employees union.

Reality check   At the request of the Senior Ethnologist, the Senior Management Group and the Manager of Personnel agreed to recognize the traditional knowledge of several First Nations staff as equivalent to a master's degree for the purposes of job classification and the rate of pay. The union executive and the majority of curators are challenging this decision.

Monday, 28 February

Emergency meeting of the full Board of Directors.

Reality check   The Gay/Lesbian Alliance of People of Colour were given permission by a junior staff person to host a sexuality film festival in the museum's theatre. All of the films will have to be rated by the film classification board before being approved and no one under 18 will be admitted, in any event. One half of the Board wants the film festival cancelled immediately. The Alliance has threatened court action for censorship, along with a large demonstration, if they are not allowed to hold the event.

In light of the competing values and interests noted above, making a profit in the business world is likely to be much easier. It is the complexity of museums – these interminable shades of grey – that makes the marketplace not only less than useful as a source of guidance but also an obstacle to the trust and understanding of the broader community. Contrary to the received wisdom of the marketplace, the marketplace and its activities actually deplete trust.[10] It is the so-called third sector or civil society, occupying the space between business and government, which contains the organizations upon which the marketplace depends – these third sector organizations are neither business nor government. There is no stability without the third sector, because the markets build upon the strength of this sector. All the organizations in the third sector, including museums, generate the social capital – the networks, norms, trust and shared values – which is transferred into the social sphere and not only helps to hold society together but is also instrumental in facilitating an understanding of the interconnectedness of society and the interests within it. Social capital is born of long-term associations that are not explicitly self-interested or coerced, and it typically diminishes if it is not regularly renewed or replaced.[11]

Corporatists and marketplace ideologues believe, as do business people in general, that markets create communities when, in fact, the opposite is true. Communities create and sustain the trust upon which the marketplace is based. Museums are apparently unaware of their role and their strengths in this vital responsibility, willing to let their unique assets be subsumed under the rhetoric that would have them become businesses. This may be appealing theoretically, but it is impossible in reality, as the imperative of the marketplace cannot accommodate the real-life complexities when the final arbiter is the bottom line. The insatiable motive of the bottom line is ultimately monetary gain, in whatever guise, not collective well-being. It wasn't that long ago when the third sector was seen as a much-needed antidote to the materialism that dominated twentieth-century thinking, recognizing the third sector's emphasis on service, relationships and a sense of grounding in the larger community.[12] It is now the twenty-first century and it appears that museums are oblivious to this unfulfilled potential, while continuing to lose their way under the influence of heightened commercialism.

The anatomy of failure

The failed relationship between museums and the marketplace goes beyond the clash of values to include a litany of embarrassing and injurious contradictions and consequences, as museums drift onto the shoals of unthinking conformity. These afflictions include short-term thinking, money as the measure of worth, conspicuous consumption and business tribalism, each of which is discussed below. It is time for some independence of thought, even some well-considered rebellion to the sway of hyper-capitalism.

The 500-year business plan

The most obvious clash of values is apparent in how museums have traditionally viewed time, as compared to the marketplace. Museums are about time and are time machines in a sense, although their bias has always been for the past, not the future, unlike the classic time machine. This commitment to the continuum of time is vitally important, as the writer and philosopher, Robert Grudin, notes, 'We usually fail to understand that the present achieves full reality only when seen by those who retain the perspectives of past and future, that indeed no aspect of time is really available to us except in terms of the continuum.'[13] Depending upon the museum and its collection, be it paleontological or contemporary art, this continuum can be longer or shorter, but all museums share a long-term commitment to the objects in their care.

As a museum director, I often noted that collections management required a 500-year business plan, much to the bemusement of our corporate board members – all in an effort to operationalize the sentiment that museums keep collections 'forever.' Humankind is in dire need of a long-term perspective to counteract the short-term thinking which drives the marketplace – be it the focus on quarterly results, shareholder value, or the immediate gratification of consumerism. This is the time continuum at play, and is the special realm of museums. The commitment to the long term is an irreplaceable contribution that only museums can make, yet it is eroding under an ideology that is oblivious to its value.

The short-lived corporation

Recognizing that short-term thinking is the foundation of marketplace ideology, it is appropriate to note that the average life expectancy of multinational corporations is between 40 and 50 years, a discovery that provoked such alarm that an inquiry was undertaken to determine why.[14] The author of this work, Arie DeGeus, a senior planner at Royal Dutch Shell, concluded that the exclusive focus on the production of goods and services has doomed the vast majority of companies to rapid extinction. DeGeus also identified four traits which characterized 30 companies which have existed for 100 to 700 years. These traits are conservative financing (governing growth and evolution both effectively and frugally); sensitivity to the world around them (the ability to learn and adapt); cohesion and identity (the ability to build a community of employees who feel they belong, as well as a persona for the organization); and last, considerable tolerance, encouragement and decentralization for experiments and learning which promote change.[15]

103

Most importantly for this discussion, DeGeus concludes that, 'The twin policies of managing for profit and maximizing shareholder value, at the expense of all other goals, are vestigial management traditions. They no longer reflect the imperatives of the world we live in today. They are suboptimal, even destructive – not just to the rest of society, but to the companies that adopt them.'[16] Yet, these twin policies continue to grow in status and influence, and have now entered the museum boardroom in the guise of quantitative measures, earned revenues, excess consumption, hollow imitation and 'the customer is always right' mantra. On the contrary, DeGeus sees companies as living organisms, existing for their own improvement, to fulfil their potential and become as great as they can be – just as human beings exist to survive and thrive. Why should museums be any different? DeGeus' book, now a business classic, has apparently escaped the attention of both the for-profit and non-profit sectors, and much tension and conflict can now be expected to accompany the rearguard action to rid museums of their outmoded belief system.

Money as the measure of worth

Underlying the pervasive power of short-term thinking is the new orthodoxy of money as the measure of worth, and herein lies another significant clash in values. This orthodoxy has so imbued our everyday lives that we seem oblivious to it, and it is no wonder that it now pervades the museum world. Psychologist Mihaly Csikszentmihalyi notes that:

> The most important functions of society, which used to be relatively independent of the market, have now become servants of Wall Street. From managed health care to agribusiness, from the media to genetic research, from education to music and entertainment, the intrinsic value of these institutions has been overshadowed by their valuation on the market.[17]

Indeed, even warfare has once again been privatized, and mercenaries are now employed from Iraq to Africa, including the provision of logistical support for government armies.[18]

In the museum world, the extent to which money has cast its spell is visible in recent remarks delivered at the Midwinter Meeting of the Association of Art Museum Directors in January of 2008.[19] John Wetenhall, an art museum director, introduced a panel discussion on the performance of art galleries by referring to the three means of competition as taught by management schools – price, quality or differentiation. He added speed and flexibility to the holy trinity and noted 'how quickly we can deliver results affects how many accomplishments we may pursue.'[20] He rightly questioned the need for continuous institutional growth, and noted that a mature art gallery can be likened to a 'mature industry', otherwise known as 'a cash cow, valued for spinning off quarterly dividends to shareholders – the stuff of so-called widow and orphan stocks.'[21]

A curious and telling choice of language, to be sure. Art galleries do, indeed, have 'dividends', including the quality of the art shown, the richness of cultural programming,

and the associated learning and personal experiences. But why entomb these qualities in the vacuous language of commerce? Is this meant to legitimize the work of
art galleries in the competitive marketplace, or to satisfy colleagues and trustees
who are already immersed? I would hope that art gallery directors are capable of
using language that is more natural and more appropriate than commercial dogma.
Perhaps it is more difficult now, with the marketplace elephant in the room.

This juggernaut of market forces cannot be blamed on the business community
alone, although it is definitely the prime mover. Society as a whole must also assume
responsibility, for intentionally or not, we have all developed a taste for comfort,
excess and the highest possible return on investment in the shortest amount of
time. As difficult as it may be to concede, the marketplace now provides much of
our ostensible happiness and sense of worth, and museums are not immune. This
has not gone unnoticed, and there is obvious concern in the museum community
about the advent of money as the measure of worth. Veteran museum executive Tom
Freudenheim writes that 'The money worm has burrowed into museum foundations
in the last five decades, weakening structures already challenged by power politics,
relevancy issues, and contemporary anxieties.'[22] He further notes that 'the idea of a
museum ... as a money-making machine is frighteningly pervasive.'

Similar anxieties are also emerging from the UK, where the Museums Association
(MA) notes that more and more museums are adopting the short-term, money focus
characteristic of business. The MA's landmark report, which will be discussed in a
later chapter, questions the sustainability of museums that occupy energy-hungry
buildings, have expanding collections, and continually destroy old exhibitions with
little reuse or recycling, while also promoting international tourism that involves
energy-consuming travel.[23] All in the service of the marketplace, of course.

Fighting fog with fog

Alas, even the debilitating effects of marketplace ideology have been insufficient
to mobilize the museum community to rise to its own defence. The result has been
the insidious imposition of quantitative performance measures based on money as
the measure of worth (attendance, number of exhibitions, earned revenues, cost per
visitor and so forth), in the absence of any substantive evaluation or comment by
the museum community itself. There was, however, a flurry of interest in performance measures throughout the 1990s, but none of the ensuing published papers,
conference sessions or actual strategic plans led to any consensus (local, national
or international) on which types of measures are appropriate, including the mix
of quantitative and qualitative. Without such dialogue and evaluation, museums
have once again chosen passivity and isolation, bereft of any influence to counteract
the dominance of simplistic, commercial indicators. To relinquish the definition of
performance measures is dangerous, as these measures are, in effect, professional
standards. For museums to claim professional status and then decline the setting of
standards has created a debilitating trajectory governed by external forces. One can

only assume a tacit belief on the part of museums that they would remain immune to the societal demand for accountability.

The need to involve the museum community in its own performance assessment has not gone away, however, and will continue to grow, as performance measurement systems themselves are problematic and require intelligence and discipline to design and monitor. This is underscored by research in Austria where, in 2002, the eight national museums became responsible for their own budgets.[24] The ministry retained ownership of the collections, but the museums assumed operational control, and are required to report a number of key figures to measure their performance. Based on interviews with museum managers, curators, artists, and government officials about their experiences, the researchers concluded that:

> neither museum managers nor ministerial agencies are satisfied with the existing reporting system. They are all aware that the performance measurement systems actually can be compared to shooting clay pigeons in the fog. Both groups try to find the solution in a continuous elaboration of the key figures in use, which results in an inflation of numbers. As numbers lack the capability to provide full transparency, it is the attempt to fight 'fog' with more 'fog'.[25]

'Shooting clay pigeons in the fog', and 'fighting fog with fog', are not exactly bold inducements to forging an intelligent performance management system for museums. In the absence of a deliberate approach to measurement in North America, however, the imposition of money as the measure of worth will continue, either until museums confront its essential meaninglessness, or the marketplace collapses from its own excesses. Based on museum inertia to date, my money is on the latter.

Culture as consumption

Both short-term thinking and money as the measure of worth are key ingredients in another contemporary museum phenomenon – culture as consumption. Again, it is helpful to look at what museum directors are saying to each other, and to their constituencies, for an indication of how deeply consumption has pervaded the museum scene. In a 2007 address to the Empire Club of Canada (which includes some of Canada's most influential professional, business, labour and government leaders), William Thorsell, Director and CEO of Toronto's Royal Ontario Museum (ROM), spoke of the museum as the new agora. He noted that architecture is the most public of arts and 'cultural institutions have a responsibility to be vigorous patrons of architecture, pushing boundaries and empowering genius.'[26] Thorsell is committed to this sentiment and recently opened their newly renovated museum, complete with Daniel Libeskind's Crystal mentioned earlier. He sees the museum as the new meeting place, or agora, replacing the town hall and the church, and 'providing an opportunity to meet new people in an elegant setting that includes restaurants, lounges and distinctive retail.'[27]

Herein lies the other agenda, as the ROM was short CA$50 million at the time of writing to complete the CA$303 million project, as well as requiring an increase to its operating budget. Earned revenues are essential and consumers are increasingly the source, or are at least hoped to be. Thorsell concludes his address with the request 'please don't be shy about ordering that ROMtini (signature martini) in Crystal Five – Toronto's amazing new rooftop restaurant and bar. What Agora would be complete without one?'[28] Although eating and drinking have always been part of public life, this is certainly a new take on the agora of old.

What's interesting is the prominent role that consumption, in a variety of forms, now plays in defining the ostensible uniqueness of museums, usually eclipsing any reference to purpose, values or the world of the non-elite. We know the argument by now – economic necessity – born of diminishing budgets, rising costs and the need to get people's attention. Although our society remains steadfast in its allegiance to consumption, it is troublesome that so many museums are embracing commercial dogma when prescient individuals and organizations, including some museums, are loosening its grip. Some of these resilient innovators will be discussed in Chapter 5.

Surprisingly, museum excess has begun to annoy even the financial sector. In an investment commentary entitled 'Enough is Enough', William Gross, Managing Director of Pacific Investment Management Company (one of the largest fixed income managers in the world), takes issue with the growing disparity between the rich, the middle and the lower classes, and art museums emerge as one of his bellwethers. Gross writes,

> Trust funds for the kids, inheritances for the grandkids, multiple vacation homes, private planes, multi-million dollar birthday bashes and ego-rich donations to local art museums and concert halls are but a few of the ways that rich people waste money ... When millions of people are dying from AIDS and malaria in Africa, it is hard to justify the umpteenth society gala held for the benefit of a performing arts center or an art museum. A thirty million dollar gift for a concert hall is not philanthropy, it is a Napoleonic coronation.[29]

Irrespective of the rich, consumer spending on culture, including museums, has reached deeper into society, with Canadian consumers spending over CA$25 billion on cultural goods and services in 2005.[30] This spending was 5 percent higher than the combined consumer spending on household furniture, appliances and tools. Consumer spending on cultural goods and services is also over three times larger than the CA$7.7 billion spent on culture in Canada by all levels of government in 2003/04, and grew by 48 percent between 1997 and 2005, much higher than the 18 percent rise in the Consumer Price Index during the same period. This is but one example from Canada.

It appears that the so-called cultural industries, including museums, are enjoying unprecedented acceptance in our mercantile world, while the biosphere buckles under the strain. Actually, bigger is no longer better – it's becoming culpable. At the same time, there is some comfort to be had in the nature of cultural goods and services, however, as they are not the portable cigar thermidors with built-in humidification systems or the automatic watch winders mentioned in Chapter 2.

This heightened level of consumption has assumed even greater import in the broader economy, as evidenced by the 2008 International Forum on the Creative Economy devoted to 'Measuring Arts and Culture as an Economic and Social Engine of a Country's Wealth.'[31] One of the conference themes invited research on the measurement of the contribution of the arts and cultural sector to a country's economy. A second theme, 'Consumption Dynamics: Consumers Driving Change' was devoted to research that focuses on the profile of Canadian and international consumers of cultural goods and services, including trends in consumption and new roles for consumers in artistic and cultural activities. With initiatives such as these, there is little doubt that museums and their sister disciplines (the literary and performing arts) are competing for recognition as the new frontier for generating wealth.

From whom remains a mystery, however, judging by the precarious balance sheets of even the most senior museums. Museums, in fact, have grown fond of debt as the marketplace euphoria unfolds, and have turned once again to bond offerings to finance various initiatives.[32] Bond sales are not new, as the Art Institute of Chicago was doing this as far back as 1978, but the technique has now spread to smaller institutions. For example, the Holocaust Memorial Foundation of Illinois raised US$28.5 million in 2006 through a bond offering to build a museum and education centre. The Please Touch Museum in Philadelphia, where children are encouraged to handle the displays, sold US$60 million in bonds in 2006 to help expand and move to a historic site. That same year, the Telfair Museum of Art in Savannah, Georgia, raised US$8 million through bonds to help pay for new facilities. With due regard for this entrepreneurial spirit, the fact remains that bonds require the museum to pay back the interest, as well as the principal – a significant obligation as compared to donations, grants and earned revenues. Debt, consumption and growth have always been bedfellows in the world of commerce; they are now becoming familiar companions among museums.

Vanity architecture

Nowhere is culture as consumption more visible than in the realm of celebrity, vanity or simply new architecture – a widespread phenomenon throughout the museum world. China, for example, is planning to build 1,000 new museums by 2015, so that every city with a population of 100,000 or more has at least one. The newly-renovated Capital Museum in Beijing is 60,000 square metres (645,000 square feet) and as large as the Louvre Museum in Paris.[33] Celebrity architects are not a prerequisite, however, as museums are also building and renovating without necessarily employing high profile personalities. Although often likened to a renaissance, this architectural boom doesn't merit this praise, lacking as it commonly does any vigorous intellectual or creative resurgence within the museum itself. In fact, the opposite prevails, as the 'If you build it, he will come' syndrome readily diverts attention away from a consideration of purpose, values, and the requirements for long-term sustainability. If this seems unduly harsh, let's consider some implications and consequences of this contemporary bandwagon.

In pursuit of both stability and prosperity, various museums have chosen to increase their profile, popularity and earned revenues through architectural renewal, which usually strives to include some expression of sensationalism.[34] Various museums have adopted this approach, especially larger ones, although its contribution to the museum's long-term sustainability is decidedly in doubt, as well as being controversial.[35] In a research paper commissioned by the Getty Leadership Institute, museum consultant Adrian Ellis concluded that this approach is not sustainable.[36] The problem with the expansion plan, or the 'galvanizing building initiative', as the context to raise funds, refinance, and move forward, is cogently summarized by Ellis:

> this strategy ... is a form of pyramid selling or Ponzi scheme. Eventually, after the noise has died down and the new building is completed, the logic of the weakening balance sheet kicks in again. Unless the scheme was so successful that it has generated a whole new set of contributed funding opportunities, then the systemic underfinancing reappears, and in a heightened form, given the larger facility and the more ambitious programming on which the facility is premised. The museum stands faced, again, with the three options of crisis appeal, more populist programming, or obfuscatory expansion.[37]

Ellis draws several valuable and sobering conclusions, which he offers as recommendations to museum directors. He suggests that they analyse and articulate the full cost, rather than the marginal cost of program growth, in a format that allows this to be done and communicated effectively to the outside world. In addition, he suggests that museum directors think about, and articulate, the requirements for institutional growth in parallel with program growth, as well as including goals for capital structure and investment as part of their strategic planning. Ellis also asks museum leaders to 'Remember that the reason they [museums] are nonprofit organizations is not just because they are mission driven. It's not just because their mission is valued by society. It's also because the pursuit of mission is an axiomatically unprofitable activity.'[38] This is essential advice, indeed, recognizing the ubiquity of commercial dogma, and Ellis is to be acknowledged for his candor.

Similar concerns have also emerged from Western Europe, where James M. Bradburne has been writing for over a decade about museums, sustainability and the tyranny of museum architecture or, the 'edifice complex', as I prefer to call it. In a frank and highly readable article entitled 'The Museum Time Bomb: Overbuilt, Overtraded and Overdrawn', Bradburne articulates the path to potential ruin by noting that operating costs are the heart of the museum time bomb for old museums as well as new ones, as inflation continues unabated. Large buildings require larger staff and incur substantially higher operating costs, costs which are rarely, if ever, recognized by private or public funders.[39] Bradburne follows this progression to its logical conclusion – museums are required to increase earned revenues to pay the increased costs, mostly by arguing that increased visitation to the new or renovated building will generate the additional revenue. He concludes by noting that,

> After the initial burst of popularity, visitor numbers inevitably decline, leaving the new institution starved for the cash desperately needed to renew facilities

and attract new revenue. At best, the institution can limp along for a few years. At worst, the institution faces bankruptcy. In both cases the state is faced with the prospect of either refinancing the institution, or letting it go bust ... In reality, the course commonly adopted is to provide an additional injection of one-time funds conditional on becoming self-sufficient in a given time frame. All this does, however, is to emasculate the institution further, and push it further away from its initial mission. In either case, what remains is a building; another monument to short-sighted planning.[40]

The so-called 'Bilbao Effect'

It remains a mystery why the thoughtful work of Ellis and Bradburne is not more widely known and discussed in the museum community. One might conclude that there is a complicit ban on challenging the underpinnings of the 'If you build it, he will come' syndrome. Or it may be that the museum community is in a state of denial although, in fairness, this infatuation with growth and numbers is backed by a seductive poster child known as the 'Bilbao Effect.' The 'Bilbao Effect' refers to the Guggenheim Museum Bilbao (GMB), the architectural monument designed by Frank Gehry and rumoured to be the transformative agent in revitalizing the depressed industrial economy of the Basque region of Spain. In short, for urban planners, politicians, museum directors and trustees, the 'Bilbao Effect' means 'the transformation of a city by a new museum or cultural facility into a vibrant and attractive place for residents, visitors and inward investment.'[41] Alas, the 'Bilbao Effect' might well be an illusion, now that the boosterism is being replaced by evaluation and reflection.

In a recent article by Beatriz Plaza, an economist in the Faculty of Economics at the University of the Basque Country (Bilbao, Spain), we learn that the 'Bilbao Effect' is definitely not the silver bullet so fervently hoped for by those museums and their consultants in search of painless renewal. Contrary to the ardent believers who credit the GMB with transformative powers, Plaza writes that the GMB was part of a much larger economic redevelopment strategy, which included, among many other things, a new subway line, new drainage and water systems, an airport, residential and business complexes, a seaport, and industrial and technology parks. In Plaza's words, 'The icing on the cake was the construction of the GMB and additional cultural investments, such as a concert hall and a centre for young artists to promote art and cultural tourism as a means of diversifying the economy and reducing unemployment.'[42]

Plaza's quantitative and qualitative analysis is in blunt contrast to the simplistic coronation of the 'Bilbao Effect' – much heralded by directors, trustees, governments and consultants, as well as the celebrity architects themselves, as the solution to irrelevant museums, urban blight and economic renewal.[43] In summing up her analysis, Plaza could not be more explicit:

> Last, but not least ... it is inaccurate to define the Bilbao case as a culturally led regeneration process. On the contrary, Bilbao is an integral part of

a larger coherent public policy targeted at productivity and diversity, with a strong cultural component. The Basque Country was industrial in the past, and remains industrial at present, although some *'Made in the Basque Country'* goods are now heavily branded by the innovative image of the GMB.[44]

It would be unfair to reduce the 'Bilbao Effect' to branded goods, but Plaza's conclusion does bring the marketplace rhetoric into proper perspective. In addition to requiring concerted and committed civic action from all levels of government, a herculean task in any jurisdiction, the 'Bilbao Effect' embodies another nasty surprise – its undisguised dependence on tourism, especially international tourism. In fact, GMB attracts an average of 800,000 non-Basque visitors a year, compared with less than 100,000 before the GMB opened.[45] In an article entitled, 'The War on Travel', Chris Lorway points out that travel is becoming notably difficult and unpleasant as a result of post-9/11 (the terrorist attacks on New York City) security restrictions and unprofitable airlines. He quotes a cultural tourism expert who notes 'that cultural tourism as we know it has peaked and that we are moving towards a more localized cultural sector which will focus on regional artists and audiences as opposed to national and international ones.'[46] For those museums counting on the 'Bilbao Effect' to work its magic, this is a brisk touch with reality.

For example, as a result of the new requirement that all travelers to and from the Americas must carry a passport to enter or re-enter the USA, there will be 7.7 million fewer US visits to Canada between 2005 and 2008, representing a loss of CA$1.8 billion in Canadian tourism revenue. Over the same period, Canadian outbound visits to the US are projected to drop by 3.5 million, representing a loss of US$785 million in US tourism revenue.[47] Furthermore, these scenarios do not even acknowledge the rising costs of jet fuel and gasoline – the prolonged crisis that is already well under way. What are the implications for the traveling public if oil rises to US$200 or $300 a barrel? The answer is obvious – the democratization of jet travel will unravel and flying will once again become an elite activity. What will this mean for museums dependent upon national and international tourism?

There is no doubt that bold and creative buildings attract visitors and can provide meaningful visitor experiences, but these inducements are increasingly irrelevant, perhaps malevolent, in a world beset by the social and environmental pressures described earlier. The superficial truisms of the marketplace have proven to be not only inadequate as solutions, but also the source of many of our present difficulties. Are museums destined to achieve their sought-after legitimacy in the mercantile structure, just in time to witness the inevitable rejection of marketplace values by thinking people? How ironic and how unnecessary, especially when practitioners and consultants, like Ellis and Bradburne, have been waving the red flag for years. What is the meaning of this myopia? Where does it originate? Is it arrogance, introversion or a combination of both?

Business tribalism

In addition to short-term thinking, money as the measure of worth, and culture as consumption, there is another feature of the marketplace that imbues it with considerable control and influence, which is best described as the culture of business. This culture underscores the clash of values discussed in this chapter, and is a dominant factor in blinding museums to a sense of their own worth and well-being. For those museums that have no edifice complex and may be feeling smug at this point in the discussion, I note that the culture of business, irrespective of its many useful methods and techniques, possesses an influence which not only far outstrips its usefulness but is also an obstacle to the analysis and reflection required for museums to choose a different path. The cause of much of this difficulty lies in the tribal nature of business.

By tribal, I mean a particular reference group in which individuals identify with each other through common language, ritual and legend.[48] The business tribe itself is not centralized or hierarchical in its organization, and, to a great extent, is culturally and linguistically homogeneous – with English as the lingua franca and grounded in capitalist values. This tribalism sets values that orient the behaviour of individuals around common interests. There are various manifestations of this business culture, and I will focus on several that are diminishing the role of museums as social institutions. Clearly, the culture of business contributes much that is essential to our collective well-being, but that is not my concern here.

Much of the current strength and profile of the global business culture derives from the contemporary worship of business people, along with scientists, as the prescient leaders and icons of our material success. The pairing of business leaders and scientists is interesting in itself, as much of science is now in the service of business, and not in the production of knowledge for its own sake. Business leaders and scientists have now replaced nobility and the clergy as the focus of our acclaim, presumably because production and consumption are now the benchmarks of our well-being.[49] Our societal veneration of business leaders has seeded their influence far and wide, throughout every sector of society and at the highest levels of leadership, including the governance of museums. Many museums have come to resemble corporate entities, with revenues and attendance being the predominant measures of worth. Many of their boards are increasingly indistinguishable from their corporate counterparts, with too many directors being chosen for their business, legal or accounting experience.

Although such qualifications are essential, the danger lies in the growing tendency for these boards to self-select on the basis of these criteria, to the exclusion of other attributes such as cultural diversity, community connectedness and broader socio-environmental awareness. This self-selection is particularly obvious when potential board members are bypassed because they are seen to lack the necessary social or business connections, or are not wealthy in their own right. My personal experience, as well as that of colleagues, confirms that neither position nor social standing is any indication of the ability or willingness to raise money. On the contrary, the more elevated the individual, the greater the chance that he or she will be reluctant to use up their 'credit' (professional/social reputation and connections) except in the most exceptional circumstances. As well, professionals, such as lawyers, are generally averse to fundraising for fear of alienating existing or potential clients. There is nothing wrong with these personal constraints, as long as they are made explicit by board members at the outset – a rarity in the museum world. The danger lies in the tribalistic groupthink that excludes non-business people, based on the myth that they cannot add value to governance.

A lethal mixture of tribalism and loose governance led to the recent scandals that swept through a number of corporations and businesses, including Enron and WorldCom.[50] This, in turn, provoked an unprecedented concern about ethics and accountability, and the corporate and financial reformation is still under way. Suffice it to say that museums boards have always consisted of 100 percent independent directors, except in those uncommon situations where the museum director is also a board member. In addition, the role of chief executive and board chair has always been separated in museums, thus removing another conflict of interest. Museums are also not embroiled in controversies about corporate political contributions. Why, then, is corporate governance celebrated in the business literature and extolled as something the non-profit sector should emulate? Business tribalism is alive and well and teeming with hubris – there is no other explanation.

Business tribalism also has its lighter moments, if one is able to recognize it for what it is. I recall attending the opening of a centre for non-profit management, designed to impart the wisdom and techniques of business to the wayward and uninitiated. The CEO of a multinational oil company began his remarks by noting that non-profit management was an oxymoron, and that the business world could fix that. 'We know how to manage; you don't' – tribalism at its best. The centre often struggled with their non-profit clients, as the latter were subjected to business solutions from business people, who knew little or nothing of the complexities of competing values and interests in the non-profit world. As for the CEO's comment that non-profit management is oxymoronic, I am delighted to have such a fine example of business groupthink.

Me first

In addition to the narrow-mindedness of business governance, there is a darker side of business tribalism that is essentially narcissistic – the excessive and preposterous salaries that boards and CEOs pay themselves, all in the name of enhancing shareholder value. In 2006 the average pay of chief executives at Standard and Poor's 500 (an index of publicly traded companies) was US$10.5 million.[51] In 2007 chief executives of the 500 biggest companies in the US earned an average of US$12.8 million apiece.[52] Money is the obvious measure of worth for these business leaders, and their excessive salaries are conveniently maintained by a self-perpetuating system. Consultants advise their clients on salary levels while executive search firms push up the salary levels, and many of them sit on each other's pay review boards. Not surprisingly, the average chief executive's pay in the US in 2006 was 369 times as large as an ordinary worker's salary.[53] Is the CEO really this disproportionately responsible for the results of the business? The pay levels imply this, but nothing could be more ludicrous.

This corporate love affair with high salaries and abundant privileges marred the museum world recently, in the person of Lawrence Small, who headed up the Smithsonian Institution from 2000 to 2007.[54] Mr Small was hired to operate the Smithsonian in 'a businesslike manner, in keeping with his nonscientific background as an executive at Citibank and Fannie Mae.' He left under the cloud of an internal audit that showed he was paid for inappropriate and lavish expenses. In addition to being paid a salary of US$915,698 in 2007 (two and a half times more than his predecessor), Small collected an additional US$5.7 million by serving on several corporate boards while directing the Smithsonian.[55] It appears that the Board of Regents failed to exercise due diligence and this, in combination with the naïve belief that Small's background as a corporate executive would make him a better manager, created an unhappy outcome for the Smithsonian. Although this is an isolated incident (only the Smithsonian could afford Mr Small), Mr Small's tenure is an object lesson in the clash of values. It is also a stark reminder of the danger in assuming that the business community has any monopoly on competence or virtue.

Cause-related hypocrisy?

Probing more deeply into the dark side of corporate tribalism reveals another disturbing trend – the patina of philanthropy.[56] In short, various business leaders continue their pursuit of profits while employing strategies that mask their true intentions. Over the past decades, in both Canada and the USA, independent corporate foundations have been collapsed and merged with in-house marketing and communication departments to serve corporate interests – not necessarily those of local communities or the larger society. Cause-related marketing, one of the newest corporate strategies, is now revealing its real meaning. Cause-related marketing ties consumers' desires to see a social good with the corporations' desires to see higher profits. For example, 'The Product (RED)' campaign tells us that if we buy a (RED) product that a portion of the purchase price goes to help Africa cope with HIV/AIDS.

In reality, this is just one more example of the business tribe aligning its operations with its central purpose of increasing profits, except it is dressed up as philanthropy.[57] In fact, business profits are up, in part because of their association with charities. Studies show that people are more likely to buy from companies with cause-related arrangements, and that's why corporations spent more than US$100 million advertising their association with (RED), while raising under US$18 million for charity.[58] How can one avoid being cynical when these facts are revealed? Not only are these businesses boosting their profits with a ruse, they are doing it by encouraging even more mindless consumption of unnecessary stuff, which happens to be red in colour. Where is the corporate transparency and accountability? Can we really consume our way to a better world? How do corporations view the consuming public – as dupes? It's highly likely, because it appears that we are. In defense of our collective unconsciousness, I recommend that 'corporate social responsibility' be the newest oxymoron, replacing the oil executive's reference to non-profit management.

Corrosive ideology

To sum up, business tribalism has several faces, including the celebrity worship of business leaders; in-group thinking that excludes non-business people; immature corporate governance; narcissistic notions of personal worth as measured by obscene salaries; and profiteering (HIV/AIDS is an emergency, by the way) disguised as the public good. We know about these liabilities and falsehoods in our minds, if not our hearts, and they permeate our everyday lives, albeit largely unacknowledged for the damage they are doing. These faces of business are now corroding museum practice, wrapped up in the service of marketplace ideology. Museums can elect to look the other way, which seems to be the strategy of choice, or they can consider just how invasive the commercial ideology has become and change direction, as exemplified by the individuals and organizations in the next chapter.

The trouble with ideology, of any kind, is that it is a vehicle for laziness and self-deceit. Robert Grudin has aptly described its characteristics as follows:

> Ideology enables us to pass judgments on a variety of issues while lacking adequate information or analytic skill or commitment to discovering the truth. And ideology not only substitutes for information, analysis, and commitment, but also for conscience. The fact that a given action or lack of action conforms to our ideology absolves us from having to worry about it or take responsibility for it. With ideology we may appear to be well-informed, analytically skillful, inquisitive, conscientious, and morally responsible without really being so.[59]

The market values and tribalistic traits discussed above are ideological, and remain alarmingly unexamined and assumed by the museum community. Museums cannot consciously evolve without analysing their assumptions, no matter how deep and well protected these beliefs may be. Organizational self-knowledge requires that the ideology that governs purpose and values, both individually and organizationally, be made explicit.[60] It is imperative that museums embark on this journey of self-knowledge, not only to make practical sense of a beleaguered world, but also to define a meaningful contribution. Although the marketplace has narrowed the scope of museum action, they still have a choice – will museums be stewards or spectators?

Courting the corporatists: A cautionary tale

What follows is a cautionary tale about what can happen when a corporation and a large museum decide to collaborate for what was thought to be mutual gain. I am indebted to Michael P. Robinson, the former CEO of the Glenbow Museum

(2000–2008) for his candid description of these events.[61] As discussed earlier, the Glenbow Museum had adopted an entrepreneurial approach to its work, as a result of a rapid and drastic reduction in its provincial government funding. Although these initiatives began in the early 1990s, innovation and new ways of working continued with my successor, in part because provincial government funding remained modest, with only minor inflationary increases.

In the midst of studying various alternatives for renewal, Glenbow was approached by a representative of the UK celebrity architect, Norman Foster, with the idea of becoming the cultural component of a major corporate office slated for Calgary. In October of 2006, EnCana Corporation, one of the largest oil and gas companies in the world, unveiled plans to build a new 158,000 square metre (1.7 million sq. ft.), 58-story office headquarters in downtown Calgary. EnCana's CEO, along with the architects, had embraced the 'creative city' concept, and wished to promote the synergy between culture, retail and the corporation – what Robinson calls the 'cultural adjacency' model. He coined this term to describe the benefits that accrue from the presence of a major cultural facility and its various amenities. EnCana needed a prestigious, non-profit partner, while Glenbow wished to renew and expand their entrepreneurialism by moving out of their government-owned building into a new and high profile facility. The museum had outgrown its building, which had always been devoid of architectural appeal. The partners were willing, and the court-ship began.

For the next year and a half, Glenbow's CEO, senior staff and Board of Governors spent the lion's share of their collective time preparing a space and program plan for EnCana, which included travel to the UK to meet with the architects, employing a consultant to assist with the planning, meetings with provincial cabinet ministers and federal members of Parliament, as well as the preparation of a case for support to test the prospects of a private sector fundraising campaign to support this initiative. There were countless board meetings and special committee meetings to analyse the facts and issues surrounding the proposed move to the EnCana's EnCentre project. A special team of advisors was also assembled with legal, financial, corporate real estate and architectural expertise, to fill in where the Glenbow staff and board lacked experience and knowledge. In Robinson's words, 'I spent two years of my life on this project.'[62] By all accounts, it was indeed a thorough and well orchestrated exercise in responsible decision-making, and the board voted unanimously to negotiate their inclusion in the EnCana project. But the suitor fled before consummation, much to the surprise of the bride.

What happened? The unraveling began with the retirement of EnCana's CEO who had the vision of profit and non-profit synergy. He was replaced by a CEO whose concerns were more pragmatic. With the change in CEOs came a renewed focus on share price and shareholder value and, as noted by Robinson, 'great experiments in culture and civility do not enter this equation in quite the same way.'[63] Glenbow's original proposal required 75,000 square metres (250,000 sq. ft.) of museum space, and Glenbow was prepared to raise CA$170 million to cover these capital costs. The CA$170 million included a suggested gift of CA$25 million from the corporate partner, in recognition of the value which would accrue to the building as a result of Glenbow's visitors parking, eating and shopping in the complex. Based on their previous experience with EnCana, the Glenbow's Board and staff believed that these were reasonable negotiating points. Instead, EnCana countered with an offer of 15,000 square metres (50,000 square feet – an 80 percent reduction) and no philanthropic gift. Glenbow also wanted a condominium tenancy, whereby they would own their own space.

Unknown to Glenbow, the rules of this marketplace game had changed dramatically, with EnCana announcing its plan to sell the building and lease it back from the new owner. Ipso facto, Glenbow need not contribute the CA$170 million, but they would not have ownership of their space, and would be required to pay CA$2.8 million annually in commercial rent for one-fifth of the space they required. In addition, EnCana wanted CA$40 million in tenant improvements for the leased space. In short, EnCana was seeking a tenant, not creative philanthropy, but unfortunately failed to advise their so-called partner of this. Nor did they compensate Glenbow for the enormous effort it made to plan the prospective marriage. Glenbow's Board of Governors declined EnCana's offer.

This story, both tortuous and salutary, contains many hard-won insights and lessons, not the least of which is that when the 'elephant in the room' changes position, one has to be astute enough to avoid being crushed – this Glenbow did. Can you imagine what the new building owners might think when they discover that one of their tenants is a museum? How long would that lease last? Robinson offered several other summary observations, beginning with the counsel that it is best to choose your own partner.[64] In this instance, the suitor came to Glenbow and, in retrospect, Glenbow did not develop any criteria for the match. Instead, Glenbow spent its time and energy reacting to a partner they didn't choose. Avoiding this passive role requires defining what success looks like at the outset, and then selecting your partner accordingly. This, in turn, requires a holistic consideration of the museum's mission, purpose and values, and not fixating on the celebrity building as the solution. Sustained rigour in decision-making is essential, which means paying attention to content and substance, and not succumbing to the inevitable commercial dogma that accompanies corporatism, celebrity architecture and the search for quick fixes.

Robinson concedes that the momentum and excitement of the courtship sidetracked the key question – 'Will our mission and values be advanced by this initiative, or is it a facile solution to deeper concerns?' For Glenbow, the merits of the corporate marriage were assumed, not discussed, which is in part a reflection of the Glenbow Board's business bias. One can only hope that more museum directors, with similar accounts of corporate encounters, will be as forthcoming as Robinson. The marketplace has but one master – the bottom line – and to think otherwise is unrealistic and naïve, despite our well-disposed hopes to the contrary. Robinson's final words on the subject – 'There's no such thing as pure corporate philanthropy – it's all strategic now.'[65]

Business literacy

Having catalogued some of the real and potential consequences of marketplace ideology and commercial dogma, it is important to note that their counterpart, business literacy, is essential for any competent museum. In brief, business literacy means the staff's ability, at all levels of the organization, to fully understand the museum in all its complexity.[66] If staff understand the 'big picture', or the larger context within which the museum operates, they will have a greater appreciation of and, hopefully, a greater investment in the outcome of the work. Business literacy begins with 'open-book' management, whereby museum workers are given full budget information along with assistance in making sense of it. This approach also requires that senior management communicate fully and openly about the museum's strategic priorities, opportunities and threats. I know of several museums that do none of these things and where the director withholds financial information from staff in order to maintain power and control.

Business literacy is not only necessary for enhanced self-sufficiency in an era of scarce resources, but it is also essential to individual and organizational accountability. A working knowledge of finances/budgeting, business processes, time management, public service, project management and so forth are the foundation for enhanced effectiveness and efficiency – the purpose and outcome of business literacy. Business processes are a case in point. In a former position as a new director, I was challenged to reduce our operating costs and chose, along with our strategies, to closely examine our procedural bureaucracy – the culmination of 25 years of cumulative processes in a top-down organization. By using a business process-mapping technique obtained from a business consultant, we closely analysed how we actually did our work – challenging our assumptions and our habits. Our artifact loan procedure, for example, required over 20 separate steps and several different staff positions to complete. By identifying these time-worn bureaucratic intricacies and habits, and then scrutinizing them, we reduced the number of steps by nearly two-thirds, thus freeing up valuable time and energy for useful work. This is business literacy at its best – but it is about methods and techniques, not values.

Methods aren't values

The distinction between methods and values recalls the earlier discussion of the characteristics of long-lived companies – sensitivity to the environment, cohesion and identity, tolerance and decentralization, and conservative financing.[67] None of these defining factors have anything to do with commercial dogma or business literacy – they are values. Values are essential and enduring beliefs that articulate how an organization will conduct itself. Values also serve as guiding beacons by describing how the museum wants to treat others, as well as how it wishes to be treated. It would seem that in the pressure cooker called the marketplace, there is little time for or attention to values. Instead, values are replaced by imperatives – more visitors, more earned revenues, more collections, etc. Museums cannot claim victimhood for these quantitative measures, however, as I previously noted the museum community's collective failure to define what constitutes effective museum performance, above and beyond the bottom line.

I suggest that DeGeus' characteristics of long-lived companies might well serve as a useful departure for the consideration of qualitative, value-based, performance measures for museums. I can't help but wonder how many museums can claim to model any or all of DeGues' traits, and such an assessment would be highly revealing. Except for perhaps cohesion and identity, many museums are failing to learn and adapt, while decentralization and collaboration remain unrecognized or undeveloped. When it comes to conservative financing, museums are volatile at best, as the economic imperative of unmindful growth assumes greater influence in the museum community at large.

It is important to realize that the private ownership of natural resources; the increased centralization of power between governments and corporations; the elimination of biological and human diversity; the irrational belief that science and technology will undo or fix the problems we have created; the refusal to set limits on production and consumption; the reductionist approach to understanding life, and the concept of progress at the expense of the biosphere – all of these things are the consequences of marketplace ideology or are in the service of this ideology. Why museums would embrace commercial dogma as a strategy for the future when heightened stewardship is of paramount importance remains a vexing and essential question.

Complex portfolios

Furthermore, classical economic theory and commercial dogma do not allow for the needs of future generations, because marketplace decisions are based on the relative abundance or scarcity of things as they affect us, now. In Jeremy Rifkin's words, 'No one speaks for future generations at the marketplace, and for this reason, everyone who comes after us starts off much poorer than we did in terms of nature's remaining endowment.'[68] The marketplace notion that 'the present is all there is' is antithetical to the very nature of museums, whose existence is predicated on the stewardship of posterity. It is now imperative that this sense of the future assume greater influence in all aspects of museum work, aided and abetted by business literacy, but not beholden to the values of the marketplace. The marketplace pendulum, once the instrument of increased accountability for museums, has now swung too far.

As described earlier, museums are mixed portfolios and must continue to maintain this dynamic and seamless complexity if they are to operate effectively in the service of the public good. This means that adequate public support, whether from government, foundations or individuals, is essential to counterbalance the increasing emphasis on earned revenues. This is assuming, of course, that museums add sufficient societal value to merit this support. The simplicity of the marketplace, with its selling, buying and profit-making, simply cannot manage the complexities of a mixed portfolio – it's the bottom line at the expense of all else, including employees and the environment. As an example, the US$17,530 earned by the average Wal-Mart employee last year was US$1,820 below the poverty line for a family of four, while five of the USA's ten richest people are Wal-Mart heirs.[69]

What's wrong with this picture? If the marketplace could address the complexities of a mixed portfolio, museums would be rich, which they plainly are not. The opposite is true, in fact, and the situation continues to worsen. As the author and scholar Bill McKibben notes, 'it's extremely important to bear in mind that we're *not,* despite the insistence of our leaders, growing wealthier; that is one of several stubborn and counterintuitive facts about the world ... *Growth simply isn't enriching most of us.*'[70] For example, the wealthiest 20 percent of households in 1973 accounted for 44 percent of total US income, according to the Census Bureau. Their share jumped to 50 percent in 2002, while everyone else's fell. For the bottom fifth, the share dropped from 4.2 percent to 3.5 percent.[71] Museums have a profound choice to make about their role as social institutions. Will they honour their communities as stewards of the highest order, or become agents of marketplace dysfunction? Happily, a variety of museums have chosen to move well beyond the marketplace, and their stories are the focus of the next chapter.

5

Searching for resilience

Resilient innovators

The litany of the world's ills, combined with outmoded museum practices and the encroachment of marketplace values, are significant challenges to the future of all museums – not that the long-term survival of museums is a pressing issue anywhere. My interest lies in another direction; not in what museums think they are entitled to receive, but in the contributions they can make to address various socio-environmental issues. Admittedly, the world and its peoples have always been confronted with catastrophic events, and have managed to survive with museums on the sidelines. These catastrophes range from the 1918 influenza epidemic (which killed an estimated 20 to 40 million people worldwide), to the Second World War (which claimed over 70 million lives, making it the deadliest war in history), to HIV/AIDS. In 2007, an estimated 33.2 million people lived with the HIV/AIDS worldwide, and it killed an estimated 2.1 million people, including 330,000 children that year.[1]

We also have the catastrophic events of the distant past to ponder, such as the disappearance of the Mayan civilization, the demise of ancient Egypt and the fall of the Roman Empire – all of them the stuff of endless museum programs and blockbuster exhibitions. The stories of these collapsed societies are also popular analogues for the present, and their meaning and implications for contemporary challenges have been examined by various writers but, interestingly, not by museums.[2] For example, Jared Diamond, Ronald Wright and Thomas Homer-Dixon each demonstrate that the mismanagement of natural resources was the key factor in the demise or diminishment of the societies they write about. Although these authors are not environmental determinists (they recognize the complexities inherent in human society, including non-environmental causes such as warfare), each of them hopes that we might collectively learn from history. And the histories they reveal provide the backdrop for what will be seen as one of the greatest fallacies of our time – the idea that we can get along without natural resources, an idea that is now apparently widespread in rich countries.[3]

Many believe that our unmatched intelligence and technological hubris will enable us to separate ourselves from the natural environment and create our own solutions to the biosphere's nearly terminal distress. Time will tell, but we are running out of it as the pressures mount. As a matter of fact, the United Nations' International Panel on Climate Change (IPCC), recently awarded the Nobel Prize for its climate work, predicted the Arctic Ocean to be free of summertime ice by 2070. Later that year, another scientific panel changed that estimate to the summer of 2030. In December of 2007, the credible US Naval Postgraduate School in California indicated that there could be no – read zero – summer ice in the Arctic Ocean as early as 2013.[4] Climate change is apparently oblivious to scientific modeling.

What do museums have to do with all of this? Their relevance lies in two important distinctions between the contemporary analyses of ancient societies mentioned above and the troubled world of today. First, as the life support systems of our global precursors unraveled in the ancient past, they did so in localized contexts, with no life-threatening, global consequences. This is no longer the case, as Canada's emissions from the production of 'dirty oil' in the Alberta Tar Sands, for example, have immediate implications for worldwide carbon dioxide levels. Similarly, the American addiction to fossil fuels spreads far beyond the hallowed suburbs to influence foreign policy and armed conflict on the other side of the globe. Museums, as inhabitants of the developed world, do not themselves produce such serious consequences, but they are directly aligned with the ideology and wealth generation which produce these harmful effects. Museums are also public institutions which, in aggregate, consume a significant share of public resources, often with minimal accountability save quantitative measures.

Providing ancillary museum education and entertainment, as venerable as they are, is insufficient to address the task at hand, as the contemporary issues demanding attention are empirical, have unparalleled consequences, and require reflection and action. These issues are not about institutional self-interest, whether it be a gallery's lengthy debate to host a 'pornographic' art collection, or the bold decision to renovate an ancient permanent exhibit with high-tech interactives. As institutions in an unavoidable global web, museums are increasingly hard-pressed to assume either unspoken immunity or self-serving neutrality as the industrial era comes apart. As noted repeatedly, museums enjoy unparalleled respect and trust and it is time that this veneration be put to good use to encourage stewardship, compassion and heightened consciousness – all of which are eroding under corporatist influences and marketplace ideology.

There is a second distinction between the past and the present, as we consider the historical challenges of our fragile species. The Maya and the Egyptians had neither the hindsight nor the foresight which contemporary humankind is privileged to possess – we know where we've been and we are aware of the consequences of our actions. Although public knowledge of the consequences of our decisions grows daily, as does a sense of responsibility, very few of our political 'leaders' in North America are publicly willing to acknowledge our perilous trajectory. Many citizens are angered and wearied by their denial, but marketplace ideology and corporatism have so permeated the North American political scene that there is now a pronounced leadership vacuum, which nothing short of concerted civic action will overcome. Ronald Wright notes that, 'The concentration of power at the top of large-scale societies gives the elite a vested interest in the status quo; they continue to prosper in darkening times long after the environment and general population begin to suffer.'[5] Museums are embedded in one way or another in this 'concentration of power at the top of large-scale societies' yet, at the same time, can choose to be conscious of the dysfunction, imbalance and social consequences of concentrated power, and act. For smaller museums, the power elite is always a relative concept – privilege can be as pronounced in a rural town of 2,000 people as it can be in Toronto or London.

Will museums remain as they are as 'times darken', or will they add value above and beyond the dictates of their insular traditions, public access and economic impact? A number of individuals and organizations have weighed this question, and have developed new ways of thinking and working that transcend traditional museum practice. As a result, they are now serving the civil society (that space between the individual and government) which is in pressing need of competence and leadership, as our elected and non-elected leaders continue their infatuation with the market as the nexus of society. One doesn't read or hear much about these museums in the mainstream media, or the museum literature for that matter, because what they do lacks the sensationalism or celebrity appeal that drive the mainstream media in the grip of consumption and conformity. As far as the museum literature goes, many of these progressive practitioners are too busy to make their work more widely known. Nonetheless, these museological outliers are defining new ways of being for museums as social institutions. The people, programs, policies, organizations and collaborations described below have replaced passivity and compliance with creativity, altruism and originality, and I am pleased to provide a glimpse of nine of them in the remainder of this chapter.

Assessing relevance

I am reluctant to describe the following examples as 'best' practice, as I cannot claim to know the full range of innovation currently under way in the museum world. Instead, I consider these examples to be 'progressive', which means making use of new ideas, findings and opportunities – precisely what museums require at this point in their evolution. I will not restrict this overview to institutions, however, and will also include individuals, programs, policies and collaborations that embody creativity, commitment and heightened stewardship. It is fitting to begin with the work of an individual, Douglas Worts, as he has been concerned with the societal role of museums and galleries throughout his 25-year career as a museologist. Worts' experience is the product of deep and varied service to the museum community and, as a result, his work deserves to be better known. He was an interpretive planner and audience researcher at the Art Gallery of Ontario (AGO) until 2007, when he resigned to become an independent consultant with a focus on culture and sustainability. He is also a founding member of the Canadian Working Group on Museums and Sustainable Communities (WGMSC).[6]

Over the past decade, Worts' research has been focused on the cultural roots of our increasingly unsustainable society and, although he believes that museums have tremendous potential to become catalysts of public engagement and change leading to more sustainable lifestyles, he has been an outspoken critic of museum complacency. Combining his strong sense of stewardship with deep consternation about what he sees as the failed potential of museums and galleries as social institutions, Worts notes 'that museums suffer from the fatal flaw of having no clear vision of what they are attempting to do in cultural terms.'[7] In addition to his work as an instructor and a workshop convener, he has authored a number of articles on the role and relevance of museums, with such titles as 'On the Brink of Irrelevance: Art Museums in Contemporary Society' and 'Museums in Search of a Sustainable Future' – clear expressions of his rejection of collections and exhibitions as the principal preoccupations of museums.[8]

Of particular importance to the purpose of this book is his article entitled 'Measuring Museum Meaning: A Critical Assessment Framework' – a pragmatic guide to elevating both museum consciousness and stewardship. Worts writes that, 'although museums are normally categorized as 'cultural' organizations, they rarely plan their foundational activities or judge the success of their public programming according to the cultural health and well-being of their communities.'[9] This article offers a Critical Assessment Framework (CAF) which is intended to foster dialogue across the museum community on how museums can better address the cultural needs and opportunities of our time. The CAF consists of three lenses (the Individual, the Community and the Museum) that examine the relationship of a museum program to its community. Worts also considers this framework to be an intermediate step towards the actual development of performance indicators for cultural programming.

Worts and his colleagues (members of WGMSC) who assisted in the development of the CAF are breaking new ground in the search for qualitative measures – that no-man's-land of museum inaction. They offer a pragmatic beginning, and because of the relevance of this framework to the purpose of this book, I have included excerpts from the community lens to highlight its utility in the search for relevance.[10] The community lens focuses on the creation of public benefit, and requires that museum staff ask themselves how well their program(s) will:

- Address vital and relevant needs/issues within the community
- Engage a diverse public
- Act as a catalyst for action
- Stimulate intergenerational interactions
- Link existing community groups to one another
- Initiate or enhance long-term collaborative relationships
- Create partnerships that empower community groups
- Result in products/processes that have tangible impacts in the community.

Although this is not a complete listing of the questions, this sample provides a valuable framework for exploring community meaning and value, with the intention of catalysing action. Admittedly, this approach is a radical contrast to the typical museum program lens, which consists of questions such as 'How much will it cost?', 'How many people will attend?'; 'Will there be a catalogue?' and 'Will there be shop merchandise?' Nonetheless, the CAF is not ahead of its time, despite its relative obscurity among mainstream museums. The fact that it has not been debated, revised and put into play by practitioners is symptomatic of the widespread myopia discussed in Chapter 1. This is the museum community's loss, as Worts and his colleagues offer an alternative to passivity and unthinking core assumptions. Will it be greater output in the form of bigger collections and more exhibits, or will it be meaningful outcomes for people, communities and the beleaguered biosphere? Museums do have a choice.

Linking nature and social issues

In one of the most thoughtful mission statements I have seen, the Field Museum in Chicago, Illinois, USA, states that 'its subject matter directly relates to the great issues of the present and future: environmental and cultural diversity and their inter-relationships.'[11] In addition, the mission notes that 'We focus on critical environ-mental and cultural issues which are engaging and relevant to the public's daily lives and civic responsibilities.' This level of consciousness was apparently an offshoot of the Field Museum's strategic planning on the occasion of their 100th anniversary in 1995. The Museum concluded that it was not interested in competing with the British Museum and the Smithsonian Institution to build the world's largest collec-tions and, instead, chose to become 'interdisciplinary and relevant by creating two small initiatives: Environmental and Conservation Programs (ECP) and the Center for Cultural Understanding and Change (CCUC).'

Both initiatives are multidisciplinary, and both are meant to explore ways in which the Museum can 'direct its wealth of knowledge – in its century-strong collections, its inventory and research expertise, and its exhibits, education, and communication skills – into resolving immediate challenges in the conservation of biological and cultural diversity.'[12] These two units subsequently combined into a new organization called Environment, Culture and Conservation (ECCo), with the purpose of bringing the Museum's tradition of rigorous science to bear on practical challenges, and translate biodiversity science into conservation action that sustains wild landscapes and cultural vitality. The results have been impressive, with over 22 million acres of Andean and Amazonian lowlands protected or in the process of becoming protected, accompanied by an integrated approach to wild nature and sustainable livelihoods.

The CCUC is of particular interest, because it is also committed to public involve-ment and urban research in its own city and region – both of obvious relevance for any human history museum. The CCUC describes this commitment as follows:

> to use problem-solving anthropological research to identify and catalyze strengths and assets of communities in Chicago and beyond. In doing so, CCUC helps communities identify new solutions to critical challenges such as education, housing, health care, environmental conservation, and leadership development. Through research, programs, and access to collections, CCUC reveals the power of cultural difference to transform social life and promote social change.[13]

Figure 14 The Praise Dancers perform at a Cultural Connections event – a partnership between the Field Museum and over 20 Chicago-area ethnic museums and cultural centres. This program provides a unique opportunity to explore important questions, such as why there is cultural diversity, what is culture and what makes cultural diversity important.

Photo: copyright 2007 Sarah Sommers, ECCo, The Field Museum, C2007_246

One of the current CCUC's programs is entitled 'New Allies for Nature and Culture' and once again is grounded in cooperation and stewardship.[14] Its purpose is to 'foster collaborations between organizations working on environmental, social, and cultural issues in the Chicago region.' The CCUC had over 100 conversations with organizations throughout the region in 2007, and identified five common concerns that connect environmental and sociocultural issues, including climate change, youth programming, arts/creative practices, health and food, and economic development. This program builds on these common concerns by recognizing that the well-being of people and the earth are interrelated. Through collaboration, the CCUC and its partners intend to create a sustainable Chicago region and, 'together, change the map of the future.'

Note the commitment to sound anthropological research in combination with pressing socio-environmental issues. Contrary to conventional museum wisdom and discipline-based dogma, research and social action are not incompatible but are necessary allies. The Field Museum, one of the most highly regarded museums in North America, has managed to find a way to bring academic expertise to bear on contemporary issues without sullying its reputation as a preeminent research institution. There is perhaps no better model of interdisciplinary relevance than the Field Museum's ECCo initiative. What are museums waiting for? Size and money are not the prerequisites for this approach – thoughtful leadership and the will and courage 'to catalyze the inner capacities of human communities to achieve positive social change' are.[15] There is also much to be gained personally, according to Alaka Wali, the Director of the CCUC. She told me in an interview that, 'For me, this is my life dream come true. I am privileged to do this work, because it's a way to bring anthropology to bear on issues we all care about. It's very, very rewarding.'[16]

Baby boomers and depression

In the next 5 to 20 years, 76 million baby boomers will reach retirement and seek alternative ways to meet their personal needs.[17] A characteristic of this demographic group is the growing incidence of depression and its physiological consequences of life-threatening diseases, not to mention its impact on families and communities caring for them. With funding from the US government's Institute of Museum and Library Services (IMLS), the Morikami Museum and Japanese Gardens (Delray Beach, Florida, USA) and the Christine E. Lynn College of Nursing at Florida Atlantic University examined the effect of healing gardens and art therapy on older adults with mild to moderate depression. More specifically, the designers of the study wanted to determine if garden visits were as effective, or more effective, than art therapy in relieving symptoms of depression in older adults. This study also has much broader implications, as described in the following excerpt from the manual they produced:

> Finding cost effective, self-directed, and safe methods to alleviate depression will assist health care providers and others to facilitate health and well-being in older adults. Evidence to support the hypothesis that garden visitation alleviates symptoms of depression in the elderly would offer a means of addressing a real need in society, a means that does not rely on medication for its effectiveness.[18]

The Morikami garden is a 16-acre site landscaped in Japanese fashion and is part of the Morikami Museum. The garden is accessible by means of a meandering gravel path that circles a lake – the garden's central feature. In addition to this lake, there are a number of other water features, including ponds, streams and cascades of various heights which are overlooked by numerous places to sit and reflect. Other features include roofed gates, bridges, and a roofed rest house or contemplation pavilion. The museum complements the garden, and has been a centre for Japanese arts and culture in South Florida since its opening in 1977.[19] Among its many activities, the museum offers changing exhibitions, tea ceremonies, an educational outreach program and the celebration of traditional Japanese festivals for the public several times a year.

Participants in the research were divided into three groups. Those in group one walked in the garden individually on their own; those in group two walked in the

Figure 15 Couple enjoying the calm view of the lake at the Morikami Museum and Japanese Gardens.

Photo: courtesy of The Morikami Museum and Japanese Gardens

garden with a guide; and the third group did not visit the garden but participated in art therapy. Full details on the methodology and results of this scientific research into the therapeutic value of this garden are reported elsewhere.[20] It is heartening to note that the symptoms of depression experienced by the study participants decreased over the successive six-week study periods in 2006 and 2007, although none of the three approaches was significantly more successful in alleviating the symptoms of depression than either of the other two. The key conclusion is that walking in the garden was as successful as art therapy in relieving the symptoms of depression. Researchers also asked the participants to write stories of sadness and joy which were then analysed using special software. Notably, these stories indicated a significant difference in the severity of the participants' depression over the course of the study.

In short, the therapeutic value of the museum's garden has been clearly demonstrated. To their credit, the Morikami Museum also created a manual for developing similar public programs elsewhere, which is intended for use by museums, historic homes, botanical gardens, nature centres, and other public facilities as a guide in meeting a societal need in a nonstandard way.[21] Most importantly, the Morikami study provides scientific evidence that supports the efficacy of this kind of programming, thereby legitimizing the anecdotal evidence that museums and related organizations are capable of providing healing and therapy. There is no doubt that this pioneering study opens up a new vista of social relevance and responsiveness for those museums that are privileged to have gardens.

There are also at least two important implications of this work for those that don't. For those museums participating in the building boom, how many are aware of this work and how many have, or will, incorporate an accessible garden of any kind as part of their renewal? Second, it would be advantageous for all museum funders, especially governments and foundations, to pay attention to the farsighted vision of the Institute of Museum and Library Services (IMLS), a co-sponsor of this research.

With a mission 'to build the capacity of museums and libraries to serve their communities,' the IMLS is leading the way by supporting basic and applied research that 'raises the bar' for museums through enhanced learning and innovation.[22] The tag line at the bottom of the IMLS letterhead says it all – 'A federal agency building the capacity of libraries and museums to create a nation of learners.' If even a portion of public funding agencies were this sagacious about the potential value of museums, there would be little reason to write this book.

Committing to place

There continues to be abundant rhetoric about the importance of collaboration and partnerships to promote meaningful engagement between museums and their communities, and this book is no exception. I have argued that such partnerships are essential not only to enhancing the meaning and value of museums as social institutions but also for strengthening the civil society in the face of rampant commercial dogma. But words are cheap, as the saying goes, and there are few museum programs, if any, that are designed to impact whole communities. The work of the National Museum of Australia (NMA) and the Murray-Darling Basin Commission is a remarkable example, however, as it combines community engagement and contemporary environmental issues with the academic rigour of systematic and long-term evaluation. Even more impressive, this work has been consistently published on an ongoing basis.[23] What follows is a necessarily brief summary of this collaboration, including various hard-won insights that might well serve as beacons in the search for museum stewardship.

Increasing environmental problems in the Murray-Darling Basin in southeastern Australia, including rising salinity, declining water quality and land degradation, led to the Murray-Darling Basin Initiative. The focus of this initiative was much broader than previous environmental efforts and embraced not only entire river basins and subterranean ground water but also all the human activities that contribute to the environmental problems noted above. This more holistic perspective also required a redefinition of what constituted community, and the concept of community was expanded beyond farmers to include everyone living in the Murray-Darling Basin.

This approach also reflected international trends in natural resource management, recognizing that communities of people are as integral to ecological systems as are land and water. The NMA's involvement in this work was an outgrowth of the thinking that led to the creation of the museum in the first place, as the National

Museum of Australia Act (1980) mandated the museum to address the 'history of the interaction of man with the Australian natural environment', including the impact of human activities on ecological systems.[24] In 2002, as part of its ongoing commitment to this responsibility, the NMA and the Murray-Darling Basin Commission launched an experimental and collaborative program called the Murray-Darling Outreach Project, the purpose of which was to increase active community engagement in local environmental issues in the Murray-Darling Basin.[25]

This outreach project consisted of four different programs – two of them focused on youth education in order to build the capacity of young people to foster social and environmental change through involvement in civic activities. The other two programs, 'Basin Bytes' and 'Pass the Salt,' were concerned with the idea of 'community of place' and are described here. The 'Basin Bytes' program involved participants in digital photography, documentation and story-telling activities that explored issues of place, community and environment, including the production of an online exhibition mounted on the NMA's website. The 'Pass the Salt' program was a collaboration between the NMA and the Museum of Riverina (a regional museum), and addressed the issue of water salinity in an Australian community by profiling the personal stories of people who were affected by it. The results of this program included an online exhibition with images and stories of places, people and objects, as well as a website which included links to other community groups and detailed information on salinity. In summarizing the Murray-Darling Outreach Project, Ruth Lane, one of the senior investigators involved in the evaluation research, wrote:

> The Murray-Darling Outreach Project … sits firmly within the New Museology approach and draws on the technological capacity of the NMA to provide new online spaces for community voices. It is focused on environmental issues faced by contemporary rural and regional communities and creates new partnership arrangements between regional communities and organisations and national institutions for the purpose of building community capacity for addressing environmental change.[26]

More specifically, the evaluation research revealed a number of valuable insights that have broad applicability for any museum wishing to foster meaningful community engagement. Interestingly, none of these lessons are particularly self-evident, such as the wise observation that the process of community engagement and participation is more important than the products of that engagement.[27] Less surprising was the fact that the project's ability to influence and inspire civic engagement was dependent upon using existing community networks and structures; thereby increasing local involvement and community ownership of the program. This approach also prompted new connections among existing local networks which, in turn, contributed to the development of new forms of social capital in the long-term – a not so obvious outcome.[28]

The Murray-Darling Outreach Project also provides some valuable guidance on managing controversy, the potential for which is a constant disincentive for most museums to participate in contemporary issues. NMA staff decided to leave all the controversial material on the website, along with a disclaimer that it is a community-generated website consisting of the stories and opinions of individual participants. Most importantly, the NMA's commitment to include criticism and advocacy honours community voices, rather than limiting them, and thereby builds capacity for broad-based civic engagement.[29] This is a powerful message for all government-owned museums, as the responsibility of all good government is to encourage community views, politically sensitive or otherwise, in public arenas. The NMA has demonstrated, contrary to conventional wisdom among museums, that controversy and criticism can be managed intelligently and constructively.

There are many cogent signposts to be gleaned from the work of the NMA, and I will conclude with one more example which is strikingly relevant for the museum community. The evaluation also revealed that linking environmental issues with cultural heritage 'provided a sufficient prompt for some participants to portray local places in unusual ways, giving some support to ... the potential of the creative arts to promulgate new ideas about community and ecological sustainability.'[30] The idea of 'place' is apparently a more serviceable term than 'environment', and less likely to alienate people than the scientific language of natural resource management. While museums labour under the constraints of disciplinary boundaries and ordinary mission statements, it appears that the NMA's constituents have already figured it out – nature and culture are inseparable.

In summary, the Murray-Darling Outreach Project is a valuable object lesson for all museums in search of meaning and relevance. It is also empirical, and backed up by systematic evaluation that is rigorous, transparent and shared with the museum community at large. This impressive methodology anchors the true value of this initiative, which is best summed up by the project's organizers and evaluators, who wrote, 'Museums and other cultural institutions have a considerable potential to go beyond traditional boundaries, methods, and ways of thinking, to contribute to environmental management and other higher purposes.'[31]

I can't help but note the reference to 'higher purposes'. As idealistic as it may appear, higher purposes are achievable, irrespective of sacred museum cows and commercial dogma.

Art and social justice

Art museums, especially larger ones, continue to enjoy celebrity status around the world, both in the public eye and in the media. They host spectacular blockbuster exhibitions which are major attractions for residents and tourists alike. Many art museums are also revelling in the feast of celebrity architecture, while politicians at all levels hail these facilities as essential flagships for the 'creative city.' It is also possible to enhance a museum's reputation by the quantity of tax-deductible art donations given to the institution in a year – clearly an indication of the wealth, status and privilege accruing to art museums.[32] From the outside looking in, things couldn't be better. Or, could they?

In a convincing article by veteran art museum director Maxwell Anderson, we learn that all is not well, despite the hype.[33] Anderson attributes many of the difficulties besetting art museums to the use of crude and ineffective performance measures, which make it impossible for boards and staff to set priorities, determine the museum's real contributions to society, and measure institutional success. The culprit is the old triad of success factors that continues to plague most museums – the number and marketability of exhibitions, the number of visitors, and the number of members. Anderson disassembles the meaning of these quantitative indicators, deftly pointing out their essential superficiality and uselessness. He notes, for example, that museums never compute the indirect costs of exhibitions, including salary and overtime costs and, as a result, there is rarely, if ever, a 'profit'.[34]

Anderson also develops 11 new categories of measurement that are mission-focused, long-term and verifiable – a substantial contribution to the much-needed discussion on performance measurement. Unfortunately, his framework does not recognize the aims, aspirations and issues teeming beyond the confines of the museum, and his reference to the museum's 'educational mandate' is as close as he gets. That's fine for traditional practice, but it does not serve the need for the active stewardship and topicality that are essential to the mindful museum. For this we must journey to Scotland and have a look at an art gallery that is evolving with its community.

The Gallery of Modern Art (GoMA) in Glasgow, Scotland, is one of 11 museums run by Culture and Sport Glasgow on behalf of Glasgow City Council. Glasgow Museums is the largest civic museum service in the UK, with three million visits (free of charge) each year.[35] GoMA opened to the public in 1996 and was soon suffering from a paradoxical reception. It was loved by the public and unloved by the art world, as well as hailed and demonized for being populist. Their urban setting added a much chillier dimension, with one-third of Glasgow's citizens living in deprivation – by some measures the worst conditions in Western Europe.[36] In 1999, GoMA set out to define a new direction which would retain its audience support while including a more accurate reflection of contemporary art practice. Some may consider these to be mutually exclusive ambitions, as they often are in contemporary art museums, but GoMA took the plunge by broadening their vision to include socially excluded groups along with the best of contemporary art. GoMA's renewal happened to coincide with a major social change in the city, when Glasgow City Council agreed to take up to 10,000 asylum seekers as part of the UK government's dispersal plan to alleviate population pressure in southeast England.

The Council sought the help of its cultural agencies in assisting and integrating these displaced people, which prompted some serious reflection at GoMA. Staff were initially uncomfortable with taking on political and topical issues, and feared that their credibility would plummet even further in the art world. Nonetheless, GoMA was given the responsibility to 'reinforce Glasgow Museums' role as an agent of social change.'[37]

Coincidentally, Amnesty International approached GoMA to work on a similar project on issues facing asylum seekers and refugees. With the support of the Scottish Refugee Council, thus began GoMA's collaboration on social justice issues which is still evolving,

Figure 16 Barbara Kruger, an American feminist artist, incorporated reports of violent acts against women from Scottish newspapers into an installation at the Gallery of Modern Art in Glasgow, where visitors were immersed in her signature large graphic statements.

Photo: 2005: courtesy of Glasgow Museums and Art Galleries

having produced major exhibitions as well as outreach and education programs. For example, the program began with an artist who was commissioned to live in the most deprived areas of Glasgow where asylum seekers were being housed. The artist, Patricia Mackinnon-Day, revealed the personal histories of the people there:

> the majority were highly educated professionals. The oppression many of them had endured in their own countries had forced them to leave not only their families, but also successful careers and relatively comfortable homes. This stood in direct contrast to the popular stereotype of the refugee as a parasite, someone who comes to Britain to exploit its benefits systems.[38]

This residency resulted in the creation of art works that challenged the prevalence of generalizations, which then led to the development of a major program with two principle aims. The first was 'Sanctuary: the exhibition,' consisting of the works of 34 highly regarded artists from 15 countries who explored global issues such as migration, displacement, torture, identity and concepts of 'home.' The intent was to raise awareness of the plight of asylum seekers and refugees worldwide, in order to redress local public perception. The second program, 'Sanctuary: the project,' was an outreach program focused on highlighting the issues facing people from elsewhere coming to live in Glasgow, including access to local services.

The public reaction to this unprecedented initiative has been salutary and positive, with attendance figures increasing annually since the project began, including more visitors with diverse backgrounds than ever before.[39] A survey also revealed strong public support for the issues raised, laying to rest the sacred cow that museums and topicality are a dangerous mix. In fact, the success of this program has created its own legacy in the form of three further programs, including violence against women and sectarianism in Glasgow and Scotland. In 2009, GoMA also plans to explore the issues faced by the lesbian, gay, bisexual and transgender communities.

In summary, this gallery's remarkable journey into the realm of social justice has joined the best in contemporary art practice with social change and the creation of more compassionate communities. This experience has also had a profound effect on both the vision and the management of the gallery, as GoMA has adopted the core values of 'quality and equality.' This means that their inclusion and access work is not an add-on but an intrinsic part of everything they do.[40] I am particularly struck by the consciousness and empathy this gallery exhibited when it recognized the dichotomy of a large and busy city thriving on culture, investment and international tourism, set against appalling statistics for the health and welfare of much of its population. GoMA had a choice, as all art galleries do, to pay attention and act. It did; many do not. Perhaps GoMA reflects a European perspective which, when contrasted with North America, is seemingly more cognizant of the social and environmental contexts within which individuals and public institutions live. As mentioned earlier, Europeans use about half as much energy per capita as Americans do and produce far less carbon. It would seem that North American museums and galleries remain largely oblivious to the opportunities for social stewardship, much as the larger society remains oblivious to unbridled consumption.

Less abstract than values, effective leadership is a key for a mindful museum, and GoMA's heightened awareness is less of a revelation knowing that the Head of Arts and Museums for Culture and Sport Glasgow is Mark O'Neill – one of the more thoughtful museum directors. As for the staff of GoMA, they note that their foray into contemporary arts and human rights 'is actually the best thing that could have happened to us.'[41] Marketplace ideologues and practising cynics will argue that only government galleries, reliant on the tax payer, are able to address such issues as social justice, as they have no commercial appeal. Perhaps, but museums and galleries must first challenge themselves to determine where the truth lies. We simply don't know at this time, as museum practice has been too hidebound to test the sustainability of making a difference.

Authenticity and money – an unlikely mix

There are several examples of resilience in the museum world that are neither individuals nor institutions, but nonetheless contribute mightily to the overall welfare of museums – economically, professionally and intellectually. These examples are

one-of-a-kind, and demonstrate that creativity and consciousness are also the property of those who serve the extended museum community. The first of these is the
Economuseum Network, which was founded in Quebec, Canada, in 1992 and is a
decidedly new take on the meaning of museums, heritage and the marketplace.[42]
An economuseum engages in the small-scale production of crafts and foods in a
workshop setting, with a focus on the preservation and perpetuation of traditional
skills and authentic craftsmanship, ranging from bronze metal working to embroi-
dery; from glassblowing to the production of paper using seventeenth-century techniques. Economuseums not only promote the products of local craftspeople, but they
also create employment and promote what is commonly called intangible cultural
heritage – knowledge, skills, values and practices. They also differ significantly from
standard retail operations, including those of mainstream museums, with the shop
owners providing the public with information on skills, techniques and production
processes.[43]

In fact, there are six components to being an economuseum, which demonstrate
the rigour and uniqueness with which this network retails traditional knowledge
in a marketplace setting.[44] These components include a public reception area with
space that commemorates some aspect of cultural heritage; a production workshop which is visible to the public and equipped with educational resources; an
exhibition space providing interpretation of the particular craft from a historical
perspective; an exhibition area that interprets the adaptation of the traditional
product to contemporary needs; a public area that provides resource materials for
visitors who want to learn more about the craft, and a shop for selling the products. These components constitute far more rigorous merchandising standards than
can be seen in museum shops (with their crowded spaces, T-shirts and calendars),
yet these economuseum prerequisites do not appear to be obstacles to the growing
success of this network.

Although I was unable to access any revenue figures (economuseums are privately-
owned small businesses), the system is thriving with separate economuseum
networks in Quebec, the four Atlantic provinces of Canada, and Ontario (under
development), as well as an international network. Over the next three years, the
network will expand into five northern European countries, underwritten by €1.6
million in funding from the European Union and a county council in Norway.[45]
Thirteen new economuseums will be created in Norway, Iceland, Northern Ireland,
the Republic of Ireland and the Faroe Islands. Canada already has 48 of them in
the networks mentioned above, and more are under development.

There is much to ponder in the success of this enterprise, founded by Canadian
architect and ethnologist Cyril Simard, who envisioned a community of people
preserving traditional trades and knowledge by developing culturally innovative
tourism products. Note the reference to 'tourism products', not museum products.
The implications go far beyond tourism, however, as the necessity to preserve traditional know-how grows in lockstep with our increasing inability to solve the many
problems that our blind faith in technology has created. Traditional knowledge and
techniques, be they indigenous or of the dominant society in origin, are harbingers
of long-term sustainability as the wisdom of past adaptations is rediscovered. This

Figure 17 Women making a patchwork quilt at La Maison de Calico, the Quilting Economuseum in Pointe-Claire, Quebec, Canada.

Photo: courtesy of International ECONOMUSEUM Network Society

alone is sufficient reason for the museum community to consider the possibilities of economuseum partnerships, or at least to consider the value of the economuseum approach, in the quest for relevance. Museums are the custodians of the objects that economuseums celebrate, produce and sell, and the potential for synergy is impossible to ignore.

Perhaps most importantly, the economuseum may be a prototype of that elusive hybrid organization that must be invented if museums are to contend with the fallout of hyper-capitalism. Although in purpose and intent economuseums are small businesses, they part company with the marketplace because of their concern for integrity, knowledge, and intelligent consumption. In fact, the Economuseum Charter of Values states: 'we act in compliance with lasting respect for the principles of sustainable development, equitable work practices, the conservation of our intangible heritage and cultural identities.'[46] This is a rare and complex blend of competing values and interests, and a mix that commercial dogma cannot accommodate. This alone makes the Economuseum Network worthy of attention – a twenty-first-century marriage of enduring values and unabashed pragmatism.

Leading the pack

The second example in my search for resilience within the broader museum community is the Museums Association (MA) of the UK – the oldest museum association in the world, although its age belies its contemporaneity.[47] It dates back to 1889, when it was founded by a small group of museums and galleries to look after their own interests.

Unlike many museum associations, the MA is entirely independent of government funding and is supported by individual, institutional and corporate members. Its mission is multifaceted and includes providing information through conferences, its website and publications; lobbying government on behalf of UK museums; setting ethical standards; and providing professional development programs for members. The MA immediately distinguishes itself by offering two unique services unheard of in North America – and in the rest of the museum world, I suspect.[48]

The first of these is the Benevolent Fund, the purpose of which is to alleviate the financial distress of MA members and their immediate dependents. Support for childcare, respite care, school fees, special equipment for disabled living, and nursing home fees are all eligible. This program is a refreshingly humane and inventive counterpoint in an era of underpaid museum workers, the rising cost of living, and the expendable employee. The other program deserving mention is the Monument Fellowships, intended to capture the unrecorded collections-related knowledge held in the minds of retired museum professionals. Recall the Curator in the Prologue and her angst about incomplete collection records and the information that is never recorded. I had no idea when I wrote that lament that anyone in the museum community was addressing the ongoing departure of curatorial memory. The MA's fellowship program offers financial support to recently retired, or about to retire, collection specialists to enable them to share their unrecorded collections-related knowledge at their former place of work, especially with their successors. These fellowships support not new research but rather the recording of existing knowledge that might otherwise be lost.

The MA concluded that with all the demands on curatorial time, much of the collections work was left undone, with the most telling of consequences – when experienced curators leave their museums much of their collection knowledge, accumulated over decades, leaves with them. This is a universal problem in museums but, to my knowledge, the MA is the first association to speak frankly and plainly about it, and to move beyond the platitudes.

The Museums Association does much of its work through what are called 'campaigns', ranging from developing salary guidelines, to highlighting the low pay in the museum sector for employers and funding bodies, to encouraging people from under-represented backgrounds to take up a career in museums and galleries. There is a decidedly activist intent in the choice of the word 'campaign', as well as in the MA's overall work – a clear indication of the benefit of independence from government. Independence of thought and action are qualities that more museum associations could pay attention to if they intend to move beyond the inertia of the status quo, weighed down as it is with passivity and habit.

The MA's latest foray into relevance concerns sustainability and includes a discussion paper published on their website entitled 'Sustainability and museums: your chance to make a difference', as well as a shorter version that was printed and sent to all members.[49] In addition, there were follow-up meetings with members in the summer of 2008, culminating in their annual conference in the fall where the museum community's reaction to the discussion paper and community consultations will be reported. This process had not yet been completed at the time of writing, so I will conclude this discussion with several observations on the purpose and intent of the discussion paper. It starts with the premise that sustainability means meeting the needs of the present without compromising the ability of future generations to meet their own needs. The MA recognizes the importance of inter-generational equity, and sees sustainability in its broadest sense – social, environmental and economic. With this as the starting point, 11 draft sustainability principles are included in the discussion paper, which embody what museums must do 'to flourish sustainably.' Some examples include:

- Manage collections well, so that they will be a valued asset for future generations, not a burden.
- Make the best use of energy and other natural resources and minimize waste, setting targets and monitoring progress towards them.
- Contribute responsibly to the social, cultural and economic vitality of the local area and wider world.
- Respond to changing political, social, environmental and economic contexts and have a clear long-term purpose that reflects society's expectations of museums.
- Join with other museums, and other organisations, in partnerships and mergers, where it is the best way of meeting their purpose in the long term.

These draft principles are offered for evaluation and discussion by the membership, as are 28 questions which range from 'Do you agree that museums need to think about sustainability?', to 'How could your museum be a socially responsible enterprise?', to 'How might your museum reduce the financial and energy cost of each visit?'[50] The discussion paper is as seamless as a good conversation, with these questions interspersed in a benignly provocative manner.

This sustainability initiative is a bold attempt to galvanize action, at a time when boards and practitioners alike are in need of compelling motivation to broaden their perspectives as social institutions. This broader conversation about the role of museums in the greater scheme of things is long overdue, and it will require the sort of leadership inherent in the Museum Association's discussion paper and consultative process. How many local, provincial, state, regional, national and international museum associations have embraced sustainability issues as forthrightly as the UK Museums Association? How many of them are breaking new ground with their policies and programs, or simply plowing up old ground in thrall to comfort and conformity?

Academics in action

Museum studies departments are playing an increasingly important role in the evolution of museum practice and their continued growth is silent testimony to the need for enhanced method, theory and training.[51] For a glimpse of their global distribution, museum studies departments can be found in universities and colleges in every state in the USA, and in Australia, Canada, Japan, Mexico, New Zealand, Sweden, South Africa, Switzerland, Turkey and the United Kingdom. These programs offer various qualifications, including diplomas and undergraduate degrees with a museological specialization, as well as master's and doctoral degrees, and students may choose to study online, in residence, or both.

One of the more prominent programs is the Department of Museum Studies at the University of Leicester in the UK and, by any standard, this is an active and committed group of scholars, teachers and researchers.[52] With 15 core academic staff (14 with PhDs), 22 distance learning associate tutors and 29 PhD students in 2008, this department has steadfastly maintained its dual mission of teaching and research, which is grounded in a commitment to working with museums, galleries and related cultural organizations internationally in the interests of developing creative museum practice. The department's website is worth examining for its own sake, as it reveals a rich and substantive trail of teaching and research activities, including a blog devoted to the ruminations of their PhD students. In addition to academic programs in museum studies, art museum and gallery studies, digital heritage, interpretation, and representation and heritage, the department publishes the *Museological Review* edited by students and an online electronic journal entitled *Museum & Society*. This department is equally adept at sharing its work and that of others, and hosts two highly recognized book series about museums, including the *Leicester Readers in Museum Studies* and *Museum Meanings*, both published by Routledge.

This is the foundation for the department's innovative Research Centre for Museums and Galleries (RCMG), and it is this organizational entity which is of particular interest in this overview of progressive practice. The RCMG was established in 1999 in 'response to the growing need for research and evaluation within the sector, in particular around the relationship between museums, galleries and their audiences.'[53] One of the strengths of the RCMG is its autonomy as a distinct research group within the Department of Museum Studies, which allows them to assemble customized research teams by drawing not only on existing RCMG staff but also on departmental staff, other Leicester academics, external researchers, specialists and consultants, including the international community. This model encourages cross-fertilization and collaboration within and outside the museum sector – a vital tonic in the insular world of museums. The RCMG has two research themes that are particularly germane to the purpose of this book, including 'the social role and impact of museums and galleries' and 'the museum's potential to engage with contemporary social issues (in particular, through collections, exhibitions and displays).'[54]

One of the RCMG's current research projects, both initiated and managed by them, is 'Rethinking Disability Representation' (RDR). This is a large-scale, experimental

Figure 18 The Rethinking Disability Representation Project included the 'Life Beyond the Label' exhibition at the Colchester and Ipswich Museum Service. This exhibition included large photographs of disabled people with labels written onto their faces. The purpose was to make visitors think about the people behind these labels and give disabled people the opportunity to define themselves.

Photo: courtesy of Julian Anderson and the Research Centre for Museums and Galleries

project which is developing new approaches to the interpretation of disability and the representation of disabled people's lives within museums and galleries.[55] More specifically, the RDR project has 'set out to challenge commonly held perceptions of impairment as limitation and to interrogate disablist attitudes, experiences and barriers, both historically and within contemporary society.'[56] Unlike sexism and racism, however, disablism is not in contemporary dictionaries and refers to discriminatory, oppressive or abusive behaviour arising from the belief that disabled people are inferior to others.[57]

In pursuit of this cutting-edge, social advocacy mission, the RCMG is collaborating with nine galleries and museums across the UK, as well as with a think tank of experts in the disability field. The museum projects involve exhibitions and educational programs which are intended to offer visitors alternative and non-prejudicial ways to think about disability, while enhancing their understanding of disabled people's histories and experiences. Each museum or gallery project is unique, but each of them shares a philosophy and approach created by the think tank of disabled activists, artists and cultural practitioners, as well as representatives from the museum and gallery world. Among its members are the Director of Disability Awareness in Action and the Director of the UK Museums Association. In addition, many of the projects have been developed through consultation and partnership with disabled people in the museum's particular community. Drawing on the broader community for expertise that the museums themselves do not have is fundamental to the intellectual and social integrity of this project.

A large-scale, qualitative and quantitative evaluation of the RDR project was under way in 2008, including in-depth interviews, focus groups and comment cards, with the focus on the ways in which visitors responded to the exhibits and educational sessions at the nine partner museums. The evaluation results were not available at the time of writing, but it is clear that the nine projects have prompted considerable discussion among visitors, as well as new ways of thinking about disability.[58]

In summary, the RCMG's 'Rethinking Disability Representation' project is close to a textbook example of what can be achieved when academic rigour and sensibility are combined with the know-how of competent and community-minded museums. The mix of research expertise, social relevance and inspired museum practice is an undeniably powerful recipe for the collective good. With this in mind, what is the ultimate purpose of the significant amount of time and money museums spend on audience research: to help them get better at what they are already doing well – education and entertainment? Perhaps a more socially aware agenda could augment this traditional preoccupation, assuming that the research design includes non-museum experts and the citizens' chorus as part of the plan. For museums to forgo this opportunity is to accept the ideology that sees them only as one more purveyor of conformity and consumption. The RCMG has quietly and effectively broken rank with the status quo by combining disciplinary expertise with the counsel of citizens. Both the Department of Museum Studies and the RCMG are role models for unlocking the synergy between museum practitioners and museums academics. The wheel does not have to be reinvented.

Why resilience?

The reader may wonder why I have chosen to use 'resilience' to characterize these examples of innovative and progressive museum practice. I do so because resilience means 'the ability to recover from or adjust easily to misfortune or change.'[59] Resilience also suggests a frame of mind that is not bound by deadening routine, habit, or traditional practices. Most importantly for museums, becoming resilient allows systems and organizations to absorb large disturbances without changing their fundamental natures.[60] Resilient systems are supple, agile and adaptable – concepts seldom associated with museum practice, at least up until now. Recognizing the litany of biospheric issues and tectonic stresses outlined in Chapter 2, planetary change is well under way with a host of known and unknown consequences for museums, ranging from increased utility costs to the possible curtailment of public funding. Within this continuum of consequences are the enormous lost opportunity costs if museums remain satisfied in the marketplace rather than using their resources, intelligence and trusted societal status in the interests of enhanced and creative stewardship. Fostering institutional resilience may soon become the number one strategic priority for museums as events unfold, as it is the foundation for both renewal and prosperity. Survival, as the museum scholar Stephen Weil was fond of noting, is not a purpose.[61]

Exploring resilience

All of the preceding examples of individuals, programs, and organizations merit attention for their efforts at becoming resilient and, collectively, they exhibit various characteristics that both create and define resilience. To begin with, resilience is enhanced by 'loosening some of the couplings inside our economies and societies', in the words of Homer-Dixon.[62] For museums, this means a serious appraisal of the current growth model based on building expansions, expensive exhibitions, growing collections and increased operating costs, coupled with the relentless imperative of visitor consumption in order to augment the earned revenues that are required to support the increased costs, and so on and so on. This vicious cycle is unsustainable as discussed earlier, and decoupling may be the only solution. The best approach is to avoid this addictive pattern in the first place.

Resilience is also thwarted by the disciplinary boundaries, organizational hierarchy, insularity and insecurity which plague many museums. Practitioners at all levels must become much more comfortable with leaving their buildings and seeking out the knowledge and experience that they themselves are lacking. Yes, there are always one hundred and one pressing internal excuses that support compartmentalization and isolation, but crossing cultural, social and ideological barriers is the very essence of resilience. I once thought that this insularity was the result of a certain arrogance; now I also see it as a lack of self-confidence among museums, stemming in part from a practised unfamiliarity with the wider world. Resilience also means that there is no one solution or strategy for successful adaptation and institutional success.[63] This is really the idea of the museum as a mixed portfolio, discussed in Chapter 5, restated. Museums will increasingly need to operate on multiple fronts, conceding attention to marketplace revenues while embracing new initiatives like those described in this chapter.

The strength which ensues from a mix of sound business practices and social responsibility is qualitatively no different than the strength which emerges from species diversity in an ecosystem. For a museum to judge its performance on attendance and/or collection growth is analogically identical to monoculture food production, where only one crop is grown. This is not resilient; it's a high risk strategy because that one crop may fail – just like blockbuster exhibitions commonly do. Yet every day we see museum boards, executives, troops of consultants and architects decreasing resilience by promoting more growth, bigger buildings, and increased costs. This is brittleness, not resilience, and the implications of this approach are even grimmer, in the words of Homer-Dixon:

We need to exercise our imaginations so that we can challenge the unchallenge-able and conceive the inconceivable. Hunkering down, denying what's happening around us, and refusing to countenance anything more than incremental adjust-ments to our course are just about the worst thing we can do.[64]

Resilient values

Clearly, enhanced resilience is as important for museums as it is for any other twenty-first-century organization. Our collective well-being requires that all organizations (private, public, non-profit or for-profit) contribute concepts, ideas, plans, and alter-natives for a better and more stable world, not to mention assistance in coping with the fears, constraints and issues we have already created. A surge of innovation, creativity and experimentation is urgently needed, and it is heartening to see that the individuals and organizations featured in this chapter are contributors. To assume that the majority of museums may somehow sit this one out is the embodiment of self-deception. The 'long emergency' is now well under way, and will require no less than the shift from our 'high-entropy culture', the purpose of which was to create material abundance and satisfy every human desire, to a 'low-entropy world' that minimizes energy flow.[65]

In our high-entropy culture, we have celebrated material progress, efficiency and specialization, and joined this with an unalloyed hubris that places our species at the centre of the universe. In addition, reality is now defined as what can be meas-ured, quantified and tested. Fossil fuels have allowed this spectacular florescence of technological growth, but these days are numbered.[66] In contrast, the inevitable low-entropy world will recognize that excessive materialism and consumption are maladaptive and constitute an unacceptable assault on the biosphere. In addition to this core distinction between high- and low-entropy cultures, there are numerous other values inherent in the low-entropy age we are entering, and it is exciting to see that the progressive practices outlined in this chapter embody various values that distinguish a low-entropy culture.

Jeremy Rifkin, in a groundbreaking book that is nearly 30 years old, explores the implications of the laws of thermodynamics for our current way of life, including the values that characterize a low-entropy world.[67] His book is a readable and insightful account which I highly recommend, but the details need not concern us here. What's important is Rifkin's characterization of low-entropy values, which I will use to frame this concluding overview of exemplary museum practice.

As noted repeatedly, materialism and unbridled consumption are destructive of both nature and culture, and the work of Douglas Worts, the National Museum of Australia and the UK Museums Association reveal a commitment to confronting unthinking consumption and its implications for environmental sustainability – a major tenet of a low-entropy society. The low-entropy future will also see a renewed respect for the importance of quality work and the importance of high quality work places. In our high-entropy society, where work has become the means to consume, and where efficiency and profit are of primary concern, work often lacks purpose and value. Whether it is an assembly line or a sweatshop, corporate hierarchy and specialization rule the day.

In contrast, we get a glimpse of low-entropy work cultures at the Center for Cultural Understanding and Change, the Morikami Museum and Japanese Gardens and the Department of Museum Studies at Leicester. Each of these organizations demonstrates the meaning of high quality work – grounded in expertise yet leavened by genuine empathy for intractable issues that impact on individuals and communities. In all cases, the hierarchy is minimal, self-organization is present, responsibility is decentralized, and the scale is relatively small. Large, centralized organizations of any kind are increasingly dysfunctional, contributing more to inertia and disorder than they do to leading the way. Another key value of low-entropy organizations is a renewed emphasis on the importance of public duties and social responsibilities.

In a low-entropy world, the capitalistic emphasis on self-interest and private gain is replaced by a greater sense of the collective good. The neo-liberal and neo-conservative rhetoric that 'a rising tide raises all ships' is recognized for what it is – another smoke screen for the protection of privatized interests. In contrast, we have the social justice work of the Gallery of Modern Art (GoMA) in Glasgow, and the Economuseum Network, with its unique commitment to the preservation of knowledge in the retail world.

Most of the examples in this chapter also share another key value of a low-entropy society – an explicit respect for the interrelatedness of people and the natural world. Industrial capitalism, and indeed the so-called knowledge economy, continue to be based on a separation from the natural world so profound that nature is seen as a tool to be manipulated, and not as the source of all life. The consequences of this separation, which will beset us for generations, are embodied in a fourth-grade student from San Diego, California, who said, 'I like to play indoors better 'cause that's where all the electrical outlets are.'[68] There are sufficient examples in this book to confirm that museums can be key players in the integration of the natural and cultural worlds. The challenge for museums is to collectively assume this task across the board.

There are still other values of a low-entropy world that museums are ideally suited to embrace. For example, the consequences of diminishing fossil fuels will mean a pronounced shift from urban to rural sensibilities, where food is produced along with the legacy of knowledge that makes this possible. I am not referring to large-scale, industrial food production, as its future will soon be counted on two hands, reliant as it is on the fossil fuel economy. Along with this new sensibility will come a renaissance for the small community museum, resulting from the massive shift of people out of the suburbs and back to labour-intensive agriculture.[69] Community museums can offer knowledge, insight and respite, gifted as they are with volunteer community elders who serve as their organizational backbones.

In short, all of those community museums that have been undervalued and essentially ignored by bigger museums will gain newfound value as the high-entropy economy confronts its demise. It is also easy to predict, as discussed in Chapter 4, that the rising cost of jet fuel will effectively eliminate the current phenomenon of low-cost jet travel. As noted before, long-distance air travel will return to the realm of the elite, where it all began. The upside of this brisk touch with reality will be a renewed interest in local communities and their resources (including museums), for their inherent knowledge and wisdom which are essential for the low-entropy economy of the future.

Assuming responsibility

Are museums up to this task? How many have actually contemplated their role and responsibilities as the world moves from energy consumption to energy frugality? With the exception of the examples in this chapter, I venture to say – not many. Yet 28 years ago Rifkin made an observation that could serve as a touchstone for the strategic future of museums. He wrote:

> After a long, futile search to find out where we belong in the total scheme of things, the Entropy Law reveals to us a simple truth: that every single act that occurs in the world has been affected by everything that has come before it, just as it, in turn, will have an effect on everything that comes after. Thus, we are each a continuum, embodying in our presence everything that has preceded us, and representing in our own becoming all of the possibilities for everything that is to follow.[70]

Is this not the eloquent mission statement of a prescient museum? As self-professed keepers of the continuum and 'all those acts that preceded us', as well as the champions of their present and future meaning, can museums not be the harbingers of an adaptive future? Why must they limit themselves to the imposition of the status quo? The high energy paradigm, currently the foundation of our existence, must be dismantled thoughtfully and deliberately, taking into account its social ramifications and indecipherable complexities. Are museums to wait for passive bureaucracies and faltering politicians, at all levels, to point the way? If museums are reluctant to assume these responsibilities in the absence of any authority to do so, then they must ask themselves from what source they think their authority will come?[71] Because museums will never be in control of society or their communities, waiting around for the authority to act responsibly is both heedless and fraught with risk.

There are no barriers to social responsibility and relevance, and there is no one way to achieve these, as the individuals, programs and institutions described in this chapter have demonstrated. There are simply no better social institutions to assume this task than museums, grounded as they are in a diachronic view of humankind's successes and failures. The current preoccupation of museums with growing collections and audiences, while confronted with the choice of outmoded tradition or renewal, heralds the metaphorical watershed discussed in Chapter 1. Museums have also arrived at Peter Drucker's 'divide', or that point in history 'when society rearranges itself – its worldview; its basic values; its social and political structure; its arts;

its key institutions.'[72] Are museums to be active participants as these events unfold, or victims of their own myopia?

Fortunately, we have the examples described in this chapter, as well as the work of equally discerning museums unknown to me, to demonstrate that relevance and leadership are alive and well, at least in pockets of the museum community. They are heartening reminders that elite boards, big budgets and quantitative measures are not the *sine qua non* of relevance and success. On the contrary, the fruits of privilege are ultimately constraining, misleading and maladaptive, as history has proven time and again. Museums, not surprisingly, revel in marketplace success, be it high attendance, shop sales or burgeoning tax-receipted donations, but none of these things are resilient. Instead, they are brittle embodiments of a maladaptive past. Surely museums have the perspective to discriminate, and those that do can rightfully be called mindful. In fact, the mindful museum can be glimpsed on the horizon and examining its meaning and potential is the subject of the next chapter.

6

The mindful museum

Mindfulness

The word 'mindful' entered the museum vocabulary recently, albeit with a meaning that differs radically from my understanding of the concept. In an article entitled 'The Mindful Museum', American essayist Adam Gopnik writes that 'The mindful museum should first of all be mindful in being primarily about the objects it contains. Your first experience when entering the mindful museum should be of a work of art.'[1] Although Gopnik notes that he uses 'mindful' in the Buddhist sense, 'of a museum that is aware of itself, conscious of its own functions, and living at this moment', I submit that he has sorely confused the self-absorbed behaviour of museums, grounded in habit and traditional practice, with the real meaning and value of mindfulness. Ironically, the preoccupation with objects and collections is one of the primary obstacles that is preventing museums from becoming truly mindful. While I acknowledge that Gopnik is primarily concerned with art museums, this does not explain his use of 'mindful', especially with respect to its Buddhist meaning. The world of museums could do with a clearer understanding of what 'mindfulness' actually means, and this requires a brief digression into the meditation literature.

The systematic cultivation of mindfulness has been called 'the heart of Buddhist meditation.' It is a particular way of paying attention, and one of its major strengths is that it is not based on any belief system or ideology – its benefits are accessible to anyone.[2] In essence, mindfulness is moment-to-moment awareness and is cultivated by purposefully paying attention to things we ordinarily ignore. Mindfulness requires that we should always know what we are doing, and actually helps us to be more aware of events in the outside world and one's reactions to them.[3] Becoming more mindful is particularly important at this point in our evolution as a species, as the pace of life in the developed world accelerates and global stresses and strains mount – all compounded by the endless distractions of the digital revolution.

Chaotic cascades

We need only consider the dramatic changes in new technology to appreciate the new and relentless pressures of the digital age on museum work. There are computers at home and work, fax machines, cell phones, pagers, laptops, BlackBerries, high speed connectivity, email and the internet, all of which are convenient, efficient, and useful, but at a cost to mindfulness. Jon Kabat-Zinn, a professor of medicine and meditation teacher, describes the consequences as follows:

> This new way of working and living has inundated us all of a sudden with endless options, endless opportunities for interruption, distraction, highly enabled 'response ability' ... and a kind of free-floating urgency attached to even the most trivial of events. The to-do list grows ever longer, and we are always rushing through this moment to get to the next.[4]

Added to these stresses and distractions is the chaotic thinking that marks much of our everyday lives, as our brains continue their ceaseless chatter. Much of our thinking is narrow and repetitive, and based on our personal history and our habits. Our minds are filled with anxieties about the future, how we're possibly going to get everything done that needs to be done, what people said or didn't say, what we want or don't want, how will we pay the bills, do we have enough money, are we happy, will we ever be happy, are we successful, are we getting the recognition we deserve, will we ever get enough time for ourselves, and so on and so on and so on. And if that is not enough mental chatter, 'we worry about having no time, about needing more time, about having too much time, about wishing things were different, somehow better, somehow more satisfying.'[5]

Our thinking can be described as a waterfall – a continual cascade of thoughts.[6] Mindfulness is about acknowledging the power of these distractions to rob our ability to pay attention, and mindfulness meditation is the common pathway to enhanced awareness and self-knowing. Because the essence of mindfulness is knowing what you are doing while you are doing it, there is nothing mystical or extraordinary about meditating or being mindful.[7] Organizations also stand to benefit from knowing what they're doing while they're doing it and, as unlikely as it may seem, a commitment to 'being mindful' is as valuable for museums as organizations as it is for individuals engaged in meditative practice.

Museum chatter

Understandably, museums also suffer from unavoidable distractions, cascading thoughts and institutional chatter. There is the continuous preoccupation with the number of visitors, the building, security, education, food, gifts, shopping, entertainment, technology, special exhibitions and visitor demands – just a sampling of the front-of-house concerns. Then there is the internal chatter, beginning with the governing authority which may or may not be performing adequately; may have an ineffective chair; may be exercising undue or conflicting influence on the work of the museum; or may be failing to raise the necessary funding to balance the overspent operating budget. Then there is the staff, from the most senior to the most junior, who are simply human beings living out the intricacies of their lives more or less effectively, a good portion of which is done in an institutional setting. Perhaps there are also leaders and managers with 25 years of experience – the same year repeated 25 times.

Staff morale might also be low, a condition which may be endemic in museums, for the notable reason that remarkable and effective people are not necessarily comfortable or happy, and there are plenty of remarkable people working in museums. In fact, these people can be ruthless, boring, stuffy, irritating and humourless, and museums, like all organizations, are dependent upon such people.[8] Then there is the paradox of discontent, which recognizes that improvement in human affairs leads not to satisfaction, but to discontent. The psychologist, Abraham Maslow, advises managers to listen not for the presence or absence of complaints, but rather to what people are complaining about.[9] Only in healthy organizations would there be complaints about needs for self-actualization, such as 'my talents aren't being fully used around here', as compared to complaints about working conditions. This is the paradox, for only in a healthy museum, where people are involved and their talents are being used, would it occur to anyone to complain about this.

Stress

Organizational stress is another perpetual distraction, and an ever-increasing feature of organizational life that has not received the attention it deserves in the museum sector. Many museum staff, at least in North America, are understandably weary and skeptical, given the penchant for lay-offs to balance the books, the low pay, and the fact that there will be no mythical plateau where the organization can pause and say 'we've made it', and return to business as usual. There is no business as usual, or an idealized past for that matter, contrary to the wishful thinking of most museum administrators and workers. The resulting stress must be seen as an inherent danger, nonetheless, and be confronted organizationally with intelligence and caring. That being said, we are all familiar with the stress that results from individuals who needed to work out their anxieties long ago, with their parents, in fact, and not with their colleagues. Empathy is clearly required, but it is best not to confuse these foibles with the overall health of a particular museum.

Negative people

Stress is also a factor in the 'negative people syndrome', another source of institutional chatter and perpetual ruminations. There is always a certain amount of negativism afloat in even the most exemplary museum, and it can be salutary in counteracting complacency and providing an inadvertent source of humility for those that are paying attention. Overall, however, staff negativity is a bane, and can translate into constant complaining, hostility and a notable lack of generosity of spirit among colleagues. It can also lead to compliance and passivity, both deadly hurdles to creativity and action. Although the negative voices are unfortunately the loudest, it is important to acknowledge that skepticism and questioning are integral parts of a well-functioning museum. The essential task lies in continually determining whether the negativism is self-serving or of benefit to the organization. More chatter: more distractions. Which leads me to the last example of unrelenting chatter – the ambiguity that envelopes all museums, whether or not they are mired in habit or awakening to resilience.

Ambiguity and paradox

Ambiguity should not be feared, however, contrary to the dictates of the marketplace. Marketplace disciples spend vast amounts of time and energy seeking control over their internal and external environments, in order to enhance the bottom line. For corporations in general, they succeed to the extent that they can exercise sovereignty over people's lives through marketing, hidden trade agreements, preferential government treatment, globalism and so forth, all of which provide them with unacknowledged public support for their corporate self-interests. Free trade and private enterprise have to be two of the more oxymoronic terms of the twenty-first century, as evidenced by the recent Bush administration in the USA, where the American people have essentially been robbed by self-interested corporatists dressed up in political clothing.[10] The museum world is far more complex, with few privileged connections and no history of influence peddling with which to bolster one's fortunes.

Museums have no choice but to confront the ambiguity, complexities and paradoxes which make them what they are, many of which have been noted in this book. Paradoxical questions and imperatives abound – 'Is the customer always right?'; 'Are museums sustainable without significant contributions of public funding?'; 'Are there too many museums?'; 'What is the purpose of a competent museum?', and 'What role should tradition play in an effective museum?' In light of all this ambiguity, museum boards and staff have laboured long and hard to 'avoid surprises' and, admittedly, few things disturb them more than increasing complexity.[11] Questions with no ready answers are also significant management challenges in museums, and leave anxiety and discouragement in their wake.

Thinking orthogonally

We owe this preoccupation with complex details to the Newtonian hangover, where the universe is seen to be composed of small fundamental units and complex wholes are less real than their constituents.[12] This is akin to the reductionist thinking discussed in Chapter 2, and leads to fragmented thinking and the assumption that things are understandable in isolation from their contexts. The consequences of this sort of thinking are nicely summed up by Margaret Wheatley, an organizational consultant and writer:

> We still believe that what holds a system together are point to point connections that must be laboriously woven together by us. Complexity only adds to our task, requiring us to keep track of more things, handle more pieces, make more connections. As things increase in number or detail, the span of control stretches out elastically, and, suddenly, we are snapped into unmanageability.[13]

And snapped into unmindfulness, as well. All of the museum chatter discussed above, be it about governance, management, morale, stress or ambiguity, is equivalent to our cascading thoughts as individuals, and prevents museums from seeing what is actually going on in the world around them. These distractions also drown out the third agenda discussed in Chapter 3, that is the individual development, learning and transformation required to answer the crucial question of 'why' museums do what they do. Unlike individuals, museums are obviously incapable of mindful meditation as organizations, but asking the question 'why' is a workable alternative for enhancing organizational consciousness and mindfulness.

The crucial need is for the organization to recognize that much of the incessant internal chatter can be repetitive, inaccurate, disturbing, toxic and unrelenting, and to not let it subvert vision, purpose and the capacity of the museum to ponder the larger picture, clarify what is most important, and determine how it might be of real use in a troubled world. This could, in fact, be immensely liberating, and allow museums to stop taking themselves so seriously and to get out from under the pressures of having the details of their organizational plans and concerns be central to the operating of the universe.[14]

Becoming orthogonal

Although museums cannot meditate, they can become orthogonal, a rather awkward mathematical word that means 'intersecting or lying at right angles.' Its meaning, however, has been broadened to include a rotation in consciousness – orthogonally, or at right angles to conventional reality.[15] It is a matter of what one is willing to see or ignore, and to what extent one is able to ignore perceptions and remain habitually inattentive to what is really going on. Orthogonal thinking is the antidote to the constraints of conventional thinking and conditioned views, and is a vital concept for broadening individual and organizational perspectives on the world. Thinking orthogonally is also mindfulness, and is as applicable to organizations as it is to individuals. In short, it offers an alternative to the tyranny of habitual thinking and opens up new possibilities, as noted by Kabat-Zinn:

> When we inhabit this orthogonal dimension, the problems of the conventional are seen from a different perspective, more spacious than that of a small-minded self-interest. The situations we face can thus admit possibilities of freedom, resolution,

Figure 19 Ceremonialist Pete Standing Alone paints the face of museum ethnologist, Gerald Conaty, who exemplifies heightened consciousness of his professional responsibilities. The face painting was in preparation for a chieftainship ceremony in 2003 honouring Conaty's contributions to the well-being of the Kainai Nation of the Blackfoot Confederacy, Alberta, Canada.

Photo: courtesy of Robert R. Janes

acceptance, creativity, compassion, and wisdom that were literally inconceivable – unable to arise and sustain – within the conventional mindset.[16]

It is entirely reasonable to assume that museums are also capable of 'rotating their consciousness' and thereby enhance their understanding of the world. Recall the resilient museum examples described earlier – all of which signal a heretofore unorthodox engagement with reality. As discussed in Chapter 4, 'Debunking the marketplace,' many governments and corporations with vested interests are unwilling or unable to overcome the inertia and self-interest that define the status quo. Are museums, as social institutions in the civil society, capable of expanding their consciousness, recognizing their privileged position grounded in trust, respect and public support? This does not require a radical forsaking of the values and traditions that sustain museums, as an orthogonal museum can exist in its own conventional dimensionality (or consciousness), while at the same time bringing a much greater awareness to its work and its role in the greater scheme of things.

An orthogonal perspective will also entail inward and outward conflict, along with divergent and polarized views. These difficulties come with the territory and are counteracted by expanded awareness itself, which can reveal a new understanding of difficult situations, as well as the appropriate actions required.[17] Recall Glasgow's Gallery of Modern Art, whose social justice programs were launched with great staff discomfort and ended up being 'the best thing that could have happened to us.' As I noted earlier in this book, the world is simply in need of better institutions, to contribute the resilience, the intelligence and compassion to address our collective challenges. These better institutions, including museums, are orthogonal or mindful, and they have moved beyond their own self-indulgence, insecurities and anxieties to make room for new things to happen.

As the examples in Chapter 5 demonstrate, the possibilities for the museum world range from programs, to collaborations, to associations, and it is immaterial if orthogonal thinking emerges from old institutions or brand new ones. What matters is that the orthogonal museum acknowledges the need for the stewardship of the common good, commits to determining what this might require, and then acts to take care of what needs to be done. The reward will be 'unsuspected dimensions of possibility.'[18]

Museum mindfulness

With all the chatter and cascading thoughts besetting both individual museum workers and museums, thinking orthogonally and becoming more mindful might well be seen as yet another imposition on an already impossible work schedule, as well as a challenge to professionalism. There is no doubt that this way of thinking requires disciplined commitment, time and attention. As noted earlier, however, 'rotating the consciousness' of a museum does not require the wholesale discarding of conventional practice. In fact, museums can become more mindful in the course of their habitual activities. What follows are a variety of activities, techniques and considerations that can assist museum workers and their museums in heightening their collective consciousness. None of these suggestions are dramatic or expensive – they are simply different approaches to doing work that is either characteristic of all museums, or should be. The potential value of theses activities and attitudes lies in creating more space for thinking and acting with increased awareness, creativity and compassion.

Study Circles

The activity known as Study Circles was borrowed from Scandinavia and consists of small groups of people (usually 5 to 20) who meet multiple times to discuss an issue.[19] Apparently millions of people use Study Circles to increase their knowledge and understanding of a wide variety of social issues. Study Circles are supported by an organization known as Everyday Democracy, formerly the Study Circles Resource Center. This organization provides guides, books, and research 'to find ways for all kinds of people to think, talk and work together to solve problems.'[20] Study Circles don't advocate a particular solution, but welcome many points of view around a shared concern. They are voluntary and self-organizing, and are directed by a moderator or facilitator who helps to focus the discussion. Participants learn from each other, from prepared materials and from other sources such as study guides, books, guest speakers, films and field trips. The facilitator assists the Study Circle in defining and meeting its goals, as well as ensuring that people participate in the discussions. Most importantly, the facilitator or moderator is not an expert and does not teach or direct the group – he or she provides assistance and resources. The participants define their own concerns, needs and goals.

For museums, replete with many knowledgeable and motivated individuals, Study Circles are an ideal means of enhancing knowledge and awareness, with the primary cost being staff time. Because Study Circles strive for egalitarianism, they are also ideal for fostering staff-wide interaction. In my experience, the challenge will be for boards, directors and managers to suspend their authority in the hierarchy in order to listen, learn and truly participate, as Study Circles are not about formulating plans and assigning duties – they are about listening, learning and becoming informed. If managerial myopia is an impediment, it might be better for staff to 'ask for forgiveness rather than permission', as the saying goes. Staff must seriously consider proceeding on their own, as museums have little choice but to rotate their consciousness in the direction of the larger world, if they are counting on having a voice in the years ahead.

Study Circles are potentially capable of examining any issue or concern, and would be most appropriate for initiating a dialogue on the issues confronting a community, which in turn might ultimately inform the programs and services of a particular museum. Because Study Circles are small, democratic and non-expert, they can be adapted to virtually any use. And by encouraging people to develop their own ideas about issues and then to share them with others, Study Circles help people not only to become informed, but also to overcome the inertia and feelings of inadequacy that invariably accompany complex problems and thorny issues. It seems to me that any self-respecting museum would have at least one Study Circle, if not a dozen.

Strategic thinking

Strategic planning is now commonplace in museums, at least among medium to large institutions in North America, and is one of the useful results of museums becoming more business-like. Although there are as many variations of strategic planning as there are museums, all strategic planning is intended to address three fundamental questions – 'Where is the museum now (mandate, mission and challenges)?'; 'Where does it want to be in the future?'; and 'How is it going to get there?' In essence, 'strategy is about positioning an organization for sustainable competitive advantage.'[21] Despite all the time and effort invested in strategic planning, however, it appears to be largely ineffective in altering the traditional trajectories of most museums. There are exceptions, of course, such as the Field Museum mentioned earlier, and the Liberty Science Center in New Jersey, both of which determined that they wanted to be relevant and made systemic changes to become so.[22]

The failure of strategic planning to actually define innovative strategic futures for museums is puzzling, especially considering that environmental scanning (identifying external trends and issues that could affect the museum) is a key component of competent strategic planning. If environmental scanning is being done by museums, why haven't more museums awakened to the challenges of social responsibility? Irrespective of environmental scanning, an analysis of a museum's strengths, weaknesses, opportunities and threats (the so-called SWOT analysis) is also a fundamental prerequisite for any strategic plan, as it provides the context for an intelligent appraisal of the status quo. One would think that either an environmental scan or a SWOT analysis would alert museums to the realities of the external world. Apparently not, and either these analyses are not being done or the results are shelved along with many of the strategic plans themselves. It is common knowledge among museum workers that strategic plans are dutifully produced and politely ignored, in large part because the plans end up as laundry lists of additional responsibilities, unaccompanied by clear priorities and the necessary resources.

If strategic planning cannot unfreeze the tyranny of complacency, perhaps strategic thinking can. Although thinking and planning are two sides of the same coin, there is a profound distinction between the two, perhaps even a schism. Strategic planning is about the details and procedures required to implement specific actions. Planning is also about analysis – breaking down and formalizing a set of intentions into steps that can be implemented.[23] Strategic thinking, in contrast, is the process of continually asking questions, and creatively and critically thinking through the issues.[24] Critical thinking assumes that constructing and responding to questions may be more important to long-term innovation than finding the 'solution.'

Thinking strategically is ultimately the personal responsibility of every museum worker, because it is an opportunity to look at things differently, use one's imagination, break from the familiar, and uncouple from what has been done in the past. Although all of these are essential for securing a sustainable niche for museums in a rapidly changing world, they are not easily accomplished, largely as a result of the inherent inertia of our frames of reference. Along with marketplace ideology, the typical museum's frame of reference is the other 'elephant in the room', and the crowding is becoming dangerous.

Habits of mind

It is essential to be aware of our frames of reference – they stem from our habits of mind and our points of view, and are based on assumptions, beliefs, feelings and attitudes. All organizations and individuals have their frames of reference, and the purpose of strategic thinking is to critically reflect on these, to ensure that they are not impeding or preventing learning and healthy change. It is essential to question all the habits, beliefs and underlying assumptions that support museum traditions, in order to begin to imagine new and different ways of doing things. This will undoubtedly result in a certain amount of discomfort, confusion and perhaps frustration, but these feelings are not only legitimate, they are also essential to the reframing process. There are various ways to help stimulate and nurture reframing, as follows:[25]

- Use imagination – intuition, creativity, feelings and ideas are as important as logic, rationality and analysis. All are essential.
- Adopt a broad perspective – the ability to see a situation from a broad perspective is critically important, as it allows one to see things both as they are and as they might be. A broad perspective allows for possibilities.
- Tolerate ambiguity – being able to accept competing values and interests, as well as paradoxes and incomplete information, is also essential for critical reflection, because that is the way the museum world is.
- Give up control – one doesn't have to control everything, even if this were possible. The stronger the desire for control, the greater the aversion to risk-taking and experimentation.
- Ask plenty of questions – asking questions is a primary tool for testing assumptions and introducing new frames of reference.

To conclude this discussion on strategic thinking, museums must also relinquish some of their own hubris and recognize both the charm and the curse of expertise.[26] Expertise allows one to quickly identify a situation, but it can also give a false sense of knowing. We can become so complacent about what we think we know that we ignore cues and options. And along with recognizing that intransigence usually accompanies expertise must be the realization that strategic thinking and planning are as much about deciding what not to do as they are about developing new initiatives. The inability or unwillingness to say no to dated work, dated habits and new distractions is the Achilles heel of the museum world – continually blocking the coalescence of limited resources around strategic priorities.

Until museums fully embrace the meaning of positioning, priorities and sustainability, much of the emotion, imagination, intuition and reflection – special qualities of museum and arts practitioners – will be diffused or erased by the constant reshuffling of conventional practices. A pity, indeed, considering that these qualities are the mainstays of strategic thinking, and are the antidote to the preoccupation with economics, finance and purely rational thinking.

Scenario planning

Imagine that it is 2015 and your museum director has been given the power to predict the future. He tells the assembled staff that the museum will no longer exist in 2030. All public funding will have been eliminated by 2020, as all levels of government focus their efforts on mitigating climate change, conserving water, and dramatically decreasing dependence on fossil fuels. All public institutions were assessed and declared essential and non-essential, and museums, preoccupied as they were with edutainment and leisure activities, were considered non-essential. Public funding ceased, but the museum continued for another eight years by reducing the staff and operating budget by 66 percent, aided by the financial support of a handful of loyal donors. This, too, came to end, with the outmigration of the urban population, along with its suburban appendages, to rural areas. This was prompted by continual shortages of gasoline, water and electricity, and compounded by a decaying urban infrastructure with minimal public transit. The museum quietly closed its doors in 2030, one year after the permanent collection was sold at public auction and the proceeds used to assist the urban poor who were hardest hit by the escalating costs of everything. The museum building, with its environmental controls and sophisticated security system, became the electrical substation for a colossal wind farm that was eventually built to meet the city's power needs. Much to the surprise of the museum community, there was no public reaction. In fact, the opposite occurred, when a coalition of concerned citizens and public agencies issued a press release which stated 'that closing the museum was inevitable, given its reliance on public funding and its lack of interest in pressing community issues, while continuing to give tax privileges and other advantages to the city's elite.'

This is not a prediction but a story about a possible future, and this is what scenario planning is all about. It is a technique to assist with the creation of new mental models that result in powerful stories about how the future might unfold.[27] It is not about predicting the future, but rather about exploring the future based on the premise that if you are aware of what could happen, you are much better able to prepare for what will happen. In practice, scenario planning involves identifying political, economic, social and technological trends and exploring the implications of projecting them forward. As different trends are chosen and different combinations of forecast levels (high, medium and low) are combined, a whole spectrum of possibilities can be identified.[28]

In summary, scenarios resemble a set of stories, built around carefully constructed plots, and each scenario should represent a plausible alternative future. These stories can express multiple perspectives on complex events and give meaning to these events. As a participant in a community-wide, scenario-planning exercise to develop a collective vision for the small mountain town where I live, I can attest to the value of this process. There is a methodology for scenario thinking – it is highly interactive, intense and imaginative – and there is a guide written specifically for non-profit organizations, complete with an overview of key scenario thinking concepts. It is fully downloadable at no cost.[29]

The real value for museums in scenario planning is to motivate staff and board members to challenge the status quo, by asking 'what if' questions in a disciplined way. Because the future is unknowable and change is so difficult for individuals and organizations, especially museums, 'what if' questions are important catalysts for heightening consciousness. For example, what if museums are eventually declared non-essential as more pressing public spending priorities come to the fore? What if museums are unable to muddle through with their fragile menu of public money, private donations and earned revenues? What if museums decide to stop growing their collections and reallocate the resources to addressing broader community issues wherein they have expertise? What if society experiences a renaissance of social innovation and museums are counted among the potential leaders? The 'what ifs' are many, and museums may choose those with the most meaning for them.

Scenario planning is really about rehearsing the future and assessing the possibilities, coupled with the opportunity to use these insights to take action today. The only reason for not engaging in scenario planning is that there is insufficient interest and motivation within museums to break old stereotypes. If that's the case, recall the axiom – 'if you don't know where you're going, any path will do.' Bearing in mind the societal and internal complexities confronting museums, 'any path' may well prove to be perilous.

Managing holistically

One of the constant themes throughout this book is the seeming failure of most museums to truly gauge their role and responsibilities in the larger scheme of things. A medley of hesitation, introversion and self-doubt supports the museum's isolation from mainstream issues and aspirations, with the notable exception of participation in the marketplace, as discussed in Chapter 4. With the exception of those museums that are in search of resilience, the profile of many museums is now being achieved through the notoriety that accrues to consumption – sensational shows, vanity architecture, large private donations and so forth – you've heard it all before. This is not dissimilar to the situation confronting environmental scientists and resource managers in the recent past, only they have taken it upon themselves to define a new future for their work with a view to societal values, needs and participation. Museums can learn from this pioneering work and, in so doing, 'rotate their consciousness' in a more thoughtful direction.

Resource management is apparently undergoing a fundamental change in the United States, with traditional sustained yield approaches being replaced by what is called ecosystem management.[30] Sustained yield is really maximum consumption in practice, and is analogous to the burgeoning role that consumption now plays in museums. The primary goal of ecosystem management is long-term ecological sustainability, with the recognition that the socio-political context is an essential part of ecosystem management, but has been largely ignored. To achieve a more holistic and integrated perspective, ecosystem management emphasizes socially defined goals and objectives, integrated and holistic science, collaborative decision-making, and adaptable institutions. It is this recognition of the need for holistic management that highlights the current failure of museums to effectively manage their broader potential as social institutions.

I had the opportunity to attend a presentation by one of the architects of ecosystem management, Hannah Cortner, and what follows is a distillation of some of her key observations – all of which are strikingly relevant for museums.[31] Numerous considerations underlie the move to more holistic ecosystem management, all of which are directly applicable to contemporary museum management. At the outset are those thorny variables called human beings, now seen as key ingredients in ecosystem management, whereas before they were ignored in the interests of science and production. This challenge is the same for museums, and persists as a result of their inability or reluctance to share authority and responsibility with outsiders. This deficiency is directly related to the politics of expertise, where the role of the citizen is eclipsed and replaced by experts who have their own values and aspirations.

This brings to mind the question in Chapter 1 of 'how the specialists will interact with citizens, and whether the performance can be imbued with wisdom, courage and vision.' Ecosystem management is attempting to bring the 'citizens' chorus' to the table, but few such initiatives are visible in the museum world, where management is still largely seen as an obligatory task and not as a source of insight and innovation. Institutional museum perspectives still mirror the 30 years of experience syndrome – the same year 30 times over again. This is partly attributable to what Cortner calls the 'politics of interest', where agencies and organizations are captured by vested interests, authority is concentrated with them, and broader dialogue is thwarted. There is a parallel here with museums, and their increasing dependence on strategic corporate funding (not philanthropy), unrepresentative boards of directors, and hierarchical decision-making.

These are certainly formidable challenges, and ecosystem management employs various principles to address them, beginning with socially defined goals and objectives, coupled with collaborative decision building. The intention here is to make room for both experts and the public to share in a decision-making process that crosses many boundaries, be they social, cultural or economic. This principle of inclusion creates a forum for defining priorities through collective learning, and the resulting decisions are informed by science, not dominated by it. Cortner and her colleagues believe that it is the duty of scientists and scholars to also promote the ideals of democracy and citizenship, a commitment like that of the Field Museum's Center for Cultural Understanding and Change described earlier.

Ecosystem management also places great value on integrated and interdisciplinary science, a perennial need in museums, as well as on the importance of adaptable institutions. The latter are flexible, allow decentralized decision-making and are comfortable with what is called active adaptive management. This brand of management is yet another untapped source of guidance for museums, as the purpose of active adaptive management is to learn by experimentation in order to determine the best management strategy, while also involving active stakeholder collaboration.[32]

It is difficult to appreciate why museums seem inclined to sleepwalk into the future, in light of the knowledge and experience emerging from ecosystem management, which is really the attempt to nurture interconnectedness, increase knowledge and thereby evolve professional practice. The broader museum community is in dire need of all of these things, although there are admittedly impressive obstacles to developing a new museum management paradigm. These are various and include the current predilection to look to the marketplace for solving museum issues; the resulting short-term, economic thinking; the notion that risk-taking and failure are not acceptable; and the woeful lack of inter-institutional cooperation and collaboration. All of these challenges are the artifacts of convention and comfort, and can be replaced with a rotation of consciousness in the direction of ecosystem management. Indeed, a more holistic approach to management can be observed among all the examples of resilience in Chapter 5, causing one to wonder why these are exceptions and not the new paradigm?

A curator for all seasons

The following suggestion for enhancing mindfulness is perhaps less straightforward than the previous ones, as it is concerned with the purpose and role of curators. Once the very definition of museums, curators now vie with boards of directors as the museum's most popular whipping boy. Traditionally celebrated as the intellectual heart of the institution, many curators have been replaced by marketers, fundraisers and publicists in the rush to compete in the marketplace. Curatorial attrition has often been accompanied by the sentiment that curators were a liability anyway – too inwardly focused at the expense of the public; too adept at serving their own interests; too esoteric in their communications; and simply too cranky for harried administrators. All of these accusations have some basis in fact but, like all quests for easy solutions to complex problems, the vilification of curators serves no purpose.

The symbolic 'death of the curator' has been regularly noted among practitioners, with the authority of the curator often replaced by the multifunctional team, or nothing at all. As desirable as team-based work is, it can quickly become a liability for those individuals who possess deep and substantive knowledge about a particular subject – the true essence of a curator. I know one curator who grew weary of constantly being challenged by colleagues who had never made a commitment to the advanced knowledge of any subject. Egalitarianism has its downside, at least until the team matures.

While I concede the current vulnerability of curators, the rumours of their demise are much exaggerated. They continue to command status and respect in all but the most juvenile of museums, and enjoy both privilege and autonomy, especially in medium to large institutions. Curators, in fact, are one of the bastions of conventional practice. This is all to say that the role of curator requires some orthogonal thinking and a 'rotation of consciousness,' along with study circles, strategic thinking, scenario planning and holistic management. The redefinition of the curator's role is also the concern of one of the museum community's inveterate contributors, Elaine Heumann Gurian, and it is useful to report on some of her work here.[33]

In an unpublished paper entitled 'The curator's next choice', Heumann Gurian describes the traditional role of curators as 'the acknowledged voice of museum authority,' and concludes that they collectively have an important decision to make. They may choose to maintain their long-standing positions of authority, or to embrace the increasing interactivity, sharing and democratization inherent in the use of the internet – all in an effort to encourage intellectual and social engagement among citizens. Heumann Gurian fears that most museums and their curators will choose to utilize only those aspects of the new information technology that will not challenge their control of knowledge, and thus maintain their authoritative positions.[34] She attributes this conservatism to the persistence of the original vision of the curator and the contemporary training that sustains it – scholar, keeper, researcher of collections, and arbiter of taste. The matter is unresolved in her view, as follows:

> The new pressures for responsiveness by museums occasioned by the public's expectations for interactive networking might indeed lessen the requirement on curators to learn administrative skills and make their traditional focus on content and research again more prominent. This need for constant content occasioned by the interest of the public might mean that many curators become 'curators' again, but with a new focus on communicating what they know at an unfamiliar speed and encouraging an interaction with other content they do not control using the untried medium of the Internet.[35]

The wired world

There is a great deal of activity on the World Wide Web with implications for museums, including Web 2.0 and 3.0. The Web (1.0) started with sites that are authoritative content distributors, such as traditional museums, and the user experience with Web 1.0 is passive – as a viewer and a consumer. Web 2.0 consists of web-based applications with an 'architecture of participation,' in which users generate, share, and curate the content. Web 2.0 removes the authority from the content provider and places it in the hands of the user, allowing for powerful social networking. In the electronic museum world, Museum 2.0 and 3.0 are networks for those interested in the future of cultural institutions worldwide, such as museums, galleries, science centres and other collecting bodies. The future has arrived and curators now have the choice that Heumann Gurian has presented. It's not that the digital realm will somehow replace the disciplined acquisition and dissemination of knowledge and information. This task should always remain as the heart of the matter for museums, with authenticity and truthfulness as the museum's purview. The question is whether museums will choose to engage in this new frontier, or sit on the sidelines content with the noose of familiarity.

The Ontario Science Centre (OSC), an iconic Canadian institution, chose to engage and in 2008 hosted hundreds of online video fans armed with video cameras to document Canada's first YouTube party. One of the participants, 'samtwist', said that 'Filming a giant monitor of a video link of a stickam feed of people watching you film them with a camera at a science museum. Well I can safely say it doesn't get any techier than that!'[36] Substantive change in knowledge ownership is clearly in the offing, a realm claimed by museums as their birthright. Various museum scholars, including Fiona Cameron and Paul Marty, have also launched trial balloons in the literature to get the museum community to pay attention to these looming changes.[37] The OSC, Cameron and Marty are implying a 'rotation in consciousness' for the key position of curator, and there is perhaps no other position, apart from senior administrators, with more potential to influence the course of museums than that of curator. Whether it is Museum 2.0 or 3.0, Facebook or YouTube, curators must contemplate the addition of these interactives to their intellectual menus, recognizing that the intent of these innovations is to make museums more engaging, community-based, and vital elements of society.

Museum curators can claim the learned highroad and ignore such interactions as shallow and devoid of meaning, or open their collective minds to contemporary culture with enhanced mindfulness. There may not be much choice, given the unsteady position of most museums in contemporary society. Let's instead have a curator for all seasons, equally comfortable with the expressed interests of contemporary society embedded in intellectual integrity. Sound idealistic? Try persisting in isolation from the internet and see how sustainable that is. There is a caveat, however, in advocating this new mode of curatorial expansiveness, prompted by a much celebrated book entitled *The World is Flat* by Thomas Friedman.[38] With a religious belief in new technology, Friedman chronicles the 'flattening' of the world through globalization and its implications for business, institutions and nation-states.

Although Friedman provides a brilliant synthesis of global complexities, he lives in the rarefied atmosphere of business tribalism with a marginal sense of stewardship. In a book of 473 pages, only a scant nine pages are devoted to socio-environmental issues, underscoring Friedman's apparent assumption that technology will save us if only we can change fast enough. His reductionism strikes me as a stark warning for museums that the convergence of technology is not the new silver bullet. There aren't any. The democratization of knowledge is just that – it is neither a substitute for the health of the biosphere nor a reason to ignore broader issues of social responsibility.

Governing the governors

This is a true story of the board chair of an unnamed museum whose personal behaviour became an increasing liability for the institution. Because the museum had previously installed an unconventional means of monitoring the ongoing health of the board/director relationship, all was put right in the end. It is an example of how moving beyond conditioned views and conventional practice can foster mindfulness, and assist a museum in broadening its perspective on what is desirable and achievable in the realm of governance – a subject of constant scrutiny and little reform.

This board chair was accustomed to privilege and influence throughout his life, one of the primary factors in his appointment as the chair, and perhaps an explanation for the events that followed. The chair assumed his duties by first cancelling the performance reviews of the museum director, noting that the director's performance would be apparent in what the museum did or did not do. This was followed by a quiet arrangement between the chair and the museum's conservator to frame several works of art belonging to the chair, who was also an art collector. Repeated attempts to invoice the chair for these services were not acknowledged, nor were the verbal requests by the director. As a high profile citizen, the chair also served various other unrelated organizations in a voluntary capacity, one of which decided to host a major fundraising event at the museum. The chair waived the museum's rental policy for the benefit of this organization and allowed them to bring their own refreshments to the function, thereby eliminating a significant source of earned revenue for the museum. It also became known that the chair was publicly criticizing the museum's board and director at various public functions, expressing concern about the future of the museum and the competence of its leaders. This negative commentary about the museum continued in the absence of any performance review of the director, or any face-to-face meetings with the director or the board.

Although these cumulative events provoked a great deal of stress, none of it reached crisis proportions because of an uncommon administrative device known as the Director's Review Committee (DRC). The DRC was part of the director's employment contract and its membership consisted of the board chair, vice-chair, a board member and the director. The DRC served two purposes – as the forum for the regular performance reviews of the director and, uniquely, as the in-camera forum where the director was able to discuss in complete confidence any concerns or issues respecting board governance.

By special request of the director, and in the absence of the chair, the DRC convened and the director laid out the chair's activities, knowing that confidentiality would be respected. The members of the DRC then undertook a lengthy inquiry into the conduct of the chair, including several meetings with the chair, which confirmed the director's concerns. Most importantly, the chair was asked to resign by unanimous consent of the board and the director remained in his position. The reputation of the chair was protected by discreet wording in a press release, and this instance of wrongful governance became a matter of unrecorded history.

Regrettably, this is a rare example of a judicious outcome, as the tyranny of mediocre or malignant governance continues to plague even the best of museums. The typical consequence for many of these difficult governance issues is the dismissal of the director, without recourse or discussion by those involved, least of all the director. There is probably no more injurious an act than the abrupt dismissal of a director, especially in the absence of any administrative processes and board accountability. Summary dismissals and unaccountable boards are a regular feature of museum administration, and are mostly unnecessary if attention is paid to the care and maintenance of the director/board relationship with a device like the DRC. This will become increasingly important as the mindful museum seeks to break ranks with corporate orthodoxy, conventional thinking, and the board's timidity to wrestle with the status quo. In short, the museum director will simply have to be protected if a heightened museum consciousness is to be achieved. The DRC is not only a way of doing this, but also allows for truthfulness and the saving of face at the same time.

Museums for a troubled world

More opportunities

The above examples are only a glimpse of the many possibilities for enhancing mindfulness and more conscious museum work. There are many more, such as branding, which is now seen to be integral to a successful museum.[39] With few exceptions, however, most museums do not brand their values, ideas, mission or substantive contributions. They brand 'stuff' using the language of the marketplace (customer service, efficiency, entertainment, value for money and so on), and treat visitors and users as consumers and customers.[40] All of this rhetoric is imported wholly and uncritically from the marketplace, even by those proponents who claim a special knowledge of museums.

Isn't it time for museums to move beyond the language of the marketplace to create civic brands around ideas and values that are based on the answers to key questions? These questions should consider why the museum exists, what changes it is trying to effect, what solutions it will generate, and what the museum's non-negotiable values are, such as collaboration, inclusiveness, diversity, consciousness and so forth? Having answered these fundamental questions about the 'why' and the 'what', the task is then to develop a constellation of activities that both create and maintain the brand, as exemplified by the resilient museums and programs described in Chapter 5. Branding values and ideas is another means of heightening museum consciousness and moving beyond the reigning model of economic utility.

And what about the cost of collections care? Why doesn't the global museum community have a current understanding of these costs that is analysed and shared as a means of rationalization? They don't, and without such knowledge, it is impossible to allocate scarce resources intelligently in the face of new or competing priorities. Why are collection costs treated as fixed, when they are actually discretionary?

Moving from collections to public programming, where are the collaborative forums (filmmakers, videographers, artists, poets, writers, storytellers, game creators, social activists, public agencies and NGOs) working with museums to help them better understand the realm of experience design embedded in meaning, values and relevance? As suggested in Chapter 3, a variation of this creative forum should involve recognized museum and non-museum innovators, thinkers and experts in an annual think tank/think leak, with the purpose of sharing the fruits of their collaborative efforts with the broader community. The typical museum conference may offer several keynote addresses from outsiders, but the overall insularity remains a pronounced liability. It has been noted that all great change in business has come from outside the firm, not from inside, and there is no reason to assume that museums are any different.[41]

Forsaking despair

All of these innovative practices, ranging from study circles, to wired curators, to systematizing collection costs, are pathways to expanding museum consciousness and hence becoming more mindful of what is actually going on and what is actually possible. All of these ideas and practices are also grounded in the recognition that 'the conventional, consensus reality we call the human condition is itself inexorably and strongly *conditioned* in the Pavlovian sense.'[42] There is no doubt that overcoming the inertia of habit is one of the major obstacles to museum mindfulness, a condition artfully described by the late Michael Ames, Canada's distinguished museum practitioner and scholar. In one of the most memorable museum observations of all time, Ames wrote:

> It is typically easier to see what should be done which simply requires a judgement, than to get it done, which requires a more extensive analysis of the situation and the marshalling of support. Despair is thus frequently the shadow to ambition in the museum world, like devils following one in the night.[43]

Holding on to Ames' evocative image of 'devils following one in the night' for the moment, I suggest that the aids to museum mindfulness described here can be seen as instruments to light the way and minimize the shadow of despair. A slight 'rotation of consciousness' permits the possibility of forsaking despair, and replacing it with the realization that a more mindful museum is possible in the contemporary world – retaining its core characteristics of authenticity and trust, but steeped in an awareness of what it means to exercise stewardship beyond the needs of mute objects and visitor statistics.

This is stewardship of the highest order, demanding active engagement and shared authority with those individuals and communities that museums purport to serve. As Peter Drucker noted in Chapter 1, our civilization is once again between 'the old and the new', with the emerging centre of gravity being knowledge and innovation, not capital. Similarly, to assume that existing models of museum practice can somehow fulfil the requirements of the future is to invite the scorn and alienation of our descendants. As E.O. Wilson noted, 'We are creating a less stable and interesting place for our descendants to inherit. They will understand and love life more than we, and they will not be inclined to honor our memory.'[44]

Are not museums the self-proclaimed custodians of posterity, assuming that the responsibilities of today will be the gifts of the future? If so, there is an alarming disconnect between this belief and the trajectory that museums are on, which requires no less than a reinvented museum – a mindful 'hybrid' organization that incorporates the best of redeeming museum values and business methodology, with a sense of social responsibility heretofore unheard of – absent the marketplace ideology. How might we imagine a mindful, or orthogonal, museum to be?

Imagining the orthogonal

Imagining the mindful museum is a difficult task because it will be a process of invention and the future is unknowable. Nonetheless, much of this book has been devoted to identifying the current constraints in museum practice and offering alternatives. More importantly, there are those examples of resilient individuals and organizations who have already awakened to the present and are responding accordingly. Consider them to be the most advanced of the museum species, already changing and renewing before they have to, and thus avoiding decline. They will prosper because they are conscious and adaptive. Museums can no longer look to the corporate world for guidance. That has been done with the unfortunate result that museums have inherited privilege, hierarchy, tribalistic thinking and materialism, none of which serve them or the troubled world.

Nor can we look to the world of public bureaucracies as models of foresight and initiative, with the noteworthy exception of the committed individuals who work in these organizations. These individuals are incapacitated by the very nature of these organizations, which are too large, overly complex, rigid, and often self-serving because of the careerism which is their lifeblood. Many of the world's large, public bureaucracies are the dinosaurs waiting for the meteor to fall, and it's on its way in the form of global complexities that they are ill-suited to address.

The mission – why, not how

Irrespective of the many activities and programs a mindful museum may choose to adopt, all of them will have several salient characteristics in common, starting with the mission. The mission will eschew process in favour of synthesis and, instead of the typical museum commitment to 'collecting, preserving and interpreting' (the second agenda or the 'how' of museum work), the mindful hybrid of the future will recognize that processes are only the means to the end, and that disparate voices are the stuff of insight and possibilities. This is especially important now, when we suffer from dissonant voices speaking in isolation.[45] The environment is a good example of dissonant voices, which include the free-market capitalists (rooted in conventional economics where growth is everything); the environmentalists (who see the world in terms of ecosystems and focus on depletion and damage), and the synthesizers.

All museums have the responsibility and the opportunity to become synthesizers, and foster an understanding of the interconnectedness of the problems we face, both environmental and social. The mindful museum will reject all ideology and demonstrate that solutions will arise from place and culture, 'when local people are empowered and honoured.'[46] A mindful museum can empower and honour all people in the search for a sustainable and just world – by creating a mission that focuses on the interconnectedness of our world and its challenges, and promotes the integration of disparate perspectives.[47]

Rethinking the conventional

The mindful museum will also have a slate of well-considered values, but not those packaged and delivered by management consultants. Rather than self-serving values such as 'excellence in peer recognition' and 'professionalism', these values will reflect the commitment required for effective participation in the broader world. The list might include idealism, humility, interdisciplinarity, intimacy, interconnectedness, resourcefulness, transparency, durability, resilience, knowing your community and knowing your environment.

The design of the internal organization will also have to reflect an increased aware-ness, if the promise of mindfulness is to be achieved. This will preclude the popular hierarchical organization, as it has proven categorically to restrict initiative and reward passivity. Instead, the orthogonal museum will witness the fluorescence of multifunctional work groups, not the homogeneous and silo-like departments and divisions. These work groups will also persist through time, unlike temporary project teams. All of these work groups will benefit from the presence of writers, poets, artists and performers, as well as ad hoc participants from the array of agen-cies and organizations that underpin the museum's role in the community. These non-traditional staff will be a key source of the emotion, imagination, intuition and reflection that are essential to sustain the museum's mindfulness.

The organizational chart will also include one or more Rapid Response Groups (RRG), as museums are notoriously ineffective in altering their work plans to address unanticipated issues and opportunities. The RRGs will enable the mindful museum to respond more effectively to such contingencies. Sounds idealistic? It is, but without a change in how the work gets done, there can be little hope of changing what gets done. The way a museum does its work will either permit or preclude inclusive thinking, the questioning of the status quo and heightened awareness of the external world. The second agenda is still important, but not as important as the 'why.'

Increased consciousness

Assuming that any or all of these characteristics come into being, it will be one more step towards a more conscious organization. One organizational specialist, Margaret Wheatley, believes that some organizations are moving into the realm of increased consciousness, because we inhabit 'an intrinsically well-ordered universe.'[48]

Well-ordered or not (it's difficult to ignore the current human impact on the biosphere), it's too early to know if museums will commit to this path. Any progress towards increased consciousness will only unfold with decreasing hierarchy, and in the pres-ence of inter- and intra-organizational interaction and exchange. Perhaps when this is achieved, along with some of the other attributes described in this chapter, the mindful museum and post-museum, as defined by Eilean Hooper-Greenhill, will become one. She argues that it is time to move beyond the idea of the museum as a locus of authority conveyed primarily through buildings and exhibitions, and adopt a new model which she calls the post-museum.[49]

The post-museum is fundamentally different from the traditional museum and is intended to embrace a variety of societal perspectives and values, with the traditional museum perspective being only one voice among many. Perhaps most importantly, the post-museum involves intangible heritage, along with the emotions of visitors, as the post-museum is directly linked to the concerns and ambitions of communities.[50] The congruence between the post-museum and the orthogonal or mindful museum is significant, and hopefully liberating for those who might require a theoretical construct for altering the museum's traditional agenda. Various suggestions for doing so have been made in this chapter, predicated on the need for an enhanced awareness of the museum's social context.

The power of this awareness has yet to be tapped by the museum community at large, and its potential might well be limitless. For those boards and museum workers who are deeply disturbed at the thought of rethinking their role as custodians of objects, and assuming responsibilities that transcend ancillary education and entertainment – one question remains. How is it that museums, as social institutions, may remain aloof from the issues set out in this book, when all of these issues are intimately related to the purpose, mission and capabilities of museums as we know them? This is not a call for museums to become social welfare agencies or Greenpeace activists, but rather to heighten their awareness and deliberately coalesce their capabilities and resources to bring about change, both internally and externally. It has been noted that 'There is no power for change greater than a community discovering what it cares about.'[51] Will communities continue to care about museums in their current guise? Will museums discover what they care about? Or are museums at risk? These questions are the subject of the next and final chapter.

7

Museums: Stewards or spectators?

I am hoping that the preceding chapters have made it clear that there are many reasons why communities should care about their museums, albeit more for their unfulfilled potential than for the conformity, imitative excesses and conventional practices examined in this book. However, does the museum community itself actually care about its broader, non-museum relationships – a genuine and necessary question? Furthermore, why should they care? Although there are no ready answers to either of these questions, the indications are not heartening and reflect the litany of intractable challenges confronting museums. Among these many issues, as noted before, are the preoccupation with revenues and attendance as the measures of worth; little or no diversification in the traditional visitor profile; the insularity and fragmentation of the museum community; the belief or assumption that the marketplace creates communities; and the belief that nature exists to serve the interests of people.

Certainly, these issues are not the exclusive domain of museums, as the consequences of marketplace ideology haunt all sectors of global society. Nonetheless, the convergence of all these issues has created a watershed of either opportunity or crisis for museums. One could argue that this decision point is self-imposed, however, as there is no obvious demand for museum accountability from any part of society, except fiscally by public and private funders. Recall that in the contemporary literature on global challenges, museums never make the index, much less the title or the table of contents, either as friend or foe. Perhaps anonymity is bliss, but it is akin to irrelevance, the implications of which will be considered in this chapter.

A brief retrospective

Although museums are essentially invisible to the social critics and public intellectuals anxious about the future, I sense that museums are tacitly included in the thoughts of at least one of them. Wendell Berry, farmer and essayist, notes that all the institutions that serve the community are publicly oriented, but do not concern themselves with issues of local economy and local ecology on which community health and integrity must depend. Further,

Nor do the people in charge of these institutions think of themselves as members of communities. They are itinerant, in fact or spirit, as their careers require them to be. These various public servants all have tended to impose on the local place and the local people programs, purposes, procedures, technologies, and values that originated elsewhere.[1]

As harsh as this may sound, there is an undeniable familiarity in Berry's words for any museum director who has served in more than one position, and there are many of us. Choosing opportunity or crisis will require the deliberate consideration of reflections like Berry's – if museums are to avoid the role of hapless victim of funding cuts and apathetic communities. Hapless victim is a role that museums have comfortably assumed from time to time, but it will become increasingly difficult or impossible to claim in the future. Museums have, in fact, done much to create the fragility which besets them, not only because of governance and managerial myopia but also as a result of the current inclination for arguing the economic value of museums above all else. There have been striking exceptions to this lack of foresight, however, and it's not as if museum workers have always failed to adopt a broader perspective.

Delving into the past, albeit briefly, is instructive, and might also help to steel the museum community's resolve to move beyond its current servitude to the status quo. What follows is a brief discussion of several past examples that demonstrate once again that the museum community is perfectly capable of thinking and acting with acuity and foresight. A generation ago, Canadian and American museum workers were deep in thought about some big issues.

Think tank at the lake

After fourteen months of planning, a conference entitled '2001: The Museum and the Canadian Public' was held at one of Canada's finest retreat centres in Lake Couchiching, Ontario. The year was 1976 and more than 145 museum workers participated, with as many as half of the participants under the age of 35 – an intentional criterion set by the conference organizers.[2] The meeting consisted of presentations and discussion groups, all of which were structured around a past/present/future time frame. The conference topics included an overview of the development of museums in Canada and the airing of contemporary museum problems, as well as an opportunity for self-criticism provided by a panel of museum professionals who gave their views on contemporary issues. The last two days were designed to encourage thought about future priorities for museums, including a strategy for future museum operations.

Of particular interest are the opening remarks of the Conference Chair, Peter Swann, who emphasized the uniqueness of this meeting by noting that 'to my knowledge [this meeting] has never before been attempted – five days for museum professionals to think exclusively about the future.'[3] His observations ranged from the prescient to the critical, and he exhorted participants to 'plan constructively to meet our increasing obligations to society', despite the fact that 'museum people ... tend to look at the past rather than the future.' With an uncanny grasp of the future, Swann presaged the stranglehold of quantitative measures 33 years ago when he said, 'Again, if you do not decide what you want to do, you most certainly will be told – for better or worse and possibly worse – by those who provide the funds.' He concluded his remarks with a quote from Albert Camus, who wrote, 'The strongest temptation of man is the temptation of inertia.' To this comment on inertia, Swann added the complacency of the Canadian museum community.

All of the discussion and debate were distilled into 42 'Recommendations for Action', with the understanding that they would be examined further.[4] The recommendations cover a broad range of topics including professionalism, training, exhibitions, social and cultural responsibilities, museum policy, inter-museum liaison and architecture. All of them are noteworthy, especially the recommendation that museums and their professional staff commit themselves to 'a greater extent' to current social, economic and environmental issues and involvement in their communities. In addition, 'in view of the energy crisis and the projected rapidly escalating cost of energy consumption', it was recommended that museums give urgent consideration to the use of alternative sources of energy in new and existing buildings. As a brand new museum director attending this conference, it was a heady and daunting gathering and, in retrospect, stands as testimony to a heightened and collective consciousness which has yet to be replicated a full generation later. What has actually happened in response to all this forward-thinking and conscious reflection? Very little, in fact, at least with respect to the more progressive recommendations.

An early wake-up call

Museum workers in the USA were also conscious and engaged in the early 1970s, and their aspirations found expression in a book entitled *Museums and the Environment: A Handbook for Education,* published by the American Association of Museums. This edited volume evolved in response to the needs expressed by museums for resources with which to interpret environmental problems, and to initiate or expand environmental exhibits and education programs. Underlying this publication was the recognition that 'museums are admirably equipped through their diverse collections, their expertise in display … and their vast clientele, to play an important role in making the public aware of environmental problems as well as of the means for their solution.'[5] There are three overarching themes that unify this book, including man and the environment, population, and environmental pollution. There is also abundant information on the design and development of ecological exhibits, as well as a section containing specific instructions on how to build display cases. This book is remarkably substantive, providing theory, method and themes as the context for a 'how-to-do-it guide' for effective and economical exhibits and programs on ecological stewardship.

The penultimate chapter is surprisingly contemporary, as it addresses the emerging role of museums in environmental education. Of particular note is a section on museums and the ecological imperative, which is basically a manifesto on the need for ecologically sustainable museums. The writing was far ahead of its time, with its emphasis on creating green spaces, recycling, reducing water use, heat recovery, proper insulation, and so on. The museum of the future is to be built in harmony with the land, or not to be built at all.[6] The final chapter is concerned with programs of action and addresses a range of essential considerations, such as how to involve the community, the role of local experts, developing an apprenticeship program and cooperating with other museums. This chapter even includes several pages of important environmental problems that must be acted upon, including toxic food, the lack of privacy and the destruction of the night sky by excessive artificial lighting.

The section on the consequences of museum activism is remarkable, and concludes with the blunt observation that environmental outdoor education in museums is 'part of a sophisticated fight against public apathy, government bureaucracy, corporate greed, trustee timidity, college and university aloofness, and some cherished but essentially outworn idols, eg., gross national product.'[7] Could any museum work be more relevant now than this 38-year-old book? Its obscurity in the museum literature is disturbing, considering that the book's contributors were all senior practitioners from mainstream museums and related organizations. It appears that they were simply too far ahead of their time – they still are.

Scholars, agitators and communities

In addition to these organizational initiatives, there is also the work of individuals who are mindful of the present, and I want to mention two examples. The late Stephen Weil, practitioner and scholar, was articulate in his aversion to self-serving museums, and left a legacy of articles and books that offered alternatives.[8] His thoughts and values are best summarized in one of his typically penetrating questions – 'If our museums are *not* being operated with the ultimate goal of improving the quality of people's lives, on what other basis might we possibly ask for public support?'[9] This question continues to reverberate, with only marginal attention being paid to its contemporary implications. As highly regarded as Weil is, I detect no groundswell of approbation among practitioners to ensure that his questioning is constantly held in view. Perhaps many museum directors have never read his work, a liability, I fear, that is widespread among harried senior managers.

There is also the recent volume on *Museums and Their Communities*, edited by Sheila Watson, a lecturer in the Department of Museum Studies at the University of Leicester.[10] This edited collection explores the evolving relationships between museums and the communities they represent and serve, and considers the challenges and opportunities of community engagement. There is much to learn here, from the theoretical to the practical, which can guide the mindful museum in its quest for meaning and relevance. It's clear that there is no lack of method, theory, ideas and experience with which to nurture a more substantive role for mainstream museums in contemporary society, yet the relationship between museum studies research and the community of practice remains obscure, perhaps even unacknowledged by many practitioners.

To return to the question posed at the beginning of this chapter, there are clearly practitioners and academics who do care about the museum community's broader relationships. For the others, the failure to act upon the available knowledge and insight underlying this imperative lies elsewhere, seemingly in a collective inability or unwillingness to generate and sustain a critical mass of purpose and will. Thought and action are largely uncoupled in the museum world – a primary cause of the drift into irrelevance. So are morality and effective strategies, for that matter.[11]

The consequences of ignoring the present

It is increasingly vital that museums generate the requisite purpose and will to participate more consciously in the world around them, as the warning signs of our collective vulnerability continue to accumulate. Recall the tectonic stresses and global problems discussed in Chapter 2, which are further exacerbated by additional evidence that our civilization is living beyond its means.[12] There is growing chaos in natural systems, for example, with more frequent natural disasters as a result of eroding environmental resilience. More money and labour are now being spent for activities that were once provided by nature, such as water purification and flood control. Capital and labour are also being used by governments and corporations to gain access and defend resources that are concentrated in fewer and increasingly hostile regions. And so on.

All of these complexities can be distilled into a rather simple model of what could transpire if these events continue to unfold. Jeremy Rifkin notes that 'our modern economy is a three-tiered system, with agriculture as the base, the industrial sector superimposed on top of it, and the service sector, in turn, perched on top of the industrial sector.[13] Each sector is totally dependent on more and more non-renewable energy – fossil fuels. Rifkin posits that, as the availability of this energy diminishes, the public and private service areas will be the first to suffer, because services are 'the least essential aspect of our survival.' In short, an economy with limited energy sources will be one of necessities, not luxuries or inessentials, and will be centred on those things required to maintain life. Where do tourism, edutainment, museum shops, permanent collections and blockbusters fit in this looming adaptive model?

Museums are a public service, and the extent to which they will weather the above scenario is difficult to predict. It is immediately obvious that reducing energy consumption and avoiding large and consumptive building footprints are prerequisites, making the current museum building boom even more bizarre. Energy-efficient buildings, however, are only one ingredient in a meaningful future. Along with the willpower required to reduce consumption is the greater need to transform the museum's public service persona defined by education and entertainment to one of a locally-embedded problem-solver, in tune with the challenges and aspirations of the community. Is this idealistic? Yes, woefully so, considering the path to irrelevance many museums are seemingly content to tread. The trajectory looks something like this: privileged societal position of trust and respect = assumed authority = group-think by boards and staff, i.e. 'we know what's best for you and us' = museum complacency = isolation from the needs, values and aspirations of local communities = incremental irrelevance at a time of increasing urgency.

In a world of pressing local and national issues, it is no more than common sense to expect that public funding will eventually go to environmental, social and economic priorities. Museums, based as they are on a business model of consumption, edutainment and ancillary education, will no longer be sustainable in this context. Many are not sustainable now. Will museums continue to believe that tradition and status will exempt them from increasing irrelevance, or will they seize the opportunity to assume responsibility as gifted and privileged social organizations? Unfortunately, there are indications that this decision point is not yet on the museum radar screen.

Irrelevance

Government indifference to the Canadian museum community provides a stark case study of the consequences of perceived irrelevance by elected leaders. In a democratic country, one can assume that this indifference also reflects the electorate's sentiments. For decades, the Canadian Museums Association (CMA) has laboured long and hard to increase the amount of federal government financial support for Canadian museums.[14] Their efforts were to culminate in a new federal museums policy in 2006, as well as in an increase of CA$75 million to support the nation's museums. Instead, the government rejected both the funding increase and the new museums policy, despite the repeated promises by the then Minister of Canadian Heritage to bring in a new policy and new investment for all of Canada's 2,500 museums. The federal government did announce in 2006, however, a commitment to spend an additional CA$100 million over the next five years on the refurbishment of the federal museum buildings in Ottawa. Late in 2008, the government announced a CA$3 million reduction to a capacity building program for all the other Canadian museums and galleries.[15]

It should be noted that the federal government currently spends roughly CA$205 million per year on the four national museums in Ottawa, with another CA$22 million slated annually for the newest national museum – the Canadian Museum for Human Rights.[16] Roughly CA$20 million is distributed to the rest of Canada's 2,495 museums, although this is only an estimate, as funding for museums is also provided by various other federal programs. Neither the CMA nor federal officials were able to provide a global figure for museum funding in Canada. Predictably, federal politicians claim that the funding for the National Museums is proof of their substantive support for Canadian museums, despite the unconscionable discrepancy in the actual allocations between the federal museums and all the others. At the time of writing, the much needed museums policy remains a chimera, as the government of the day concerns itself with the war in Afghanistan, the politics of climate change and the toxic fragility of capital markets.

The lack of federal government support is nonsensical, given the facts and figures surrounding the role of museums in Canadian society.[17] Canada's museums employ

24,000 people full- and part-time (the Canadian oil and gas sector employs 33,000 workers), and are supported by 55,000 volunteers and 600,000 members and supporters – for an annual economic impact of CA$17 billion. These facts have apparently had no impact on past and current federal governments, even in light of their marketplace bias. Two conclusions can be gleaned from this impasse. First, the CMA's strategy of lobbying the federal government for enhanced funding is bankrupt and must be replaced with a fresh view of reality and a new strategy. Second, museums have generally failed to establish and communicate their broader worth to elected officials and society at large.

A *failure to communicate*

The failure of museums to communicate their value was also noted in 2005 by the Department for Culture, Media and Sport (DCMS – UK's museum funding agency) in a public consultation document entitled *Understanding the Future: Museums and 21st Century Life*.[18] This paper examines the contribution that museums and galleries can, and should, make to a modern democracy, and notes that museums 'cannot be immune from sweeping international, cultural, technological and social changes.' In addition, 'the sector needs to demonstrate that it is cohesive, innovative and visionary ... and acts as a unified sector, with a common direction and purpose, whilst not losing the benefits of its inherent eclecticism.'[19] Although this document was developed with the assistance of several museum professionals, it is troublesome that a government department had to initiate this inquiry. This forced the museum community to react to a directive about its meaning and value, rather than initiating this essential inquiry themselves. This is glaringly unstrategic.

Fortunately, various museum associations have recently embarked upon demonstrating their worth, including the recent launch of the American Association of Museums' Center for the Future of Museums. This is the museum field's first national think tank that brings together innovative leaders and practitioners, as well as representatives of other sectors, to explore ways to serve the public and prepare museums for the challenges of the future. Together, they will conduct research, publish and present recommendations to advise funders, policymakers and museums themselves.[20] This initiative is precisely what was called for in Chapter 6, and should become a standard operating procedure for all museum associations. The UK Museums Association's national sustainability consultation, also discussed in Chapter 6, is another example of the search for legitimacy in a changing world. In Canada, the Canadian Museums Association has invited museums to join a national media campaign with Kellogg Canada in 2009 to put promotional coupons on three million cereal boxes.[21] Each of these initiatives represents a different approach to articulating the worth of museums, and it is too early in their development to assess their relative success.

In short, the status quo for most museums is devoid of substance. The economic value of museums has been demonstrated time and again, complete with record-breaking attendance at international shows. To what end? Nor does a certain future lie in glitzier infrastructure and the creative city rhetoric that 'more is better.' The architectural shamans come and go, leaving capital and operating deficits in their wake. And political lobbying continues to be a sinkhole for scarce resources and self-respect. As Douglas Worts recently noted, 'Culture needs to be understood as to how we live our lives, and not what we do in our leisure time.'[22] The trappings of consumer society must give way to critical reflection in museums, based on the collective recognition of the dangers in passivity and the many opportunities to act otherwise. For museums, change has become discontinuous, and the past is no longer the guide to the future. Judging by the growing fragility of the global museum community, museums have little to lose by moving beyond the status quo and embracing a mindful mission.

Collapse

The increasing fragility of museums is, of course, the prerequisite to collapse, but the idea of 'museums collapsing' may itself be redundant, if not overly dramatic. Irrelevance is a sufficient *coup de grâce* for a public institution, however slow the process may be. Museums that actually fail and disappear are still a very small minority, although many might well classify as lifeless – apathetic and unresponsive. Nonetheless, collapse is always possible, if not on a large scale, then perhaps one museum at a time. James Bradburne, a veteran practitioner with a global perspective, has described the current potential for collapse as 'the museum time bomb', and much of what has been written in this book parallels his thinking.[23]

His cogent analysis of the tautologies underlying current institutional thinking should be required reading for all museum workers and boards of directors. Bradburne concludes that museum education and entertainment, the choice of museums for decades, are both dead ends. He notes that museums with traditional educational missions are finding that the public purse is questioning its return on investment. For those museums that have joined the leisure industry of edutainment, he notes that funding authorities are increasingly reluctant to fund entertainment. Bradburne puts a fine point on his overall concern, as follows:

> 'It is clearly time to 'bell the cat' and declare that in their present form, most museums are not sustainable. The museum market is over-saturated, the operating costs are high relative to earned revenue, and productivity (however defined), cannot be enhanced by one-time infusions of technology. Most vulnerable are middle-aged, middle-sized institutions that are unable to generate sufficient operating revenue to remain attractive to the visiting public, thus slowly suffocating for lack of visitors and funding. As long as public funding continues to decrease – a likely scenario given the increasing demands on the public purse and decreasing revenue – museums must face a future where their survival depends on earned revenue.'[24]

A future dependent upon earned revenues is indeed the recipe for collapse, because it is simply unachievable, even for those 'superstar' museums that depend upon international visitation. As discussed earlier, jet-based tourism is in for a brisk touch with reality. There are others who share Bradburne's anxiety, resulting in a small, but vocal literature, decrying museum indifference to the warning signs around them. In an article entitled 'Can We Afford the Audience?', Magnus von Wistinghausen confirms the anxiety of many museum workers by noting the paradoxical imperative to maintain and increase audiences. This treadmill is a high risk scenario in his view because 'Most museums operate with a sizeable structural deficit, mostly hidden by a combination of chronic underinvestment in core infrastructure (building mainte- nance, collections management, staff salaries) and the occasional cash injection from capital and other large projects.'[25]

The popular press has expressed similar concerns in an article entitled, 'Who Now Will Save Our Museums?'[26] Although this newspaper article deals with the 2005 strike action at London's Science Museum, it recognizes some hefty issues, such as the outsourcing of curatorial functions to commercial organizations – a trend that is apparently alive and well in the museum world. This is yet another whiff of collapse, best summed up by museum consultant, Adrian Ellis, who notes in this article that, 'We have too many museums with big bodies and small brains, whereas what a museum really needs is a big brain.' Is that clear enough?

All of these things may be harbingers of a museum shake-up but, for now, wide- spread collapse requires a leap of imagination. It is also noteworthy that the majority of those who challenge museum myopia are not mainstream museum practitioners but work outside the constraints of organizational conformity. This is oddly remi- niscent of a story about the Battle of the Little Bighorn, that most famous action of the American Indian Wars, when the Lakota and the Northern Cheyenne decimated the US Seventh Cavalry.[27] As the story is told, after the battle a squaw (sic) drove a sewing awl through General George Custer's ear and into his skull so that he might hear better in the next world. Let's hope, metaphorically, that museums will not suffer the same fate, because by then listening will be too late.

Renewal – denial is not an alternative

If the idea of collapse is premature, yet museums grow more fragile as the signs of their irrelevance multiply, what choice do they have in light of their self-inflicted challenges and the tyranny of marketplace ideology? I submit that renewal – rethinking, replacing, and rejuvenating – is the only alternative, despite the hackneyed use of this concept in all aspects of our lives. There is much lip service paid to this ageless and vital concept in organizations, but very little actual renewal. This is because authentic renewal is a tough and burdensome process, not a silver bullet, and is conveniently ignored by most museum workers as yet another managerial bandwagon – trendy, but unnecessary. In effect, all people, organizations and societies start slowly, grow, prosper and decline.

Organizational decline, however, is not inevitable if one is willing to challenge assump- tions and conventional practices, because this kind of thinking is the precursor to renewal. Renewal is also profoundly paradoxical, because it requires change at a time when 'all the messages coming through to the individual or the institution are that everything is fine.'[28] The fact that most museums think that everything is fine is the most salient reason for widespread renewal, but the commitment remains out of mind. The burden of proof thus rests with those who would advocate its importance, and that is the purpose of the remainder of this chapter. As uncertain as the future is, I offer six reasons why museums can, and must, transform. Disguised as they are by conformity and habit, the singular qualities and capabilities of museums still outweigh the heavy baggage of conventional practice and passive self-interest.

Museums are free to choose and act

> Negotiating modernity requires creativity.[29]

This observation by author and environmentalist, Bill McKibben, stands as a challenge to all museums to help create the future, grounded in their unique blend of the past and the present. Museums, unencumbered with the public policy responsibilities of government and the compulsive bottom lines of corporations, are agenda-free at the moment, with the exception of their tacit agenda that serves mainstream consumer society. But there is no future in this fickle relationship. The time has come for a particular 'museum agenda', predicated on mindfulness and wherever that leads. It was noted in the Introduction that museums are some of the most free and potentially creative work environments in the world, and that there are few other organizations which offer more opportunities for thinking, choosing and acting in ways that can blend personal satisfaction and growth with organizational goals.

Museums are also in a postion to adopt an agenda framed in consciousness, and it is only museum groupthink that perceives this as dangerous. For those boards and executives who claim a lack of autonomy with which to chart their own course, I suggest that addressing the issues outlined in this book requires both courage and a leap of faith. I am hopeful that any initiative to do so will be fully acknowledged as the ensuing contributions become apparent. Don't wait around to be asked to do so – you will be waiting for a long time.

Museums are seed banks

> All I can say is that we are mistaken to gouge such a deep rift in history that the things old men and old women know have become so useless as to be not worth passing on to grandchildren.[30]

Novelist Charles Frazier wrote this, perhaps in reaction to modernity, but his words also evoke the enduring value of museums. The 'gouge' and the 'rift' can be healed with the collective memory that museums contain, despite the arrogance of the technological present that disavows much of the scientific, traditional and local knowledge that chronicles our species. Modernity has also led to the loss of knowledge of sustainable living practices that have guided our species for millennia, as discussed in Chapter 2. Museums are the repositories of the evidence of our adaptive failures and successes, not to mention the chroniclers of our creativity and pathos. In this sense, museums are akin to the biological seed banks that store seeds as a source for planting, in case seed reserves elsewhere are destroyed.

If seed banks are gene banks, then museums are tool, technology and art banks – curating the most distinctive trait of our species – the ability to make tools and things of beauty. And to this priceless legacy we must add the trove of natural history specimens sitting dormant in the world's museums. Richard Fortey, a prescient paleontologist at London's Natural History Museum, has suggested that 'Museums might now be considered the conscience of the world.' He notes that their permanent collections 'will be the only way to understand and monitor what we're doing to the world.'[31] It's a troubled story.

The need to revisit this cumulative knowledge and wisdom may come sooner than expected, as the destruction of the biosphere renders industrial technology increasingly malevolent. The record of material diversity contained in museums may have a value not unlike biodiversity, as we seek adaptive solutions in an increasingly brittle world. Collections will be the key to examining the relevance of this material diversity in contemporary times, and will distinguish museums as the only social institutions with this perspective and the necessary resources. In this respect, museums are as valuable as seed banks. This, alone, is sufficient cause for renewal, if museums would only realize their obligations to the future, beyond the rhetoric of 'How can we know where we're going if we don't know where we've been?' For many museums, it still seems that any path will do.

Museums are diversity personified

> … globalization requires a high degree of standardization and homogenization. One of the great problems of the twenty-first century will be finding out where the tolerable limits of this homogeneity are, beyond which they would produce a backlash …[32]

Unbeknown to Eric Hobsbawm, the preeminent historian who made this observation, the humble museum is one of the problem-solvers. This is because the world's museums, despite their incredible diversity, all exist as part of a vast and informal global network. The meaning of the word 'museum' enjoys explicit name recognition everywhere, irrespective of language, and museums populate the world. There are 22,500 museums in Canada, the USA and the UK alone, and the World Bank estimates there are about 40,000 museums worldwide, which strikes me as an underestimate.[33] It's as if there is a global museum franchise, only it is self-organized, has no corporate head office, no board of directors, no global marketing expenses, and is trusted and respected. Is this not the dream of every marketplace ideologue?

This informal network exists by virtue of the apparently universal need for museums, and its inherent diversity will be a significant antidote to the globalized homogenization that Hobsbawm fears. With a global presence grounded in individual autonomy and diversity, yet united in purpose and tradition, this vast network of museums has untold potential for nurturing both museum and societal renewal. The challenge will be for museums to collectively acknowledge that this critical mass of museums offers the hope of heightened mindfulness on an unprecedented scale, especially when it is imbued with the will to act.

Museums are the keepers of locality

> Perhaps the most critical social condition for sustainability is a shared commitment to community cohesion (both local and global) and a sense of collective responsibility for the future.[34]

Like most of the individuals who worry about ecological collapse, Wackernagel and Rees, the fathers of the Ecological Footprint quoted above, see local communities as the key to intelligent adaptation. No one would dispute the fact that most of the world's museums are expressions of locality and community, and the world is full of museums because they are spawned by communities of all sizes and shapes. Museums also enjoy a certain intimacy in their communities, unlike universities, which are acknowledging their perceived aloofness and are struggling to overcome it. The ubiquity of museums and the familiarity they enjoy are the building blocks of renewal, especially as the need increases to seek ingenuity and solutions on a smaller scale – in communities.

Wendell Berry writes that 'the real work of planet-saving will be small, humble and humbling' and that problem solving will require individuals, families and communities.[35] The UK's Department for Culture, Media and Sport consultation paper, *Understanding the Future: Museums and 21st Century Life* noted that, while globalization brings new opportunities for travel, cultural diversity and access to information, it also disperses communities and erodes traditions. This creates a greater need for community roots and values, and enhances the role of museums 'by virtue of their unique ability to connect the local to the global and ... place personal beliefs within more general and universal truths, and historical settings.'[36]

Writing of his work in Latin America, archaeologist Charles Stanish makes the value of community museums abundantly clear:

> scholars have become much more aware of the power of small, community-based museums to affect people's daily lives positively. In the past two decades or so, 'site museums' have emerged as one of the principal means by which indigenous peoples and their descendants have resisted many of the negative cultural effects of globalization. These museums are small, but they are powerful.[37]

Are mainstream museums paying attention to the possibilities of moving away from the economic paradigm, and replacing it with the value they bring to communities for exercising responsible citizenship? If the answer is yes – renewal is inevitable.

Museums are the bridge between the two cultures

> The distinction between the two cultures of science and the humanities ... thus persists. Until that fundamental divide is closed or at least reconciled in some congenial manner, the relation between man and the living world will remain problematic.[38]

This divide, noted by E.O. Wilson, is a formidable and increasingly destructive tension in Western societies. It was brought to the attention of the world in two famous essays by C.P. Snow entitled *The Two Cultures: And a Second Look,* wherein Snow described the dangerous split between the humanities and the scientific community.[39] Snow argued in 1959 that Western society had become seriously fragmented, with scientists and non-scientists failing to communicate and working at cross-purposes, with no place where the two cultures could meet.[40] Various consequences of this ever-increasing divide were discussed earlier in Chapter 2, including reductionism, dualism, the irrational belief in technology, and the alarming disparity between the rich and poor, and Snow's writing reflects all of these concerns. Canada's public intellectual, John Ralston Saul, also condemns the cult of expertise and specialization, and writes that 'Such intellectual splintering explains some of academia's passivity before the crisis of the society they ought to be defending.'[41]

Intellectual splintering also underlies museum passivity when, in fact, museums are one of the few knowledge-based institutions equipped to bridge the divide between the two cultures that continues to fragment our world-view. Although museums have borrowed the disciplinary boundaries of the academy, they are not bound to them for purposes of institutional identity and advancement. The very nature of any human, natural history, science or art museum demands interdisciplinarity and holistic thinking, because they embrace multiple subjects and points of view, all of which are intimately interconnected with the biosphere. Disciplinary boundaries and intellectual silos are mostly in the service of those who benefit from them – academics and scientists in universities and research institutes. Museums are not universities, and for museums to assume this cloak is to deny their professed role as interpreters, presenters and public communicators.

This, however, is not to dismiss the important science under way in a variety of museums, examples of which were noted earlier in this book. Rather, my purpose is to open another door for renewal, framed in the possibility of museums becoming the meeting place for the two cultures that is currently lacking. In the process, museums might well create a 'third culture', along with other mindful individuals and organizations, by parting company with academic convention and offering a less fragmented understanding of human presence in the biosphere. Museums are not only particularly suited for this renewal – the troubled world and its citizens are crying out for this leadership.

Museums bear witness

> One thing worth defending, I suggest, is the imperative to imagine the lives of beings who are not ourselves and are not like ourselves: animals, plants, gods, spirits, people of other countries and other races, people of the other sex, places – and enemies.[42]

This is Wendell Berry again, in pursuit of our collective responsibility to become more conscious and caring. I am indebted to Marjorie Schwarzer, professor and chair of museums studies at John F. Kennedy University, for cementing the connection between Berry's aspirations and the relevance of museums. I can do no better than quote Schwarzer directly, who responded with the following when I questioned her about the value of museums in contemporary society:

> If not for the museological impulse, there would be NO memorials, NO resources and NO caretakers of the remnants of the kinds of history that our society's more evil impulses seek to destroy ... I'm saying all of this because I do raise this question: despite all of the missed opportunities perpetuated by poor and unethical museum practice, would the world be a better place without museums?[43]

Berry and Schwarzer are talking about bearing witness – an unsung role for museums but one that is unmistakably present. One need only recall the work of the International Coalition of Sites of Conscience as a powerful reminder of the need to remember past struggles for justice and to address their contemporary legacies. The scope for bearing witness has expanded exponentially in recent times, however, and now includes an increasingly damaged biosphere, as well as the seemingly infinite catalogue of human rights conflicts and issues. Are not museums founded on 'imagining the lives of beings who are not ourselves'? All museums specialize in assembling evidence based on knowledge, experience and belief, and in making things known – the meaning of bearing witness. It is puzzling that so fundamental a trait is languishing from disuse, obscured by the press of the marketplace and the timidity to assert its value.

Undertaking museum renewal, with an expanded sense of what is important, is simply building on tradition, as museums already bear witness to the intricacies of existence as a matter of course. What's missing is an expanded consciousness that embraces all those sentient beings who are not ourselves, and making clear the interconnectedness that we continue to ignore. This may not even be renewal – but a newfound understanding of what should always have been a core purpose of museums. In summing up this discussion about the imperative of renewal, it is worth noting that the six reasons discussed above – museum autonomy, museums as seed banks, diversity, locality, bridging the two cultures and bearing witness – are not only reasons for undertaking renewal, but they are also individual missions in their own right. Take your pick.

In praise of museums

This book has sampled the growing complexity in biospheric affairs and the reluctance of the museum community to muster the innovation and ingenuity to address the issues and challenges that relate directly to them, especially considering the unique knowledge and resources that they possess. The fundamental question is – what social institutions exist to address these challenges, recognizing the growing ineffectiveness of government bureaucracies and the wreckage of the corporate profit agenda? Even universities are becoming the handmaidens of corporatists, with science in the interests of consumerism driving many university research budgets. Museums, it is argued here, are one of the few social institutions with vast potential for proactive and effective community engagement.

But this book is not about a new business model for museums – it is about going beyond business models to reappraise the museum mission itself. Business models are about processes and the means to the end, including collecting, preserving and exhibiting. This book is ultimately about the ends. In fact, the endless talk of business and business models has become tiresome and harmful. This preoccupation with the 'how' is diverting museums from the real task at hand, which is to become mindful of what is actually going on in the world around them, and then redefining their missions to reflect this new sensibility and purpose in appropriate ways.

The world is in need of intellectual self-defence, everywhere, as an antidote to the mindless work of marketers, corporate balance sheets, and money as the measure of worth. Museums, as public institutions, are morally and intellectually obliged to question, challenge, or ignore the status quo and officialdom, whenever necessary. With the exception of museums, there are few, if any, social institutions with the trust and credibility to fulfil this role.

It is also time to honour this trust and broaden the purpose of museums to encompass critical thinking, mindfulness and social responsibility. Human adaptation lies at the heart of the current global challenges and mindful museums can help. The role of the museum as emotional refuge in the storm – a place for reflection and contemplation in the world of mass marketing and superficiality – is increasingly essential. But it's no longer enough, because the habit of skeptical passivity serves no one – instead, it is dangerously self-serving in an age of tectonic stresses.

Long live the museum

Paradoxically, despite their inherent conservatism and adherence to convention, museums have survived for thousands of years, unlike the bulk of business enterprises. Museums have evolved through time, from the elite collections of imperial dominance, to educational institutions for the public, and now to the museum as 'mall.'[44] The mall is the culmination of marketplace dominance, over-merchandised and devoted to consumption and entertainment. Although the 'museum as mall' is now being dressed up as the new agora, this is only semantic camouflage that fails to hide the looming time bomb of increased operating expenses, political indifference and empty missions.

There is an important lesson in this historical trajectory, however, and it resides in the ability of museums to learn and adapt as circumstances require, however slowly. This ability is one of the characteristics of the long-lived companies discussed in Chapter 4, and can be described as organizations remaining 'in harmony with the world around them' and reacting in a 'timely fashion to the conditions of society around them.'[45] Although we have no explicit record of museums giving prominence to societal considerations, their development over time mirrors such concerns, as their missions changed to suit the times. Whether or not museums themselves led this change is immaterial.

Now, and in tandem with the rest of the developed world, museums have arrived at the dead end of materialism. This turning point for museums has evolved slowly, in the manner of the cabinet of curiosities becoming educational resources, but there is now much greater urgency to hasten renewal. Remarkably, museums have retained their core work of collecting, exhibiting and interpreting, irrespective of all of these historical iterations – a clear demonstration that core practices need not be relinquished as the environment changes. The choice now is between more of the same, or embracing mindfulness in pursuit of greater societal relevance. The sustainability that museums seek cannot be achieved through education, entertainment and connoisseurship, but by sustained public benefit through the quality of the work they do, sustained community support through the commitment of the local community, and an appropriate degree of financial commitment by the main financial stakeholders.[46] Competent governance, organizational effectiveness, sound financial management and multi-year planning are critical, but they are all the means with which to achieve sustainability – they are not ends in themselves.

This book has argued that a heightened sense of stewardship, grounded in mindfulness, is the foundation for a sustainable future for museums and that it is within the grasp of every museum to embrace greater consciousness in all that they do. From the curiosity cabinet to the mall; from the post-museum to the mindful museum – museums have demonstrated their capacity to adapt. Judging by the state of the troubled world and the need for urgent adaptation, museums are needed now more than ever before.

Not surprisingly, society is not even cognizant of the museum's unique potential, much less demanding its fulfilment. This is ideal, for it permits museums to engage in deliberate renewal of their own design, but the time to do so grows short. Marketplace ideology, capitalist values and corporate self-interest are clearly not the way forward, having conclusively demonstrated their financial fragility and moral bankruptcy. Resistance and independence of thought are essential to renewal, as is the quality of hope. And there's some plain truth about hope that bears repeating, in the words of James Kunstler:

Figure 20 Children – the hope of things to come. Lawrence Menacho, Priscilla Baton and Lucy Ann Menacho at the Willow Lake hunting camp, Northwest Territories, Canada, 1974.

Photo: courtesy of Priscilla B. Janes

> Hope is not a consumer product. You have to generate your own hope. You do that by demonstrating to yourself that you are brave enough to face reality and competent enough to deal with the circumstances that it presents. How we will manage to uphold a decent society in the face of extraordinary change will depend on our creativity, our generosity, and our kindness ...[47]

I suggest that upholding decency at a time of extraordinary change will also require a new breed of museums grounded in consciousness of the world around them – renouncing complacency and fulfilling their latent potential as community organizations of the highest order. Anything less foreshadows irrelevance, decline and the possibility of collapse.

Notes

Epigraph

1 J. Kabat-Zinn, *Coming to Our Senses*, New York: Hyperion, 2005, pp. 602–3.

Foreword

1 Elaine Heumann Gurian is a consultant and advisor to a number of museums and visitor centres, and lectures worldwide on many graduate programs in museum studies.

Prologue

1 This account is based in part on J.E. Brown, *The Spiritual Legacy of the American Indian*, New York: The Crossroad Publishing Company, 1989, p. 124, and G. Blondin, *Yamoria – The Lawmaker,* Edmonton: NeWest Publishers Limited, 1997.

2 This account is taken from R.R. Janes, *Archaeological Ethnography among Mackenzie Basin Dene*, Canada, Technical Paper No. 28, Calgary: The Arctic Institute of North America, The University of Calgary, 1983.

3 The languages spoken by the Indians of the western Canadian subarctic belong to a language family known as Athapaskan. Those who speak the various dialects of Athapaskan are called Athapaskans or Dene (den´ay). Dene is the Athapaskan word meaning 'man or person', and the Athapaskans of the Northwest Territories have indicated a preference for the use of Dene.

4 A.McF. Clark, *The Athapaskans: Strangers of the North*, Ottawa: National Museum of Man, National Museums of Canada, 1974.

5 This quotation is taken from R. Buckminster Fuller, *Grunch of Giants*, New York: St. Martin's Press, 1983, pp. xx–xxi.

1 Museums and irrelevance

1 C. Handy, *The Age of Paradox*, Boston: The Harvard Business School Press, 1994, p. 183.

2 J. Ralston Saul, *The Doubter's Companion*, Toronto: Penguin Books Ltd., 1994, p. 25.

3 W.W. Lowrance, *Modern Science and Human Values*, London: Oxford University Press, 1986, p. 209.

4 I am indebted to James M. Bradburne for alerting me to various international initiatives to rethink traditional museum and science centre practices, including promoting public interest and intelligent debate about the benefits and liabilities of science in modern society (personal communication, September 2008). For example, see the work of Jorge Wagensburg, Director of the Museum of Science in Barcelona, Spain, available online at <http://ec.europa.eu/research/rtdinfo/37/print_article_62_en.html> (accessed 20 October 2008). See also Holland's new Metropolis Science and Technology in Amsterdam, where experiential exhibitions address environmental issues such as the consequences of transporting oil at sea; available online at <http://www.esp.uva.nl/oceaan/visit.htm> (accessed 20 October 2008).

Experimentation is also under way in the non-scientific museum world, as exemplified by the Palazzo Strozzi in Florence, Italy. Completed in 1538, Palazzo Strozzi is one of the finest examples of Renaissance domestic architecture. It is now being revitalized, including a Centre for Contemporary Culture. Palazzo Strozzi pays particular attention to 'visible listening' – the recognition that culture is made of many voices and the importance of making different voices visible.

5   M.A. Grubbs (ed.), *Conversations with Wendell Berry*, Jackson, Mississippi: University of Mississippi Press, 2007, p. 17.

6   C. Keating, T. Robinson and B. Clemson, 'Reflective inquiry: a method for organizational learning', *The Learning Organization* (3), 1996, 35–43.

7   This popular expression is commonly misquoted as 'If you build it, they will come.' See '100 movie quotes', Wikipedia. Available online at <http://en.wikipedia.org/wiki/Movie_quotes> (accessed 14 October 2008).

8   With thanks and apologies to Yogi Berra, the baseball philosopher, who once noted that 'if fans don't come out to the ball park, you can't stop them.' Available online at <http://rinkworks.com/said/yogiberra.shtml> (accessed 29 November 2007).

9   R. Sandell, *Museums, Prejudice and the Reframing of Difference*, London and New York: Routledge, 2007, p. 6.

10   Handy, *The Age of Paradox*, p. 183.

11   R.F. Nelson, 'How Then Shall We Live?', *The Post-Industrial Future Project Working Paper No. 2*, Canmore, Alberta, 1989, p. 45.

12   R. D. Stacey, *Managing the Unknowable: Strategic Boundaries Between Order and Chaos in Organizations*, San Francisco: Jossey-Bass Inc., Publishers, 1992, p. 11.

13   Stacey, *Managing the Unknowable*, p. 4.

14   N. Postman, 'Museum as dialogue', *Museum News* (69), 1990, 55–8.

15   Available online at <http://www.countercurrents.org/us-sikand171105.htm> (accessed 4 December 2007).

16   M. Cappelletti, P. Richard, D. Ross, A. Sanchez, M. Wallace and S. Weil, 'Round table discussion on exhibiting controversy', *Museum News* (November/December), 1989, 62–6.

17   Available online at <http://www.csun.edu/science/health/docs/tv&health.html> (accessed 4 December 2007).

18   L. Moore, 'Seven little hints', *Lawrence Today* (81), 2000, 23.

19   R. Fritz, *Creating*, New York: Fawcett Columbine, 1991, pp. 74–5.

20   Fritz, *Creating*, p. 76.

21   E. Hobsbawm, *On the Edge of the New Century*, New York: The New Press, 2000, p. 160.

22   P.F. Drucker, *Post-Capitalist Society*, New York: HarperCollins Publishers, 1994, pp. 1–8.

23   R.R. Janes, 'Museums, corporatism and the civil society', *Curator: The Museums Journal* (50/2), 2007, 219–37.

24   G. Lord, 'Museums and sustainability: Economy, culture and community', Lord Cultural Resources Planning and Management. Available online at <http://www.lord.ca/Media/Artcl_MSustainability-EconomyCultureComm-GL-Irish.pdf.> PDF (accessed 5 November 2007).

25   K. Coffee, 'Audience research and the museum experience as social practice', *Museum Management and Curatorship* (22/4), 2007, 379.

26   D.C, Korten, *When Corporations Rule the World* (2nd edn), Sterling, Virginia, USA: Kumarian Press, 2001. See also A. Shah, 'The rise of corporations', *Global Issues: Social, Political, Economic and Environmental Issues That Affect Us All*. Available online at <http://www.globalissues.org/article/234/the-rise-of-corporations> (accessed 16 October 2008).

27   Hobsbawm, *On the Edge of the New Century*, p. 167.

28   A. Kaplan, *The Conduct of Inquiry*, San Francisco: Chandler Publishing Company, 1964.

29   R. Gross, *The Independent Scholar's Handbook*, Berkeley: Ten Speed Press, 1993, pp. 164–70. Available online at <http://www.sfu.ca/independentscholars/ISbook.pdf.> (accessed 8 November 2007).

30   Gross, *The Independent Scholar's Handbook*, p. 170.

31   F. Conroy, 'Think about it: Ways we know and don't', *Harper's Magazine* (277, November), 1988, 68–70.

2 A troubled world

1 For several powerful overviews of the world's challenges, the reader should see T. Homer-Dixon, *The Ingenuity Gap* (Toronto: Vintage Canada, 2001); T. Homer-Dixon, *The Upside of Down: Catastrophe, Creativity, and the Renewal of Civilization* (Toronto: Alfred A. Knopf, 2006); B. McKibben, *The End of Nature* (New York: Random House, 2006) and E.O. Wilson, *The Future of Life* (New York: Vintage Books, 2003).

2 J. Heath and A. Potter, *The Rebel Sell: Why the Culture Can't Be Jammed*, Toronto: Harper Collins, 2004, p. 206.

3 N. Postman, *The End of Education: Redefining the Value of School*, New York: First Vintage Books Edition, 1996, p. 101.

4 M.A. Grubbs (ed.), *Conversations with Wendell Berry*, Jackson: University of Mississippi Press, 2007, p. 95.

5 M. Woodhouse, *Paradigm Wars: Worldviews for a New Age*, Berkley: Frog, Ltd., 1996, pp. 432–5.

6 W.W. Lowrance, *Modern Science and Human Values*, London: Oxford University Press, 1986, p. 209.

7 R. Wright, *A Short History of Progress*, Toronto: House of Anansi Press Inc., 2004, p. 3.

8 T. Homer-Dixon, *The Upside of Down: Catastrophe, Creativity, and the Renewal of Civilization*, Toronto: Alfred A. Knopf, 2006, pp. 11–12.

9 H. Henderson, 'Making a living without making money', *East West Journal*, March, 1980, 22–7.

10 Descriptions of the Copenhagen Consensus Center and its work are available online at <http://www.copenhagenconsensus.com/Default.aspx?ID=788> and <http://pp.copenhagen consensus.com/Statistics.aspx> (accessed 20 November 2007).

11 D. Cameron, 'The museum, a temple or the forum', in G. Anderson (ed.), *Reinventing the Museum: Historical and Contemporary Perspectives on the Paradigm Shift*, Walnut Creek, California: Altamira Press, 2004, pp. 61–73.

12 Cameron, 'The museum, a temple or the forum', p. 72.

12 G. Morgan, *Images of Organization*, Newbury Park, California: Sage Publications, Inc., 1986, p. 133.

14 M. Wackernagel and W. Rees, *Our Ecological Footprint: Reducing Human Impact on the Earth*, Gabriola Island, Canada: New Society Publishers, 1996.

15 M. Pollan, *The Omnivore's Dilemma: A Natural History of Four Meals*, New York: Penguin Books, 2006, p. 306.

16 E. O. Wilson, *Consilience: The Unity of Knowledge*, New York: Alfred A. Knopf, 1998, pp. 282–3.

17 See the Global Footprint Network. Available online at <http://www.footprintnetwork.org/webgraph/graphpage.php?country=canada> (accessed 6 October 2008).

18 B. McKibben, *Deep Economy: The Wealth of Communities and the Durable Future*, New York: Henry Holt and Company, LLC, 2007, p. 222.

19 See the Global Footprint Network. Available online at <http://www.footprintnetwork.org/gfn_sub.php?content=national_footprints> (accessed 20 November 2007).

20 McKibben, *Deep Economy*, p. 115.

21 See McKibben, *The End of Nature*.

22 B. McKibben, 'Pie in the sky: Solutions to problems you never knew you had', *Orion* (March/April), 2006, 14–15.

23 Recent research indicates that the roots of our unbridled consumption go back to the late 1920s, when the US Secretary of Labour and his corporate cohorts defined a strategic shift for American industry – 'from fulfilling basic needs to creating new ones.' See J. Kaplan, 'The gospel of consumption: And the better future we left behind', *Orion* (27, May/June), 2008, 38–47.

24 Woodhouse, *Paradigm Wars*, p. 22.

25 J. Zernan, 'Greasing the rails to a Cyborg future', *Adbusters* (35, May/June), 2001, 88.

26 United Nations Development Program, *Human Development Report*, New York: Oxford University Press, 1998, p. 37. Available online at <http://hdr.undp.org/en/media/hdr_1998_en.pd> (accessed 7 December 2007).

27 Canadian Museum of Civilization, *Summary of the Corporate Plan (2006–2007 to 2010–2011) and Summary of the Operating and Capital Budgets (2006–2007)*, Gatineau, Quebec: Canadian Museum of Civilization. Available online at <http://www.civilization.ca/societe/corpsm06/corp06e.pdf> (accessed 28 January, 2008).

28 S. Morel (Vice-President, Exhibitions and Programs, Canadian Museum of Civilization), via email, October 2007. This was a follow-up to an interview with Sylvie Morel at the Canadian Museum of Civilization on 24 September 2007.

29 Canadian Museum of Civilization, *Summary of the Corporate Plan (2006–2007 to 2010–2011) and Summary of the Operating and Capital Budgets (2006–2007)*, p. 9.

30 National Gallery of Canada, *Inside Out: Annual Report 2005–06*, Ottawa: National Gallery of Canada. Available online at <http://www.gallery.ca/files/ANNUALREPORT_06.pdf> (accessed 7 December 2007).

31 Canada Science and Technology Museum Corporation, *Corporate Plan Summary 2006–2007 to 2010–2011*, Ottawa: Canada Science and Technology Museum Corporation. Available online at <http://technomuses.ca/app/filerepository/F22DB621B0DC407280BF9E3CAFA7ECAB.pdf> (accessed 7 December 2007).

32 Canadian Museum of Nature, *A New Beginning: 2006–2007 Annual Report*, Ottawa: Canadian Museum of Nature. Available online at <http://nature.ca/pdf/ann06–07nature_e.pdf> (accessed 7 December 2007).

33 G. Anderson (ed.), *Reinventing the Museum: Historical and Contemporary Perspectives on the Paradigm Shift*, Walnut Creek, California: Altamira Press, 2004, pp. 1–7.

34 Royal BC Museum, *Annual Report 2006–2007*, Victoria: Royal BC Museum. Available online at <http://www.royalbcmuseum.bc.ca/Content_Files/Files/RBCMuseumAR0607.pdf> (accessed 7 December 2007). See also Royal BC Museum Corporation, *Service Plan 2007/08–2009/10*, Victoria: Royal BC Museum Corporation. Available online at <http://www.royalbcmuseum.bc.ca/Content_Files/Files/ServicePlan2008–09–09–10.pdf> (accessed 7 December 2007).

35 R.J. Hebda, 'Commentary: Museums, climate change and sustainability', *Museum Management and Curatorship* (22/4), 2007, 329–36.

36 The Manitoba Museum, *Value and Benefit*, Winnipeg: The Manitoba Museum. Available online at <http://www.manitobamuseum.ca/gi_value.html> (accessed 7 December 2007). It should be noted that the Manitoba Museum's values include respect for diversity, active stewardship and environmental responsibility, but none of these values appear on the museum's website: Claudette Leclerc (CEO), via email (September 2008).

37 Royal Ontario Museum, *Dawn of the Crystal Age*. Available online at <http://www.rom.on.ca/crystal/index.php> (accessed 14 December 2007).

38 Royal Ontario Museum, *Countdown to the Crystal: Annual Report 2006/2007*, Toronto: Royal Ontario Museum. Available online at <http://www.rom.on.ca/about/pdf/reports/2007.pdf> (accessed 10 December 2007).

39 Nova Scotia Museum: The Family of Provincial Museums. Available online at<http://museum.gov.ns.ca/> (accessed 10 January 2008).

40 P. Marty, 'Museum websites and museum visitors: Before and after the museum visit', *Museum Management and Curatorship* (22/4), 2007, 337–60.

41 A. Kaufman, 'Ten steps to successful reinvention', *Cultural Capital*, Spring, 2008, 1–4. Available online at <http://www.lord.ca/Media/CulturalCapital-Spring2008.pdf> (accessed 5 July 2008).

42 Western Development Museum, *Saskatchewan Western Development Museum: Strategic Plan (2007–2012)*, Saskatoon: Western Development Museum. Unpublished Strategic Plan on file at the Western Development Museum, Saskatoon, Canada.

43 The Imperial War Museum's *Sustainable Development Policy Statement*. Available online at <http://london.iwm.org.uk/upload/pdf/SustainablePolicyStatement.pdf> (accessed 5 July 2008).

44 Maurice Davies, Deputy Director of the Museums Association (United Kingdom) via email (February 2008). The Museums Association developed a discussion paper entitled 'Sustainability and Museums' that was posted on their website and mailed to all members. This distribution was followed by a series of discussion meetings throughout the United Kingdom. This process culminated in a report on the sector's reactions to the discussion paper at the MA's annual conference in the fall of 2008. The outcome of this process was not available at the time of writing.

45 Global Security.org provides details on the current conflicts and wars throughout the world. Available online at <http://www.globalsecurity.org/military/world/war/> (accessed 29 January 2008).

46 See the Global Issues website for complete details on international arms spending. Available online at <http://www.globalissues.org/Geopolitics/ArmsTrade/Spending.asp> (accessed 29 January 2008).

47 See 'Primates: Extinction threat growing for mankind's closest living relatives'. Available online at <http://www.sciencedaily.com/releases/2007/10/071026095223.htm> (accessed 31 January 2008).

48 J. Abramovitz, 'Ecosystem conversion spreads', in *Vital Signs*, New York: WorldWatch Institute and W.W. Norton and Co., 1997, pp. 98–9.

49 E.O. Wilson, *Creation: An Appeal to Save Life on Earth*, New York: W.W. Norton & Co., Inc., 2006, p. 27.

50 'Biodiversity and its value', *Biodiversity Series, Paper No.1*, Canberra: Department of the Environment, Water, Heritage and the Arts, Australian Government. Available online at <http://www.environment.gov.au/biodiversity/publications/series/paper1/index.html> (accessed 5 February 2008).

51 'Biodiversity and its value.'

52 Wilson, *Consilience*, p. 293.

53 A. Shah, *Global Issues: Social, Political, Economic and Environmental Issues That Affect All of Us*. Available online at <http://www.globalissues.org/EnvIssues/Biodiversity.asp> (accessed 6 February 2008).

54 Wilson, *Consilience*, p. 294.

55 Wilson, *Creation*, pp. 77–78.

56 Wilson, *Creation*, pp. 77.

57 I am indebted to Joanne DiCosimo, President and Chief Executive Officer of the Canadian Museum of Nature (Ottawa, Canada) for bringing the Buffon Symposium and the ensuing declaration to my attention. *The Buffon Declaration* is available online at <http://sssssssmct.gov.br/upd_blob/0021/21746.pdf> (accessed 5 July 2008).

58 See the *Encyclopedia of Life* website for details. Available online at <http://www.eol.org/index> (accessed 5 July 2008).

59 J. H. Kunstler, *The Long Emergency: Surviving the End of Oil, Climate Change, and Other Converging Catastrophes of the Twenty-First Century*, New York: Grove Press, 2005, p. 130.

60 C. Handy, *The Age of Paradox*, Boston: Harvard Business School Press, 1994, p. 77.

61 Wilson, *Creation*, p. 91.

62 W. Davis, *Light at the Edge of the World*, Vancouver: Douglas and McIntyre Ltd., 2001, pp. 1–14.

63 Davis, *Light at the Edge of the World*, p. 6.

64 H. Kane, *Vital Signs*, New York: Worldwatch Institute and W.W. Norton and Company, 1997, pp. 130–1.

65 Davis, *Light at the Edge of the World*, p. 7.

66 Davis, *Light at the Edge of the World*, p. 189.

67 For details on the implications of global capitalism for indigenous peoples, see the summary of Richard H. Robbins' book, *Global Problems and the Culture of Capitalism*. Available online at <http://faculty.plattsburgh.edu/richard.robbins/legacy/chap_9_intro.html> (accessed 5 July 2008).

68 Survival – The Movement for Tribal Peoples. Available online at <http://www.survival-international.org/info> (accessed 6 October 2008).

69 A. Johnson, 'The death of ethnography', *The Sciences* (27), 1987, 24–30.

70 'Indigenous Peoples and Globalization Program.' Available online at <http://www.ifg.org/programs/indig.htm> (accessed 5 July 2008).

71 See the summary of this exhibition. Available online at <http://london.iwm.org.uk/server/show/ConWebDoc.1425> (accessed 5 July 2008).

72 'Survival: People and their land.' Available online at <http://www.glasgowmuseums.com/showProject.cfm?venueid=0&itemid=51> (accessed 5 July 2008).

73 International Coalition of Sites of Conscience. Available online at <http://www.sitesofconscience.org/about-us/en/> (accessed 5 July 2008).

74 *Task Force Report on Museums and First Peoples*, Ottawa: The Assembly of First Nations and the Canadian Museums Association, 1992.

75 E. Scott and E.M. Luby, 'Maintaining relationships with native communities: The role of museum management and governance', *Museum Management and Curatorship* (22/3), 2007, 265–85.

76 T. Homer-Dixon, *The Ingenuity Gap*, Toronto: Vintage Canada, 2001, pp. 79–80.

77 Wilson, *Consilience*, p. 54.

78 Woodhouse, *Paradigm Wars*, pp. 11, 15.
79 Woodhouse, *Paradigm Wars*, p. 14.
80 Homer-Dixon, *The Ingenuity Gap*, pp. 31, 241.
81 U. Franklin, *The Real World of Technology*, Toronto: House of Anansi Press Limited, 1999, pp. 84–5.
82 Franklin, *The Real World of Technology*, pp. 65–7.
83 Wilson, *Consilience*, pp. 290–2.
84 McKibben, *Deep Economy*, pp. 26–8.
85 C. Taylor, *The Malaise of Modernity*, Toronto: House of Anansi Press Ltd., 1991, p. 5.

3 It's a jungle in here

1   W. Phillips, 'The three agendas', Management Briefing, Quality Management to a Higher Power. Available online at <http://www.qm2.org/mbriefs/32.html> (accessed 23 May 2008).
2   Phillips, 'The three agendas', p. 2.
3   Phillips, 'The three agendas', pp. 2–3.
4   A. Bullock and S. Trombley (eds), *The New Fontana Dictionary of Modern Thought*, London: HarperCollins Publishers, 1977, p. 414.
5   See also the work of Kevin Coffee: 'Cultural inclusion, exclusion and the formative roles of museums', *Museum Management and Curatorship* (23/3), 2008, 261–79. He notes that 'inclusivity and exclusivity are neither abstract nor absolute qualities; they can only be measured according to specific socio-cultural relationships. Key among these is the ideological performance of the museum as exemplified in its collections and programming activities, and by the specific narratives privileged by the museum and shared with specific sub-groups, classes or strata within the population as a whole' (p. 271).
6   T. Lenoir, 'Separated by birth', *The Sciences* (July/August), 1993, 38–42.
7   T. Lenoir, 'Separated by birth', 42.
8   K. Coffee, 'Cultural inclusion, exclusion and the formative roles of museums', 261.
9   'Nightmare on 53rd Street', in Readings, *Harper's Magazine* (316, January), 2008, 20–3. See also M. Elligott, 'Tentative and confidential: Exhibition X', *Esopus* (9, Fall), 2007, 132–45.
10 'Nightmare on 53rd Street', 20.
11 'Nightmare on 53rd Street', 23.
12 G. Hardin, *Filters Against Folly: How to Survive Despite Economists, Ecologists and the Merely Eloquent*, New York: Viking Penguin, Inc., 1985, p. 63.
13 Canadian Museums Association, 'Canadians and their museums: A survey of Canadians and their views about the country's museums', March, 2003. Available online at <http://www.museums.ca/media/Pdf/surveyanalysis2003.pdf> (accessed 26 May 2008).
14 F. Cameron, 'Contentiousness and shifting knowledge paradigms: The roles of history and science museums in contemporary society', *Museum Management and Curatorship* (20/2), 2005, 213–33.
15 K. Coffee, 'Audience research and the museum experience as social practice', *Museum Management and Curatorship* (22/4), 2007, 377–89, 383.
16 N. Postman, *The End of Education: Redefining the Value of School*, New York: Vintage Books, 1996, p. 59.
17 R.K. Greenleaf, *Servant Leadership*, Mahwah, NJ: Paulist Press, 1977, p. 61.
18 R.R. Janes, *Museums and the Paradox of Change: A Case Study in Urgent Adaptation*, Calgary, Canada: Glenbow Museum and the University of Calgary Press, 1997 (2nd edn), pp. 195–7.
19 M.P. Robinson, 'The duty of succession planning', *Museum Management and Curatorship* (20/1), 2005, 81–3.
20 R.I. Goler, 'Interim directorships in museums: Their impact on individuals and significance to institutions', *Museum Management and Curatorship* (19/4), 2001, 385–402.
21 Greenleaf, *Servant Leadership*, p. 63.
22 For details on Museum Director's Roundtables, see Qm2's website. Available online at <http://www.qm2.org/roundtables.html> (accessed 27 May 2008).
23 Greenleaf, *Servant Leadership*, pp. 64–5.
24 See J. Rounds, 'On the uses of museum studies literature: A research agenda', *Curator: The Museum Journal* (50/1), 2007, 135–46. In this valuable article on museological research, writing and reading, Rounds notes that 'We need more sophisticated ways of thinking about

museums as organizations, and about the field of museums as an institutional system. Perhaps if we were armed with such advanced understanding, we would be able to figure out how to design what we really seem to need' (p. 145).

25 Greenleaf, *Servant Leadership*, p. 65.
26 R. Farson, *Management of the Absurd: Paradoxes in Leadership*, New York: Simon and Schuster, 1996, p. 144.
27 Greenleaf, *Servant Leadership*, p. 63.
28 J.P. Kotter, 'What leaders really do', *Harvard Business Review* (68), 1990, 103–7.
29 Farson, *Management of the Absurd*, p. 108.
30 S. Weil, 'From being about something to being for somebody: The ongoing transformation of the American Museum'. In R. Sandell and R.R. Janes (eds), *Museum Management and Marketing*, Oxford: Routledge, 2007, p. 45.
31 R.D. Stacey, *Managing the Unknowable: Strategic Boundaries Between Order and Chaos in Organizations*, San Francisco: Jossey-Bass Inc., Publishers, 1992, pp. 1–2.
32 Stacey, *Managing the Unknowable*, p. 2.
33 Stacey, *Managing the Unknowable*, pp. 3–7.
34 J. H. Kunstler, *The Long Emergency: Surviving the End of Oil, Climate Change, and Other Converging Catastrophes of the Twenty-First Century*, New York: Grove Press, 2005, p. 122.
35 K. Scott, *Funding Matters: The Impact of Canada's New Funding Regime on Nonprofit and Voluntary Organizations*, Ottawa, Canada: The Canadian Council on Social Development, 2003.
36 M. Robinson, email (August 2006).
37 J. Kluger, 'Intelligent organizational design', *Platform*/AEA Consulting, 5 (1), April, 2006, p. 1. Available online at http://www.aeaconsulting.com/ice_print.php?id=1468> (accessed 22 October 2008).
38 D. Griffin and M. Abraham, 'The effective management of museums: Cohesive leadership and visitor-focused public programming'. In R. Sandell and R.R. Janes (eds), *Museum Management and Marketing*, Oxford: Routledge, 2007, pp. 104–41.
39 Janes, *Museums and the Paradox of Change*, p. 275.
40 Janes, *Museums and the Paradox of Change, passim*.
41 R.B. Lee and I. DeVore (eds), *Man the Hunter*, Chicago: Aldine Publishing Company, 1968, p. 3.
42 Lee and DeVore, *Man the Hunter*, p. 3.
43 M. Ames, 'Thirty-one propositions on changing museums: An introduction to the Glenbow case study'. In R.R. Janes, *Museums and the Paradox of Change: A Case Study in Urgent Adaptation*, Calgary, Canada: Glenbow Museum and the University of Calgary Press, 1997 (2nd edn), pp. 2–3.
44 J.M. Roberts, 'Three Navaho households: A comparative study in small group culture', *Papers of the Peabody Museum of American Archaeology and Ethnology*, Cambridge, Massachusetts: Peabody Museum of American Archaeology and Ethnology, 1951, p. 83.
45 S. Leka, A. Griffiths and T. Cox, 'Work organisation and stress: systematic problem approaches for employers, managers and trade union representatives', *Protecting Workers' Health Series No. 3*, Geneva World Health Organization. Available online at <http://www.who.int/occupational_health/publications/en/oehstress.pdf> (accessed 30 May 2008).
46 Stacey, *Managing the Unknowable*, p. 6.
47 J. Jaworski, *Synchronicity*, San Francisco: Bennett-Koehler Publishers, 1998, p. 109.
48 G.T.Conaty and B. Carter, 'Our story in our words: Diversity and equality in the Glenbow Museum'. In R.R. Janes and G.T. Conaty (eds), *Looking Reality in the Eye: Museums and Social Responsibility*, Calgary, Canada: The University of Calgary Press and the Museums Association of Saskatchewan, 2005, pp. 43–58.
49 M. Gallant and G. Kydd, 'Engaging young minds and spirits: The Glenbow Museum School'. In R.R. Janes and G.T. Conaty (eds), *Looking Reality in the Eye: Museums and Social Responsibility*, Calgary, Canada: The University of Calgary Press and the Museums Association of Saskatchewan, 2005, pp. 71–84.
50 C. Locke, 'Internet apocalypso', in C. Locke, R. Levine, D. Searls and D. Weinberger, *The Clue Train Manifesto: The End of Business as Usual*, New York: Perseus Publishing, 2000, chapter 1. Available online at <http://www.cluetrain.com/apocalypso.html> (accessed 15 January 2009).
51 Janes, *Museums and the Paradox of Change*, pp. 223–4.

52 K. McLean, 'Do museum exhibitions have a future?', *Curator: The Museum Journal* (50/1), 2007, 109–21.

53 McLean, 'Do museum exhibitions have a future?', 110.

54 McLean, 'Do museum exhibitions have a future?', 118.

55 'Exhibiting controversy', *Museum News* Round Table, November/December, 1989, p. 63.

56 R. Ferguson, 'The burden of proof and the alchemy of content: Leadership brands and sustainable organizations', presentation to the Government of Canada's Annual Meeting of the Networks of Centres of Excellence, Gatineau, Quebec, Canada, December 5, 2007, p. 1. Available from the author at robferguson@knowledgemarketinggroup.com.

57 Ferguson, 'The burden of proof and the alchemy of content', p. 2.

58 McLean, 'Do museum exhibitions have a future?', 119.

59 Ferguson, 'The burden of proof and the alchemy of content', pp. 6–7.

60 Mid-Atlantic Association of Museums, 'Inaugural Symposium on Creating Exhibitions' Program, Philadelphia, Pennsylvania, April 5–7, 2008. Available online at <http://www.midatlanticmuseums.org/Documents/maam_ce_2008_brochure.pd> (accessed 5 June 2008).

61 Janes, *Museums and the Paradox of Change*, p. 223.

62 Wosk Centre for Dialogue. Available online at <http://www.sfu.ca/dialog/> (accessed 5 June 2008).

63 The Dana Centre – About Us. Available online at <http://www.danacentre.org.uk/> (accessed 7 October 2008).

64 Interview with Kathleen McLean. Available online at <http://www.informalscience.org/community/interview/kathymclean.html> (accessed 5 June 2008).

65 S. Keene, email (June 2008).

66 S. Knell, 'Museums, reality and the material world', in S. Knell (ed.), *Museums in the Material World*, Oxford: Routledge, 2007, p. 26.

67 Quoted in S. Keene, *Fragments of the World: Uses of Museum Collections*, Oxford: Elsevier, Butterworth-Heinemann, 2005, p. 5.

68 M. Schwarzer, *Riches, Rivals and Radicals: 100 Years of Museums in America*, Washington, DC: American Association of Museums, 2006, p. 71.

69 S. Keene, *Collections For People: Museums' Stored Collections as a Public Resource*. London: University College London, Institute of Archaeology, Section 2, 2008. Available online at <http://www.ucl.ac.uk/~tcrnske/files/report/> (accessed 8 October 2008); and S. Carter, B. Hurst, R. Kerr, E. Taylor and P. Winsor, *Museum Focus: Facts and Figures on Museums in the UK*. London: Museums and Galleries Commission, Issue 2, 1999, p. 22. Available online at <http://www.ndad.nationalarchives.gov.uk/CRDA/12/DD/5/8/quickref.html?jump=1> (accessed 8 October 2008); and S. Keene, email (June 2008).

70 G. Anderson (ed.), *Reinventing the Museum: Historical and Contemporary Perspectives on the Paradigm Shift*, Walnut Creek, California: Altamira Press, 2004, pp. 1–7.

71 Schwarzer, *Riches, Rivals and Radicals*, p. 71.

72 Keene, *Fragments of the World*.

73 Knell, 'Museums, reality and the material world', p. 13.

74 The full text of the *Declaration of the Importance and Value of Universal Museums* is contained in the International Council of Museums Thematic Files. Available online at <http://icom.museum/universal.html> (accessed 10 June 2008).

75 C. Sandis, F. Bell, N. Curtis, B. Murphy, and A. Snodgrass, 'Two tales of one city: Cultural understanding and the Parthenon sculptures', *Museum Management and Curatorship* (23/1), 2008, 5–21.

76 Snodgrass, 'Two tales of one city', 18–19.

77 Snodgrass, 'Two tales of one city', 19.

78 M. Anderson, 'Prescriptions for art museums in the decade ahead', *Curator: The Museum Journal* (50/1), 2007, 9–18, 14.

79 M. Kimmelman, 'What price love? Museums sell out', *The New York Times* (late edn), 17 July 2005, section 2, p. 1, col. 1.

80 See *Museum Watchdog*. Archaeological Institute of America. Available online at <http://www.archaeology.org/online/interviews/gill.html> (accessed 15 June 2008).

81 Knell, 'Museums, reality and the material world', p. 23.

82 Details on Samdok are available from the Nordiska Museet. Available online at <http://www.nordiskamuseet.se/> (accessed 13 June 2008).

83 Knell, 'Museums, reality and the material world', p. 26.
84 L. Brandon and G. Wilson, 'The Canadian Museums Association research summit: A report', *Museum Management and Curatorship* (20/4), 2005, 349–58, 350.
85 Brandon and Wilson, 'The Canadian Museums Association research summit', 351.
86 N. Merriman, 'Museum collections and sustainability', *Cultural Trends* (17/1), 2008, 3–21.
87 K.S. Thomson, 'Museums: Dilemmas and paradoxes', *American Scientist* (86/6), 1998, 522.
88 H. Klutschak, *Overland to Starvation Cove: With the Inuit in Search of Franklin* (trans. and ed. William Barr), Toronto: University of Toronto Press, 1987, pp. 72–3.
89 P. Ainslie, 'A collection for the millennium: Grading the collections at Glenbow', *Museum Management and Curatorship* (19/1), 2001, 93–104, 93.
90 Ainslie, 'A collection for the millennium', 102.
91 Ainslie, 'A collection for the millennium', 103.
92 P. Ainslie, *The Deaccessioning Strategy at Glenbow: 1992–1997*, Calgary, Canada: Glenbow-Alberta Institute, 1995, p. 6.
93 Janes, *Museums and the Paradox of Change*, pp. 30–42.
94 Museum of New Zealand Te Papa Tongarewa Website, *Te Papa: About Us/What We Do – Our Concept, Act, Mission and Corporate Principles*, 2005. Available online at <http://www.tepapa.govt.nz/TePapa/English/AboutTePapa/AboutUs/WhatWeDo/> (accessed 27 October 2008).
95 *Te Papa: About Us/What We Do*, 2005, p. 8.
96 Te Papa National Services, *A Guide to Guardians of Iwi Treasures Issue 8*, Wellington, New Zealand: Museum of New Zealand Te Papa Tongarewa, June 2008. Available online at <http://www.tepapa.govt.nz/NR/rdonlyres/392E5CBE-93B2-4934-A9B9-E0FE4994E63D/0/Iwi.pdf> (accessed 27 October 2008).

4 Debunking the marketplace

1 M. Kingwell, *The World We Want: Virtue, Vice, and the Good Citizen*, Toronto: Viking, 2000, p. 184.
2 J. Ralston Saul, *The Unconscious Civilization*, Concord, Canada: House of Anansi Press, 1995, p. 2.
3 Ralston Saul, *The Unconscious Civilization*, p. 190.
4 E. Hobsbawm, *On the Edge of the New Century*, New York: The New Press, 2000, p. 35.
5 Hobsbawm, *On the Edge of the New Century*, p. 106.
6 R.R. Janes, *Museums and the Paradox of Change: A Case Study in Urgent Adaptation*, Calgary, Canada: Glenbow Museum and the University of Calgary Press, 1997 (2nd edn).
7 *Glenbow Annual Report 2000*, Calgary, Canada: Glenbow Museum, 2000, p. 7.
8 *Glenbow Museum Annual Report, 2006–2007*, Calgary, Canada: Glenbow Museum, p. 23. Available online at <http://www.glenbow.org/media/AR2007-Glenbow.pdf> (accessed 26 June 2008).
9 F. Capra, *The Turning Point: Science, Society and the Rising Culture*, New York and Toronto: Bantam Books, 1983, p. 397.
10 J. Rifkin, 'The end of work'. Public address on behalf of the Volunteer Centre of Calgary, Palliser Hotel, Calgary, Alberta, Canada, November 13, 1997.
11 A. Bullock and S. Trombley (eds), *The New Fontana Dictionary of Modern Thought*, Hammersmith and London: HarperCollins, 1999, p. 798.
12 J. Rifkin, *The End of Work*, New York: G.P. Putnam's Sons, 1996, p. 246.
13 R. Grudin, *Time and the Art of Living*, New York: Houghton Mifflin Company, 1982, p. 18.
14 A. DeGeus, *The Living Company: Habits for Survival in a Turbulent Business Environment*, Boston: Harvard Business School Press, 1997, p. 1.
15 DeGeus, *The Living Company*, pp. 5–9.
16 DeGeus, *The Living Company*, pp. 15–16.
17 M. Csikszentmihalyi, *Good Business: Leadership, Flow and the Making of Meaning*, New York: Viking Penguin, 2003, p. 189.
18 Hobsbawm, *On the Edge of the New Century*, pp. 12–15.
19 J. Wetenhall, 'Impossible job: The changing role of the museum director'. Available online at <http://www.getty.edu/leadership/compleat_leader/downloads/aamd08wetenhall.pdf> (accessed 2 July 2008).
20 Wetenhall, 'Impossible job', pp. 3–4.

21 Wetenhall, 'Impossible job', p. 5.

22 T. Freudenheim, 'Fifty museum years, and then some', *Curator: The Museum Journal* (50/1), 2007, 55–62, 55, 60.

23 M. Davies and H. Wilkinson (2008), *Sustainability and Museums: Your Chance to Make a Difference*. London: Museums Association. Available online at <http://www.museumsassociation.org/asset_arena/text/al/sustainability_web_final.pdf> (accessed 2 July 2008).

24 T. Gstraunthaler and M. Piber, 'Performance measurement and accounting: Museums in Austria', *Museum Management and Curatorship* (22/4), 2007, 361–75.

25 Gstraunthaler and Piber, 'Performance measurement and accounting', 373.

26 W. Thorsell (2007), 'The museum as the new agora', p. 3. Available online at <http://www.rom.on.ca/about/pdf/agoraspeech.pdf> (accessed 3 July 2008).

27 Thorsell, 'The museum as the new agora', p. 5.

28 Thorsell, 'The museum as the new agora', p. 5. In fairness, I note that the Royal Ontario Museum recently hosted a forum on 'International Intervention in Genocidal Situations', which was subsequently aired in December 2008 on the 'Ideas' radio program (Canadian Broadcasting Corporation). This kind of substantive discussion lies at the heart of the true agora.

29 W. Gross (2007), 'Enough is enough', p. 1. Available online at <http://www.pimco.com/LeftNav/Featured+Market+Commentary/IO/2007/IO+August+2007.htm> (accessed 3 July 2008).

30 *Consumer Spending on Culture in Canada the Provinces and 15 Metropolitan Areas in 2005* (2007), pp. 1–8. Ottawa: Hill Strategies Inc. Available online at <http://www.hillstrategies.com/docs/Consumer_spending2005.pdf> (accessed 3 July 2008).

31 *International Forum on the Creative Economy*, 17–18 March 2008. Ottawa, Canada: The Conference Board of Canada. Available online at <http://www.conferenceboard.ca/documents.asp?rnext=2567> (accessed 3 July 2008).

32 S. Beatty, 'Museums learn to love debt', *The Wall Street Journal Online*, 30 March 2007. Online. Available online at <http://online.wsj.com/article_email/SB117521262951653880-lMyQjAxMDE3NzM1MDIzMTAyWj.html> (accessed 3 July 2008).

33 A. Ellis, 'The impact of globalization on the cultural sector'. Arts Administration Graduate Student Association, Drexel University, May 22, 2007, p. 16. Available online at <http://www.drexel.edu/westphal/pdf/aadm/TheImpactofGlobalization.pdf> (accessed 30 September 2008). See also V. Dickenson, Commentary: 'A trip to China: Observations and Reflections', *Museum Management and Curatorship* (22/3), 2007, 237–45.

34 N.Grattan, (ed.), 'New museums', *MUSE* (XXIV/3), 2006, 10–11; and C. Hume, 'Arts story: Cultural vacuum', *The Toronto Star* (26 August 2000), 1–5; and C. Hume, 'A fragile renaissance: Toronto's big-name architecture is rising against perilous landscape. Once the fever subsides, how we will afford our culture?', *The Toronto Star* (9 October 2005), p. H1.

35 A. Hudson, 'New! Improved! The rhetoric of relevancy in a construction boom', *MUSE* (XXIV/3), 2006, 38–41.

36 A.Ellis (2002),'Planning in a cold climate', research paper prepared for the Directors' seminar: 'Leading retrenchment'. Los Angeles, California: The Getty Leadership Institute. Available online at <http://www.getty.edu/leadership/compleat_leader/downloads/ellis.pdf> (accessed 7 July 2008).

37 Ellis, 'Planning in a cold climate', p. 21.

38 Ellis, 'Planning in a cold climate', pp. 22–3.

39 J.M. Bradburne, 'The museum time bomb: Overbuilt, overtraded, overdrawn', *The Informal Learning Review*, 65, 2004, 4–13. Available online at <http://www.bradburne.org/downloads/museums/InstitutioninCrisisWEB.pdf> (accessed 7 July 2008).

40 Bradburne, 'The museum time bomb', 34.

41 G. Lord and M. Sabau, 'The Bilbao effect: From poor port to must-see city', *The Art Newspaper* 184, 2007, pp. 32–3. Available online at <http://www.lord.ca/Media/TheArtNewspaper32–33Museums.pdf> (accessed 7 July 2008).

42 B. Plaza, 'On some challenges and conditions for the Guggenheim Museum Bilbao to be an effective economic re-activator', *International Journal of Urban and Regional Research* (32/2), 2008, 506–16, 507.

43 Lord and Sabau, , 'The Bilbao effect: From poor port to must-see city', pp. 32–3.

44 Plaza, 'On some challenges and conditions for the Guggenheim Museum', p. 514.

45 Plaza, 'On some challenges and conditions for the Guggenheim Museum', p. 506.

46 C. Lorway, 'The war on travel', *Platform*/AEA Consulting 5(3), 2007, pp. 7–8. Available online at <http://www.aeaconsulting.com/sites/aea/images/1815/aea_1815.pdf> (accessed 21 October 2008).

47 Lorway, 'The war on travel', p. 7.

48 R.B. Lee and I. DeVore (eds), *Man the Hunter,* Chicago: Aldine Publishing Company, 1968, p. 188.

49 M. Csikszentmihalyi, *Good Business: Leadership, Flow and the Making of Meaning,* pp. 6–10.

50 *Wall Street Reform,* Online NewsHour. Available online at <http://www.pbs.org/newshour/forum/july02/b_ethics4.html> (accessed 8 July 2008). See also Joe Knight's 'Lessons from the orgy of corporate greed', The Business Literacy Institute. Available online at <http://www.business-literacy.com/joeknight/corporategreed.html> (accessed 10 July 2008).

51 S. Stern, 'Fat-cat pay rate shows no signs of moderation', *National Post,* 1 November 2006, p. WK 5.

52 S. DeCarlo, 'Top paid US CEOs', *Forbes*, 7 May 2007. Available online at <http://www.cbc.ca/money/story/2008/05/06/fforbes-toppaidceos.html> (accessed 8 July 2008).

53 Stern, 'Fat-cat pay rate shows no signs of moderation', p. WK 5.

54 Editorial, 'The Smithsonian Challenge', *The New York Times*, 28 March 2007. Available online at <http://www.nytimes.com/2007/03/28/opinion/28wed3.html?_r=1&ex=1175745600&en=84ad07fa9de6b7b5&ei=5070&emc=eta1&oref=slogin> (accessed 8 July 2008).

55 R. Pogrebin, 'Smithsonian ex-chief criticized in report', *The New York Times,* 21 June 2007, pp. 1–2. Available online at <http://www.nytimes.com/2007/06/21/arts/design/21smit.html> (accessed 8 July 2008).

56 M. Rosenman, 'Blog: The patina of philanthropy', *Stanford Social Innovation Review*, 11 April 2007, 1. Available online at <http://www.ssireview.org/opinion/entry/the_patina_of_philanthropy/> (accessed 8 July 2008).

57 Rosenman, 'Blog: The patina of philanthropy', 1.

58 Rosenman, 'Blog: 'The patina of philanthropy', 1.

59 R. Grudin, *The Grace of Great Things: Creativity and Innovation,* New York: Houghton Mifflin Company, 1990, p. 220.

60 Grudin, *The Grace of Great Things,* pp. 220–1.

61 Interview with Michael P. Robinson, 3 December 2007, Canmore, Alberta, Canada: transcript, pp. 1–9.

62 Interview with Michael P. Robinson: transcript, p. 4.

63 Michael P. Robinson, *President's Report, November 22, 2007,* Calgary, Alberta, Canada: Glenbow Museum, p. 5.

64 Interview with Michael P. Robinson: transcript, p. 7.

65 Interviews with Michael P. Robinson: transcript, p. 6, also 30 October 2008 (telephone).

66 M. Morris, 'Organizational health', *NEWStandard* (1)3, The American Association of Museums, Washington, DC, 1998, p. 4.

67 DeGeus, *The Living Company*, p. 9.

68 J. Rifkin, *Entropy: A New World View*, New York: The Viking Press, 1980, p. 134.

69 C. Jeffrey, 'A look at the numbers: How the rich get richer', *Mother Jones*, May/June, 2006, p. 1. Available online at <http://www.motherjones.com/news/exhibit/2006/05/perks_of_privilege.html> (accessed 10 July 2008).

70 B. McKibben, *Deep Economy: The Wealth of Communities and the Durable Futur*e, New York: Henry Holt and Company, LLC, 2007, p. 14.

71 P. Nyhan and S. Skolnik, 'America's income gap grows; Rich get richer', *Seattle-Post Intelligencer,* 17 August 2004, p. 1. Available online at <http://seattlepi.nwsource.com/local/186625_incomegap17.html> (accessed 10 July 2008).

5 Searching for resilience

1 For statistics on the 1918 influenza epidemic, see 'The influenza pandemic of 1918', available online at <http://virus.stanford.edu/uda/> (accessed 16 January 2009); for an overview of Second World War statistics see Wikipedia, available online at <http://en.wikipedia.org/wiki/

World_War_II> (accessed 16 January, 2009), and for details on the HIV/AIDS pandemic, see Wikipedia, available online at <http://en.wikipedia.org/wiki/AIDS_pandemic> (accessed 16 January 2009).

2   See J. Diamond, *Collapse: How Societies Choose to Fail or Succeed*, New York: Viking Penguin, 2005; Thomas Homer-Dixon, *The Upside of Down: Catastrophe, Creativity, and the Renewal of Civilization*, Toronto: Alfred A. Knopf, 2006; and R. Wright, *A Short History of Progress*, Toronto: House of Anansi Press Inc., 2004, p. 3.

3   T. Homer-Dixon, *The Ingenuity Gap*: Toronto, Canada: Vintage Canada Edition, 2001, pp. 31, 241.

4   M. Tidwell, 'Snap! The terrifying new speed of global warming and our last chance to stop it', *Orion* 27, May/June, 2008, 18–19.

5   R. Wright, *A Short History of Progress*, p. 109.

6   See the Douglas Worts website for biographical details. Available online at <www.geocities.com/dcworts> (accessed 16 July 2008).

7   Douglas Worts, email (December 2007).

8   See the Douglas Worts website for details on his publications.

9   D. Worts, 'Measuring museum meaning: A critical assessment framework', *Journal of Museum Education* 31, 2006, 41–8.

10 D. Worts, 'Measuring museum meaning', p. 45.

11 Mission Statement of the Field Museum. Available online at <http://www.fieldmuseum.org/museum_info/mission_statement.htm> (accessed 17 July 2008).

12 Telephone interview with Alaka Wali, Director of the Center for Cultural Understanding and Change and John Nuveen Curator of Anthropology at the Field Museum, April 2008. Canmore, Alberta, Canada. See also 'From Experiment to Commitment', in *ECCo Annual Report 2005*, pp. 6–7. Available online at <http://www.fieldmuseum.org/research_collections/ecp/pdf/ECCoAR05.pdf> (accessed 17 July 2008).

13 Center for Cultural Understanding and Change website. The Field Museum. Available online at <http://www.fieldmuseum.org/ccuc/default.htm> (accessed 17 July 2008).

14 'New Allies for Nature and Culture', Center for Cultural Understanding and Change website. The Field Museum. Available online at <http://www.fieldmuseum.org/ccuc/allies.htm> (accessed 17 July 2008).

15 'From Experiment to Commitment'.

16 Telephone interview with Alaka Wali.

17 Baby boomer is a term used to describe a person who was born during the post-World War II baby boom between 1946 and the early 1960s. Following the Second World War, several English-speaking countries, including the United States, Canada, Australia, and New Zealand experienced a marked increase in the birth rates, commonly referred to as the baby boom. See Wikipedia, available online at <http://en.wikipedia.org/wiki/Baby_boomer> (accessed 21 July 2008).

18 R. G. McCaffrey, 'The effect of public garden visitation on older adults with depression: A manual for developing a public program', 2008, p. 1. Available online at <http://www.morikami.org/clientuploads/pdf/Manual_Stroll_for_Well_Being.pdf> (accessed 21 July 2008).

19 The Morikami Museum and Japanese Gardens website. Available online at <http://www.morikami.org/index.php?src> (accessed 21 July 2008).

20 R.G. McCaffrey, 'The effect of public garden visitation on older adults with depression', pp. 1–9.

21 R.G. McCaffrey, 'The effect of public garden visitation on older adults with depression'.

22 Institute of Museum and Library Services, *Program Overview: National Leadership Grants.* Available online at <http://www.imls.gov/applicants/grants/nationalLeadership.shtm> (accessed 21 July 2008).

23 For several examples see F. Vanclay, J. Wills and R. Lane, 'Museum outreach programs promoting a sense of place'. In F. Vanclay, M. Higgins and A. Blackshaw (eds), *Making Sense of Place: Exploring Concepts and Expressions of Place through Different Senses and Lenses*, Canberra, National Museum of Australia Press, 2008; R. Lane, J. Wills, F. Vanclay, and D. Lucas, 'Vernacular heritage and evolving environmental policy in Australia: Lessons from the Murray-Darling Outreach Project', *Geoforum* 39, 2008, 1305–17; R. Lane, F. Vanclay, J. Wills and D. Lucas, 'Museum outreach programs to promote community engagement in local environmental issues', *The Australian Journal of Public Administration* 66, 2007, 159–

74; and F. Vanclay, R. Lane, J. Wills, I. Coates and D. Lucas, '"Committing to Place" and evaluating the higher purpose: Increasing engagement in natural resource management through museum outreach and educational activities', *Journal of Environmental Assessment Policy and Management* (6/4), 2004, 539–64.

24 R. Lane, F. Vanclay, J. Wills and D. Lucas, 'Museum outreach programs to promote community engagement in local environmental issues', p.163. See also F. Vanclay, M. Higgins and A. Blackshaw, *Making Sense of Place: Exploring Concepts and Expressions of Place through Different Senses and Lenses*, Canberra, Australia: National Museum of Australia Press, 2008.

25 Lane *et al.*, 'Museum outreach programs', 162–4.

26 Lane *et al.*, 'Museum outreach programs', 163.

27 Lane *et al.*, 'Museum outreach programs', 164–5.

28 Lane *et al.*, 'Museum outreach programs', 167, 170.

29 Lane *et al.*, 'Museum outreach programs', 167.

30 Lane *et al.*, 'Museum outreach programs', 170.

31 F. Vanclay, R. Lane, J. Wills, I. Coates and D. Lucas, '"Committing to Place" and evaluating the higher purpose', 560.

32 N. Tousley, 'The wrapping comes off Glenbow's The Big Gift', *Calgary Herald*, 5 August 2008, pp. 1–3. Available online at <http://www.canada.com/cityguides/calgary/story.html?id=85fc790e-ee5e-439e-861a-e78d13164a80> (accessed 30 September 2008).

33 M.L. Anderson, 'Metrics of success in art museums'. Paper commissioned for the Getty Leadership Institute, 2004. Available online at<http://www.getty.edu/leadership/compleat_leader/evalperf.html> (accessed 23 July 2008).

34 Anderson, 'Metrics of success in art museums', p. 6.

35 K. Bruce, V. Hollows, B. Harman and A. Watson, *Towards an Engaged Art Gallery – Contemporary Art and Human Rights: GoMA's Social Justice Programs*, Glasgow, UK: Culture and Sport Glasgow (Museums), 2007, p. 7.

36 Bruce *et al.*, *Towards an Engaged Art Gallery*, pp. 7–8.

37 Bruce *et al.*, *Towards an Engaged Art Gallery*, pp. 9.

38 Bruce *et al.*, *Towards an Engaged Art Gallery*, pp. 10.

39 Bruce *et al.*, *Towards an Engaged Art Gallery*, pp. 11.

40 Bruce, *et al.*,, *Towards an Engaged Art Gallery*, pp. 14.

41 Bruce *et al.*,, *Towards an Engaged Art Gallery*, pp. 15.

42 See the website of the International Economuseum Network Society. Available online at <http://www.economusees.com/iens_en.cfm> (accessed 24 July 2008).

43 For a discussion of the economuseum concept, see Wikipedia, available online at <http://en.wikipedia.org/wiki/Economuseum> (accessed 24 July 2008).

44 'The six components of an economuseum'. Available online at <http://www.economusees.com/whatisaneconomuseum.cfm#components> (accessed 24 July 2008).

45 'International News', *MUSE: The Voice of Canada's Museum Community* 26, July/August 2008, p. 14.

46 The Charter of Values of the Economuseum Network Society. Available online at <http://www.economusees.com/docs/SIE_CharteValeurs_v6.pdf> (accessed 25 July, 2008).

47 History and Mission of the Museums Association. Available online at <http://www.museumsassociation.org/ma/9783> (accessed 25 July 2008).

48 Museum Association Trusts and Funds. Available online at <http://www.museumsassociation.org/trustsandfunds> (accessed 26 July 2008).

49 M. Davies and H. Wilkinson, 'Sustainability and museums: your chance to make a difference', London: Museums Association, 2008. Available online at <http://www.museumsassociation.org/sustainability> (accessed 25 July 2008).

50 Davies and Wilkinson, 'Sustainability and Museums: Your Chance to Make a Difference', p. 20.

51 Museum Studies Graduate School Programs. Available online at <http://www.gradschools.com/Subject/Museum-Studies/262.html> (accessed 28 July 2008).

52 Department of Museum Studies, University of Leicester, United Kingdom. Available online at <http://www.le.ac.uk/museumstudies/index.html> (accessed 28 July 2009).

53 The Research Centre for Museums and Galleries, Department of Museum Studies, University of Leicester, United Kingdom. Available online at <http://www.le.ac.uk/museumstudies/research/rcmg.html> (accessed 28 July 2008).

54 Major Research Themes of the Research Centre for Museums and Galleries. Department of Museum Studies, University of Leicester, United Kingdom. Available online at <http://www.le.ac.uk/museumstudies/research/rcmg.html> (accessed 28 July 2008).

55 Rethinking Disability Representation – Project Update 1, September, 2007. Available online at <http://www.le.ac.uk/ms/research/Reports/Rethinking%20Disability%20Representation%20update%201.pdf> (accessed 28 July 2008); and Rethinking Disability Representation – Project Update 2, April, 2008. Available online at <http://www.le.ac.uk/ms/research/Reports/Rethinking%20Disability%20Representation%20update%202.pdf> (accessed 28 July 2008).

56 Rethinking Disability Representation – Project Update 2, April, 2008, p. 3. Available online at <http://www.le.ac.uk/ms/research/Reports/Rethinking%20Disability%20Representation%20update%202.pdf> (accessed 28 July 2008).

57 *Disablist Britain: Barriers to Independent Living for Disabled People in 2006*. London: Demos – The Think Tank for Everyday Democracy, 2006, p. 5. Available online at <http://www.demos.co.uk/publications/disablistbritain> (accessed 28 July 2008).

58 Rethinking Disability Representation – Project Update 2.

59 *Merriam-Webster's Collegiate Dictionary, 10th Edn*, Springfield, MA, USA: Merriam-Webster, Incorporated, 2002, p. 993.

60 T. Homer-Dixon, *The Upside of Down: Catastrophe, Creativity, and the Renewal of Civilization,* Toronto: Alfred A. Knopf, 2006, p. 283.

61 S. Weil, 'Beyond management: Making museums matter', Keynote Address at the 1st International Conference on Museum Management and Leadership – Achieving Excellence: Museum Leadership in the 21st Century INTERCOM/CMA conference held in Ottawa, Canada, September 6–9, 2000, p. 3. Available online at <http://www.intercom.museum/conferences/2000/weil.pdf> (accessed 30 July 2008).

62 Homer-Dixon, *The Upside of Down,* pp. 281–7.

63 Homer-Dixon, *The Upside of Down,* pp. 281–2.

64 Homer-Dixon, *The Upside of Down,* pp. 281–2.

65 The 'long emergency' is the phrase used by J.H. Kunstler to describe the decades ahead and the consequences of peak oil, climate change, epidemic disease, habitat destruction and so forth. See J. H. Kunstler, *The Long Emergency: Surviving the End of Oil, Climate Change, and Other Converging Catastrophes of the Twenty-First Century,* New York: Grove Press, 2005. The shift from a high-entropy world to a low-entropy world is taken from J. Rifkin, *Entropy: A New World View,* New York: The Viking Press, 1980, pp. 205–23.

66 Kunstler, *The Long Emergency*, pp. 22–60.

67 Rifkin, *Entropy,* pp. 205–23.

68 R. Louv, *Last Child in the Woods: Saving Our Children from Nature-Deficit Disorder*, Chapel Hill, North Carolina, USA: Algonquin Books of Chapel Hill, 2005, Introductory Quotation.

69 Rifkin, *Entropy,* p. 216.

70 Rifkin, *Entropy,* p. 256.

71 R.R. Janes and G.T. Conaty, 'Introduction'. In R.R. Janes and G.T. Conaty (eds), *Looking Reality in the Eye: Museums and Social Responsibility,* Calgary, Canada: The University of Calgary Press and the Museums Association of Saskatchewan, 2005, p. 12.

72 P.F. Drucker, *Post-Capitalist Society*, New York: HarperCollins Publishers, 1994, p. 1.

6 The mindful museum

1 A. Gopnik, 'The mindful museum', *The Walrus* (4 June), 2007, p. 90. This article is adapted from the 2006 Holtby Lecture at the Royal Ontario Museum in Toronto, Canada.

2 J. Kabat-Zinn, *Full Catastrophe Living: Using the Wisdom of Your Body and Mind to Face Stress, Pain, and Illness,* New York: Bantam, Doubleday, Dell Publishing Group, Inc., 1990, pp. 12–13.

3 D. Fontana, *Meditation: An Introductory Guide to Relaxation for Mind and Body,* Shaftesbury, Dorset, UK: Element Books Limited, 1999, p. 112.

4 J. Kabat-Zinn, *Coming to Our Senses: Healing Ourselves and the World Through Mindfulness,* New York: Hyperion, 2005, p. 148.

5 Kabat-Zinn, *Coming to Our Senses,* p. 607.

6 J. Kabat-Zinn, *Wherever You Go, There You Are: Mindfulness Meditation in Everyday Life*, New York: Hyperion, 1994, p. 94.

7   Kabat-Zinn, *Full Catastrophe Living*, pp. 28–9.
8   R. Farson, *Management of the Absurd: Paradoxes in Leadership*, New York: Simon & Schuster, 1996, p. 142.
9   Farson, *Management of the Absurd*, p. 93.
10 T. Frank, 'The wrecking crew: How a gang of right-wing con men destroyed Washington and made a killing', *Harper's Magazine* 317, August 2008, pp. 35–45.
11 M.J. Wheatley, *Leadership and the New Science: Learning about Organization from an Orderly Universe*, San Francisco: Berrett-Koehler Publishers, Inc., 1992, pp. 109–10.
12 M. Woodhouse, *Paradigm Wars: Worldviews for a New Age*, Berkeley: Frog, Ltd., 1996, pp. 10–11.
13 M.J. Wheatley, *Leadership and the New Science*, p. 110.
14 This is a paraphrase of a passage originally intended to describe self-indulgent and self-centred individuals. See Kabat-Zinn, *Wherever You Go, There You Are*, p. 240.
15 Kabat-Zinn, *Coming to Our Senses*, p. 350.
16 Kabat-Zinn, *Coming to Our Senses*, p. 351.
17 Kabat-Zinn, *Coming to Our Senses*, p. 351.
18 Kabat-Zinn, *Coming to Our Senses*, p. 355.
19 R. Gross, *The Independent Scholar's Handbook*, Berkeley: Ten Speed Press, 1993, pp. 169–70. Available online at <http://www.sfu.ca/independentscholars/ISbook.pdf> (accessed 15 August 2008).
20 See the website of Everyday Democracy. Available online at <http://www.everyday-democracy.org/en/index.aspx> (accessed 15 August 2008).
21 C. DeKluyver, in J. Sloan, *Learning to Think Strategically*, Oxford: Butterworth-Heinemann, 2006, p. 14.
22 E. Koster, 'The relevant museum: A reflection on sustainability', *Museum News* 85, May/June 2006, pp. 67–70, 85–91. Available online at <http://www.aam-us.org/pubs/mn/MN_MJ06_RelevantMuseum.cfm> (accessed 27 January 2009).
23 H. Mintzberg, 'The rise and fall of strategic planning', *Harvard Business Review*, January/February, 1994, 108.
24 Sloan, *Learning to Think Strategically*, p. 29.
25 Sloan, *Learning to Think Strategically*, pp. 199–216.
26 Sloan, *Learning to Think Strategically*, p. 158.
27 For a complete overview of scenario planning, see P. Schwartz, *The Art of the Long View*, New York: Currency Doubleday, 1996; and A. DeGeus, *The Living Company: Habits for Survival in a Turbulent Business Environment*, Boston: Harvard Business School Press, 1997, pp. 38–54.
28 Brefi Group Limited, 'Scenario Planning'. Available online at <http://www.brefigroup.co.uk/facilitation/scenario_planning.html> (accessed 16 August 2008).
29 D. Scearce and K. Fulton, *What If? The Art of Scenario Thinking for Nonprofits*, San Francisco: GBN Global Business Network, 2004. Available online at <http://www.gbn.com/articles/pdfs/GBN_What%20If.pdf> (accessed 26 January 2009).
30 H.J. Cortner and M.A. Moote, *The Politics of Ecosystem Management*, Washington, DC: Island Press, 1998.
31 H.J. Cortner, 'Human Dimensions in Ecosystem Management'. Presentation at *Future Landscapes in the Canadian Rockies: Integrating Human Dimensions with Ecosystem Management*. The Annual Conference of the Central Rockies Ecosystem Interagency Liaison Group, Canmore, Alberta, Canada, 13 November 2006. The conference proceedings are available online at <http://www.tpr.alberta.ca/parks/kananaskis/creilg/PDFs/CREILG_2006_Final.pdf> (accessed 17 August 2008).
32 See the *Adaptive Management Experiment* for further details on the definition of concepts. Available online at <http://www.ameteam.ca/About%20Flame/adaptive_management2.html> (accessed 28 August 2008).
33 E. Heumann Gurian, 'The curator's next choice', unpublished paper (April 2008).
34 Heumann Gurian, 'The curator's next choice', p. 2.
35 Heumann Gurian, 'The curator's next choice', pp. 12–13.
36 The 888torontomeetup. The Ontario Science Centre, Available online at <http://www.ontariosciencecentre.ca/calendar/default.asp?eventid=792&ddmmyyyy=02082008> (accessed 19 August 2008).

37 F.R. Cameron, 'Object-oriented democracies: Conceptualizing museum collections in networks', *Museum Management and Curatorship* (23/3), 2008, 229–43; and P. Marty, 'Museum websites and museum visitors: Before and after the museum visit', *Museum Management and Curatorship* (22/4), 2007, 337–60; and P. Marty, 'Museum websites and museum visitors: Digital museum resources and their use', *Museum Management and Curatorship* (23/1), 2008, 81–99.

38 T.L. Friedman, *The World is Flat: A Brief History of the Twenty-First Century*, New York: Farrar, Straus and Giroux, 2005.

39 N.G. Kotler, P. Kotler and W.I. Kotler, *Museum Marketing and Strategy: Designing Missions, Building Audiences, Generating Revenue and Resources* (2nd edn), San Francisco: Jossey-Bass, 2008.

40 R.R. Janes and G.T. Conaty (eds), *Looking Reality in the Eye: Museums and Social Responsibility*, Calgary, Canada: The University of Calgary Press and the Museums Association of Saskatchewan, 2005.

41 R. Lezner and S.S. Johnson, 'Seeing things as they really are: An interview with Peter F. Drucker', *Forbes*, 10 March 1997, pp. 122–8.

42 Kabat-Zinn, *Coming to Our Senses*, p. 349.

43 M.M. Ames, *Cannibal Tours and Glass Boxes: The Anthropology of Museums*, Vancouver: UBC Press, 1992, p. 5.

44 E.O. Wilson, *Creation: An Appeal to Save Life on Earth*, New York: W.W. Norton and Company, Inc., 2006, p. 81.

45 P. Hawken, A. Lovins and L.H. Lovins, *Natural Capitalism*, New York: Back Bay Books/Little, Brown and Company, 2000, pp. 310–13.

46 Hawken *et al.*, *Natural Capitalism*, p. 312.

47 R.R. Janes, 'Museums in a Troubled World: Renewal, Irrelevance or Collapse?', Luncheon address to the Committee on Audience Research and Evaluation (CARE), Annual Meeting of the American Association of Museums, Denver, Colorado, USA, 2008, p. 23.

48 Wheatley, *Leadership and the New Science*, p. 117.

49 E. Hooper-Greenhill, *Museums and the Interpretation of Visual Culture*, London and New York: Routledge. 2000, pp. 151–62.

50 Hooper-Greenhill, *Museums and the Interpretation of Visual Culture*, p. 152.

51 In 'Margaret J. Wheatley', Wikipedia, available online at <http://en.wikipedia.org/wiki/Margaret_Wheatley> (accessed 22 August 2008).

7 Museums: Stewards or spectators?

1 W. Berry, *Sex, Economy, Freedom and Community*, New York and San Francisco: Pantheon Books, 1992, pp. 152–3.

2 T. Poulos (ed.), *Conference Proceedings for 2001: The Museum and the Canadian Public*, Ottawa, Canada: Canadian Museums Association, 1977, pp. 2–3.

3 Poulos (ed.), *Conference Proceedings for 2001*, pp. 5–6.

4 Poulos (ed.), *Conference Proceedings for 2001*, pp. 93–5. See Recommendation F, #1 and #3; Recommendation I, #2.

5 R.N. Oliver (ed.), *Museums and the Environment: A Handbook for Education*, New York: The American Association of Museums and Arkville Press, 1971, p. vii.

6 Oliver, *Museums and the Environment*, pp. 177–82.

7 Oliver, *Museums and the Environment*, p. 191.

8 *Curator: The Museum Journal* (50/2), 2007, 185–272. This issue of the journal is a result of a conference held in honour of Stephen Weil at the University of Victoria (Cultural Resource Management Program), Victoria, British Columbia, Canada, from 13–15 September 2006.

9 S. Weil, 'From being *about* something to being *for* somebody: The ongoing transformation of the American museum', *Daedalus – Journal of the American Academy of Arts and Sciences* (128), 1999, 242.

10 S. Watson (ed.), *Museums and Their Communities*, Oxford: Routledge, 2007.

11 D. Jensen, *Endgame Volume 11: Resistance*, New York: Seven Stories Press, 2006, p. 531.

12 D. Wann, *Simple Prosperity: Finding Real Wealth in a Sustainable Lifestyle*, New York: St. Martin's Griffin, 2007, pp. 233–4.

13 J. Rifkin, *Entropy: A New World View*, New York: The Viking Press, 1980, pp. 217–18.

14   Museum Policy Information. The Canadian Museums Association. Available online at <http://www.museums.ca/en/info_resources/current_issues/museum_policy_info/index.php>(accessed 30 August 2008).

15   Information and Resources, The Canadian Museums Association. Available online at <http://www.museums.ca/en/info_resources/current_issues/alerts/index.php?pid=1218772800> (accessed 30 August 2008).

16   M.`-A. Anderson, Senior Advisor, Department of Canadian Heritage, email (September 2008).

17   Canada's Museums: Key Policy Messages. The Canadian Museums Association. Available online at <http://www.museums.ca/media/Pdf/keymessages.pdf> (accessed 30 August 2008).

18   Department for Culture, Media and Sport, *Understanding the Future: Museums and 21st Century Life: The Value of Museums,* London: Department for Culture, Media and Sport, 2005. Available online at <http://www.culture.gov.uk/reference_library/consultations/1186.aspx> (accessed 30 August 2008).

19   Department for Culture, Media and Sport, *Understanding the Future: Museums and 21st Century Life: The Value of Museums,* pp. 12, 30.

20   American Association of Museums, *Annual Report 2007,* Washington, DC: American Association of Museums, 2007, pp. 23–4. Available online at <http://www.aam-us.org/aboutaam/governance/upload/AAM_AR07web.pdf> (accessed 1 September 2008).

21   N. Grattan, Canadian Museums Association Communiqué: National Museum Campaign with Kellogg Canada 2008. Email (May 2008).

22   D. Worts, 'Rising to the challenge: Fostering a culture of sustainability' (Guest Editorial), *MUSE* (26, September/October), 2008, p. 6.

23   J.M. Bradburne, 'The museum time bomb: Overbuilt, overtraded, overdrawn', 2005, p. 22. Available online at <http://www.bradburne.org/downloads/museums/InstitutioninCrisisWEB.pdf> (accessed 31 August 2008).

24   Bradburne, 'The museum time bomb', p. 36.

25   M. von Wistinghausen, 'Can we afford the audience?', *Platform*/AEA Consulting (5/3), February, 2008, p. 6. Available online at <http://www.aeaconsulting.com/sites/aea/images/1815/aea_1815.pdf> (accessed 21 October 2008).

26   D. Sudjic, 'Who now will save our museums?', *The Observer*, 13 February 2005. Available online at <http://www.guardian.co.uk/artanddesign/2005/feb/13/art.museums> (accessed 31 August 2008).

27   E.S. Connell, *Son of the Morning Star: Custer and the Little Bighorn,* San Francisco: North Point Press, 1984. See book jacket.

28   C. Handy, *The Age of Paradox,* Boston: Harvard Business School Press, 1994, pp. 51–9.

29   B. McKibben, *Deep Economy: The Wealth of Communities and the Durable Future,* New York: Henry Holt and Company, 2007, p. 218

30   C. Frazier, *Thirteen Moons,* Toronto: Vintage Canada, 2006, p. 412.

31   J. Allemang, 'Save museums, they're the conscience of the earth,' *The Globe and Mail – Science and Ideas,* 20 September 2008, p. F8.

32   E. Hobsbawm, *On the Edge of the New Century,* New York: The New Press, 2000, p. 66.

33   Canadian Heritage Information Network, 'World Museums', email (September 2008).

34   M. Wackernagel and W. Rees, *Our Ecological Footprint: Reducing Human Impact on the Earth,* Gabriola Island, British Columbia, Canada: New Society Publishers, 1996, p. 137.

35   Berry, *Sex, Economy, Freedom and Community,* pp. 24–33.

36   Department for Culture, Media and Sport, *Understanding the Future: Museums and 21st Century Life,* p. 11. Available online at <http://www.culture.gov.uk/images/consultations/UnderstandingtheFuture.pdf> (accessed 26 January 2009).

37   C. Stanish, 'On museums in a postmodern world', *Daedalus – Journal of the American Academy of Arts and Sciences* (137, Summer), 2008, 149.

38   E.O. Wilson, *Biophilia,* Cambridge, MA: Harvard University Press, 1984, p. 49.

39   C.P. Snow, *The Two Cultures: And a Second Look,* New York: Cambridge University Press, 1959 and 1963.

40   Snow, *The Two Cultures,* pp. 9–26.

41   J. Ralston Saul, *The Unconscious Civilization,* Concord, Ontario, Canada: House of Anansi Press Limited, 1995, p. 174.

42   Berry, *Sex, Economy, Freedom and Community,* p. 82.

43 M. Schwarzer, email (July 2008).
44 A. Gopnik, 'The mindful museum', *The Walrus* (4, June), 2007, p. 89. This article is adapted from the 2006 Holtby Lecture at the Royal Ontario Museum in Toronto, Canada.
45 A. DeGeus, *The Living Company: Habits for Survival in a Turbulent Business Environment*, Boston: Harvard Business School Press, 1997, p. 6.
46 Foundation for Heritage and the Arts, *Annual Report*. Halifax, Nova Scotia, Canada: Foundation for Heritage and the Arts, 2000–2001, pp. 6–7.
47 J. H. Kunstler. 'Making other arrangements: A wake-up call to a citizenry in the shadow of oil scarcity', *Orion Magazine* (January/February), 2007, p. 1. Available online at <http://www.orionmagazine.org/index.php/articles/article/7> (accessed 4 September 2008).

Index